[美] 索恩·莱　宋晓东 编

Thorne Lay　Xiaodong　Song

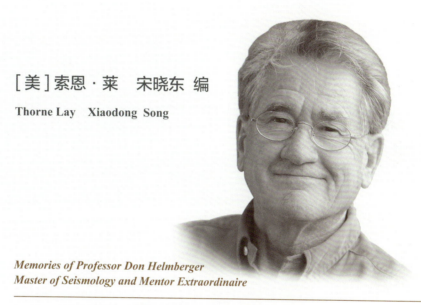

Memories of Professor Don Helmberger
Master of Seismology and Mentor Extraordinaire

追忆 唐·亨伯格教授

---- 地震学大师和非凡导师

科学出版社

北京

内 容 简 介

本书是为了纪念杰出的地震学家、从事地震学研究的研究生和研究人员的良师益友——唐·亨伯格教授。本书包括了用中英双语撰写的来自著名同事的两篇序言和一篇前言，以及亨伯格教授生前指导的学生的 19 篇文章。在这些文章中，读者可以找到他的学生参与的许多突破性成果，并体会亨伯格教授在整个职业生涯中遵循的科学哲学和指导方法。在他的指导下，多位学生已经取得了成功，并在自己的研究经历中不断践行他的理念。亨伯格教授提出的地震波形建模已成为限制从内核到地壳的地球结构以及快速量化地震时空破裂行为的关键方法，如今已在地震学科被广泛采用。这些文章证明了亨伯格教授谦逊的科研态度、永葆好奇的求知精神，以及他对解译地震记录的巨大热情，这使他深受研究生和同事们的喜爱。

本书可供地球物理学和其他领域的本科生、研究生、年轻或资深的科研人员参考阅读，相信读者都能从本书受益。

图书在版编目（CIP）数据

追忆唐·亨伯格教授 ：地震学大师和非凡导师 = Memories of Professor Don Helmberger: Master of Seismology and Mentor Extraordinaire ：英汉对照 /(美) 索恩·莱 (Thorne Lay)，宋晓东编. —北京：科学出版社，2023.5
ISBN 978-7-03-074369-5

Ⅰ. ①追… Ⅱ. ①索… ②宋… Ⅲ. ①亨利(Helmberger, Donald Vincent 1938-2020)-回忆录-英、汉 Ⅳ. ①K837.126.14

中国国家版本馆 CIP 数据核字(2023)第 000670 号

责任编辑：韩 鹏 崔 妍/责任校对：何艳萍
责任印制：肖 兴/封面设计：图阅盛世

科 学 出 版 社 出版
北京东黄城根北街 16 号
邮政编码：100717
http://www.sciencep.com

北京汇瑞嘉合文化发展有限公司 印刷
科学出版社发行 各地新华书店经销
*
2023 年 5 月第 一 版 开本：787×1092 1/16
2023 年 5 月第一次印刷 印张：15 1/2
字数：360 000
定价：298.00 元
（如有印装质量问题，我社负责调换）

Helmberger family, 1940 (Don is the little one in front as the last of 13 children)
亨伯格家族，1940 年（唐是 13 个孩子中最小的、前排的那个）

Don in Middle School, 1951
唐在初中，1951 年

Growing up in a farm, Don's pet cow, in high school, 1950s
在农场长大，唐的宠物牛，高中，1950 年代

Don at University of Minnesota , 1962
唐在明尼苏达大学，1962 年

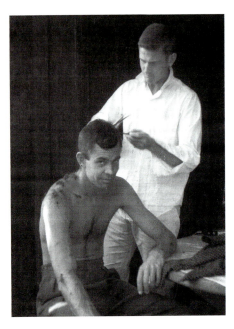

Cutting hair (for extra income) , Scripps Institute,
University of California San Diego, 1965
帮人理发（为了额外收入），加州大学圣迭戈分校
斯克里普斯研究所，1965 年

Early days at Caltech, 1970
在加州理工学院的早期，1970 年

Quarterback on the 40th birthday 1978
美式足球四分卫，1978 年 40 岁生日

Third floor office, Caltech 1970s
在加州理工学院的三楼办公室，1970 年代

Taking down a tree at home in Pasadena, 1991
在帕萨迪纳的家中砍倒一棵树，1991 年

Mendocino, California, 1991
加利福尼亚州门多西诺，1991 年

Caltech, Dabney Gardens, April 20, 1991
加州理工学院，达布尼花园，1991 年 4 月 20 日

Alaska, 2006
阿拉斯加，2006 年

Thinking ... in office piles, 2017
思考……在办公室里，2017 年

Nantes, France, 2017

法国南特，2017 年

Lecturing, Caltech, 2017

讲课，加州理工学院，2017 年

Symposium, Singapore, 2018 年 (age 80).
研讨会，新加坡，2018 年（80 岁）

Singapore 2018, age 80
新加坡 2018 年，80 岁

San Francisco, 2019
旧金山，2019 年

Foreword I

Michael Gurnis

Seismological Laboratory

California Institute of Technology

Pasadena, CA 91125 USA

(Email: gurnis@caltech.edu)

Don Helmberger was known as a seismologist, but he was also one of the greats of twentieth and early twenty-first century geophysics. I say geophysics because his seismological work and that of his students has had such a wide impact on our understanding of earth, from the inner core to the crust. Don's life, his science and his lasting impact through his many students and colleagues is an inspiration to us all. Here you will find a collection of memories and thoughts from many of Don's graduate students at Caltech's Seismological Laboratory over five decades, from his first graduate student, Chuck Langston, in the early 1970's to his final student, Voon Hui Lai, in 2020. These papers first appeared in *Earthquake Science* but are here reproduced along with the Chinese translation and a collection of photographs of Don's life as a scientist and beyond.

I knew Don not as a mentee but as a faculty colleague and close collaborator over twenty-five years. I saw the uplifting spirit he brought to so many budding young scientists as he shepherded them to being talented seismologists. I saw the patience and soft touch he brought to mentoring. Hour-after-hour I would see Don in his office, hunched over a stack of seismograms, pencil in hand, a student looking on, interrupted by long pauses as he gazed out his window at the San Gabriel Mountains.

Even before I arrived in the Seismo Lab in the mid-1980's, Don and his students drew me into the wonders of deep earth seismology. Indeed, as a first-year graduate student at the Australian National University, my advisor, Geoff Davies – a Seismo Lab alum from a decade before – realized I didn't know much about seismology and dumped a pile of books on my desk, advising that I take a look. There was a short monograph, by Bruce Bolt, with a narrative on how seismograms encoded messages of the deep earth and seismologists were akin to detectives. It was captivating, but Lay and Helmberger (1983), (discussed in Thorne Lay's chapter here) had just appeared describing new observations and seismic models of the D" layer — I was hooked. Suddenly the computational models of mantle convection I worked on were brought to life by small wiggles on a seismogram!

As several years went by, Don and I realized that there was a different way to interpret seismograms. Like many scientists outside of Don's immediate discipline, I viewed Don as an observational seismologist because, by interpreting wiggles on seismograms, he sharpened our focus on so many features in the interior (such as, up to that point, the lithosphere and upper mantle, D" and ULVZ.) But after a long discussion—I've long since forgotten on what—Don turned to me and said, "I'm a modeler." Of course, I knew that, but it was how he said it so emphatically, without qualification, that has had such a lasting impression. As recounted in these pages, it was through his deep understanding of how seismic waves propagated, that allowed Don and his students to draw such extraordinary insight from the wiggles. But Don and I started to think differently on how we could link seismograms to models – not just forward models of seismic velocities – but process-based models based first on mantle convection and then the coupling of mantle convection and mineral physics (in collaboration with our colleague Jennifer Jackson). It was through endless back-and-forth discussion, often at Seismo Lab Coffee, where we came up with the prediction of the post-perovskite phase transition and the sharp sides to the African superplume with graduate students Igor Sidorin and Sidao Ni, respectively. Don's boundless enthusiasm that science should be fun filled the walls of the Lab.

The volume is now being brought here with a new title to highlight an extraordinary legacy of Don Helmberger's, his role and impact as a mentor. Reading through the eighteen memories as well as the testimonials of his former international students, one can only feel inspired–inspired to be a better mentor and inspired to see the intellectual diversity of his students. Mentoring is much discussed these days, but nowhere can one find a richer source of material than from a true master. Don was a master mentor not just because he was a brilliant scientist, but because he was so personable, so generous to those around him. It was Don's personality and the way he connected with others which makes Don stand apart from many other successful scientists. I hope you will enjoy reading this short collection of memories as much as I did.

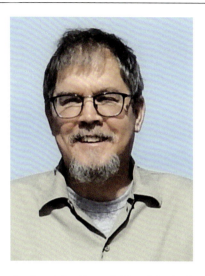

Michael Gurnis is currently the John E. and Hazel S. Smits Professor of Geophysics and Director of the Seismological Laboratory at the California Institute of Technology. He received his PhD from the Australian National University, was a postdoc at Caltech, on the faculty of the University of Michigan for five years, and since the mid-90's a close collaborator of Don Hemberger. He is the recipient of the Macelwane Medal of the American Geophysical Union, the Donath Medal of the Geological Society of America, the Love Medal of the European Geosciences Union, and the Gordon Bell Prize in Supercomputing from the Association for Computing Machinery. His webpage can be found at: http://seismolab.caltech.edu/gurnis_m.html.

序 一

迈克尔·歌尼斯

美国加州理工学院地震学实验室

唐·亨伯格是著名的地震学家，但他也是 20 世纪和 21 世纪初地球物理学领域的伟人之一。我之所以提地球物理学，是因为他和他的学生们的地震学研究对我们认识地球——从内核到地壳，产生了方方面面的影响。唐的生活理念、科学思想以及通过他的众多学生和同事所产生的持续影响对我们所有人都是一种启发。这里记录了五十多年来唐在加州理工学院地震实验室的研究生们的回忆和思考，从 20 世纪 70 年代初的第一个研究生查尔斯·兰斯顿到 2020 年的最后一个学生赖文慧。这些文章首先发表在《地震科学》英文期刊上，并于此增加中文翻译和唐的生活照片集以进行重制，展现唐不止作为一名科学家的一面。

我不是以学生身份认识唐的，而是作为一名同事和 25 年多的密切合作者。我见证了他在将许多年轻科学家培养成卓越的地震学家的过程中，带给他们的振奋精神。我看到了他在指导学生时倾注的耐心和温柔。一个钟头又一个钟头，我看到唐在他的办公室里，弓着身子面对一叠地震图，手里拿着铅笔，一个学生在看着，这一场景会被长时间的停顿打断，当他凝视着窗外的圣加布里埃尔山脉时。

甚至在我于 20 世纪 80 年代中叶进入地震实验室之前，唐和他的学生就把我拉进了地球深部地震学的奇妙世界中。事实上，作为澳大利亚国立大学一年级的研究生，我的导师杰夫·戴维斯——当时是十年前的地震实验室校友——意识到我对地震学知之甚少，就把一堆书扔在了我的桌子上，建议我看一看。其中有一本布鲁斯·博尔特写的短篇专著，讲述了地震图如何编码了地球深处的信息，而地震学家犹如侦探。这本书引起了我的兴趣，而且 Lay 和 Helmberger（1983）刚刚发表（见索恩·莱的章节），描述了 D″ 层的新观测和地震学模型——我被彻底迷住了。突然，我研究的地幔对流的计算模型通过地震图上的小扭动而变得生动起来！

几年过去了，唐和我意识到可以用一种新的方式来解释地震图。像许多没有接受过唐的直接指导的科学家一样，我觉得唐属于观测地震学家，因为通过解释地震图上的扭动，他让我们关注的许多地球内部特征（例如，到目前为止，岩石圈和上地幔，D″和 ULVZ）变得清晰。但经过长时间的讨论——我早已忘记了具体内容——唐转向我说："我是建模者。"我当然知道这一点，但正是他如此强调，才给我留下了如此深刻的印象。正如在后续篇幅中所述，正是凭借他对地震波传播方式的深刻理解，唐和他的学生才得以从波形的扭动中获得如此非凡的见解。但唐和我开始用与以往不同的方式思考如何将地震图与模型联系起来——不仅仅是地震波速的正演模拟——而是基于过程的模拟，首先基于地幔对流，然后是地幔对流与矿物物理的耦合（与我们的同事珍妮弗·杰克逊合作）。通过通常是在地震实验室的咖啡时间的反复讨论，我们分别与研究生伊戈尔·西多林和倪四道提出了后钙钛矿相变和非洲超级地幔柱的尖锐边缘的预测。唐认为科学应该是有趣的，他的热情洋溢在整个实验室内。

　　此书现以一个新的标题出版，以突出唐·亨伯格留下的非凡遗产，即他作为导师的作用和影响。阅读完这 18 段回忆以及他以前的国际学生的纪念文章，你会得到启发——如何成为一名更好的导师以及如何发现学生身上丰富多样的才能。现如今，有很多关于指导学生的讨论，但没有地方能找到比此书更丰富的教材。唐是一位大师级的导师，不仅因为他是一位杰出的科学家，更因为他是如此风度翩翩，对周围的人如此慷慨。唐的个人魅力和他与人的交往方式使他从众多其他成功的科学家中脱颖而出。我希望各位读者能像我一样享受阅读这卷简短的回忆录的过程。

　　迈克尔·歌尼斯目前是施密茨地球物理学教授和加州理工学院地震实验室主任。他在澳大利亚国立大学获得博士学位，曾在加州理工学院做博士后，在密歇根大学任教五年，自 20 世纪 90 年代中期以来一直是唐·亨伯格的密切合作者。他是美国地球物理联合会的麦凯尔温奖章、美国地质学会的多纳斯奖章、欧洲地球科学联合会的勒夫奖章和计算机协会的超级计算戈登·贝尔奖的获得者。他的主页是：http://seismolab.caltech.edu/gurnis_m.html。

Foreword II

Yun-tai Chen

University of Chinese Academy of Sciences and

Institute of Geophysics, China Earthquake Administration

I got into geophysics in the 1960s. In the autumn of 1962, I finished my undergraduate study at the Department of Geophysics, Peking University, and then I was admitted to the Institute of Geophysics, Chinese Academy of Sciences (CAS) as a postgraduate student under the tutelage of Academician Rongsheng Zeng. 60 years have passed in a blink. In the "Original Institute of Geophysics", I was not a "senior person", but I have the honor to witness and experience the development and growth of the Institute of Geophysics over the past 60 years, especially the many "fissions": at the beginning of 1966, it "fissioned" from an "Original Institute of Geophysics" into four geophysics institutes, namely the Institute of Atmospheric Physics of the CAS, the Space Center of the CAS, the Institute of Geophysics of the CAS, and the Kunming Institute of Geophysics (now merged into the Yunnan Earthquake Administration). The Institute of Geophysics of the CAS "fissioned" again in 1971 into the Institute of Geophysics of the China Earthquake Administration and the Institute of Geophysics of the CAS, and later the Institute of Geophysics of the CAS and the Institute of Geology of the CAS "fused" into the current Institute of Geology and Geophysics, CAS. Although it has undergone multiple "fissions" and multiple periods of leadership, an unwritten rule has been abided: the accumulated books and materials from the "Original Institute of Geophysics" were allocated to the corresponding institutes only when there were multiple copies. Otherwise, they would all belong to the ending geophysics institute of the "Original Institute of Geophysics" after the "fissions" - the Institute of Geophysics, China Earthquake Administration.

In those years, we could actually read not only newly published journals on geophysics and seismology from Europe, the USA and Japan, but also journals from the Soviet Union, Eastern Europe, Hungary, Czechoslovakia, German Democratic Republic and many other countries, even some important historical documents from the end of the 19th century. We could learn about the booming geophysics and seismology around the world, and also glance at the famous experts and scholars and their work contributing to the development of geophysics and seismology. Donald Vincent Helmberger (January 23, 1938 - August 13, 2020), the internationally renowned geophysicist, seismologist, member of the American

Academy of Sciences, one of the primary founders of seismic waveform modeling, was one of them.

Geophysics is a major field of earth sciences. It is a science that studies the structure of the earth and its dynamic system through quantitative physical methods. There are many branches in geophysics, and seismology is undoubtedly one of the core subjects. Earthquake-related disasters are also one of the most serious natural disasters. Ever since the pre-Qin dynasty era (some 4000 years ago), China has had a continuous recorded history of earthquakes, and the understanding of it has gradually developed from primitive understanding and nature worship to the natural law summary and scientific exploration. After the 1966 Xingtai earthquake, the country entered the exploratory stage of earthquake prediction. Our researchers experienced the great joy of the successful prediction of the Haicheng earthquake in 1975, but also suffered the heavy losses from big earthquakes such as the Tangshan earthquake in 1976 and the Wenchuan earthquake in 2008. Up to now, human beings still have not figured out the "temper" of earthquakes.

But the pace of exploration never stops. Seismic waves are the only known physical waves that can penetrate the earth's medium, lighting up the interior of the earth like a beacon. Geophysicists use various information recorded by seismic waves to explore the structure and characteristics of the earth's interior and to promote human understanding of earthquakes. The ocean of truth is endless, and Professor Don Helmberger was the lucky one who found the beautiful shell.

Don Helmberger obtained his Ph.D. in 1967 at the University of California San Diego, USA. In 1970, after serving as a faculty member at MIT and Princeton University, he moved to the famous Seismo Lab at Caltech where he was to spend the rest of his career. From 1998 to 2003 he served as the Director of the Seismo Lab. Professor Helmberger is rigorous in his research and diligent in his practice. Many of the students and postdocs he mentored have become internationally renowned seismologists and geophysicists (including several Chinese professors and scholars at home and abroad contributing to this book collection), making outstanding contributions to the development of geophysics and seismology in China.

Professor Helmberger made great contributions to the studies of the earth's deep interior and earthquake sources using creative seismological theories and modeling methods. Contributors in this special collection span the interval from his first graduate student (Charles Langston, Ph.D. 1976) to his last graduate student (Voon Hui Lai, Ph.D. 2020), including 19 articles by 23 of his graduates, postdocs or collaborators. The 19 articles cover Professor Helmberger's understanding of observed seismic data, his innovative development of Generalized Ray Theory, his methodology for 1D to 3D waveform modeling of seismograms on varies scales, his openness to exploring the model spaces that enabled breakthrough discoveries, and his valuable spiritual wealth and experience in educating students in his long-term scientific practice. From his experience with graduate students, readers can feel his inspiring and innovative spirit, his collaborative spirit of cooperation, his dedicated spirit of promotion for students, and his optimistic spirit of passion for life.

Inheritance is essential in technological innovation. I believe that every researcher, especially the younger generation of seismology researchers and practitioners, can be more or less inspired by this collection, and let the light of truth illuminate the road of exploration. I also wish the development of seismology in our country and the world can reach to a higher level, to understand the mystery of the earth and earthquakes, and to make contributions to the cause of disaster prevention and mitigation!

Yun-tai Chen, a renowned geophysicist in China. Engaged in seismology and geophysics research, especially the theoretical and applied research of seismic waves and sources. He graduated from the Department of Geophysics, Peking University in 1962 with a bachelor's degree, and graduated from the Institute of Geophysics, Chinese Academy of Sciences in 1966. In 1991, he was elected as a member of the Chinese Academy of Sciences (academician), and in 1999, he was elected as an academician of the Third World Academy of Sciences. He won the International Award of the American Geophysical Union in 2010. He used to be the director of the Institute of Geophysics of the China Earthquake Administration, the chairman of the Seismological Society of China, and the dean of the School of Earth and Space Sciences of Peking University. He is currently the honorary director of the Institute of Geophysics of the China Earthquake Administration and the honorary dean of the School of Earth and Space Sciences of Peking University.

序　二

陈运泰

中国科学院大学和中国地震局地球物理所

　　我和地球物理学结缘于 20 世纪 60 年代，1962 年秋本科毕业于北京大学地球物理系，而后考入中国科学院地球物理研究所读研究生，师从曾融生院士，倏忽间已有整整一个甲子。在"老地球所"，我算不上是一个"老（资格的）人"，但有幸目睹与经历了六十年来地球物理所的发展与壮大，特别是他的多次"裂变"：1966 年初从一个"老地球所"一次"裂变"成 4 所地球物理所，即中国科学院大气物理所、中国科学院空间中心、中国科学院地球物理研究所和昆明地球物理研究所（现已并入云南省地震局）；中国科学院地球物理研究所于 1971 年又"裂变"成中国地震局地球物理研究所与中国科学院地球物理研究所，以后中国科学院地球物理研究所与中国科学院地质研究所又"聚变"为现在的中国科学院地质与地球物理研究所。虽经多次的"裂变"、多期的各方面领导，但都遵守同一不成文的规则："老地球所"多年积累的图书资料只有当有多份时才分配给相应专业的研究所，其余统统归"老地球所"经历"裂变"后地球物理研究所的末端——中国地震局地球物理研究所。

　　在那些年，我们居然不但能够读到新出版的欧、美、日的地球物理学、地震学期刊，而且能读到苏联、东欧、匈牙利、捷克斯洛伐克、民主德国等国的地球物理学、地震学期刊，还可以查阅到 19 世纪末以来一些重要的历史性文献，对世界范围内蓬勃发展的地球物理学、地震学有所了解，对当时正在对地球物理学、地震学发展做出贡献的著名专家学者及其工作亦略知一二。国际著名地球物理学家、地震学家，美国科学院院士，地震波形建模的主要创始人之一唐·亨伯格（Donald　Helmberger，1938 年 1 月 23 日～2020 年 8 月 13 日）就是其中的一位。

　　地球物理学是地球科学的主要学科之一，是通过定量的物理学方法研究地球结构及其动态变化规律的科学。地球物理学有诸多研究分支，其中，地震学无疑是地球物理学研究的核心科学问题之一。地震引起的灾害是最重大的自然灾害之一。早在 4000 年前先秦时期，我国就有对地震历史的记载，对它的认识也从原始认识、自然崇拜，逐渐发展到规律总结和科学探索。1966 年邢台大地震后，我国进入地震预测的探索阶段。研究人员经历过 1975 年海城地震预报成功的喜悦后，也承受了 1976 年唐山地震和 2008 年汶川地震等大地震造成的重大损失。时至今日，人类依然没有摸清地震的"脾气"。

　　但是，探索的脚步从来都没有止息。地震波是目前已知的唯一能够穿透地球介质内部的物理波，是点亮地球内部的一盏明灯。地球物理学家利用地震波记载的各种信息，探索地球内部的结构与特征，推动着人类对地震的认识不断向前。真理的海洋无边无际，唐·亨伯格教授就是那个发现美丽贝壳的幸运儿。

唐·亨伯格于 1967 年获得了美国加州大学圣迭戈分校博士学位，曾在麻省理工学院和普林斯顿大学任教，于 1970 年转到著名的加州理工学院地震实验室工作，且在此度过他余下的职业生涯。从 1998 年到 2003 年，他担任该地震实验室的主任。亨伯格教授治学严谨，勤于实践，很多他曾经指导的学生已经成为国际知名的地震与地球物理学家，包括本文集中的多位国内外华人教授与学者，为我国地球物理学、地震学的发展做出了杰出贡献。

亨伯格教授在地震学的研究中利用创造性理论和建模方法，对地球深部结构和地震震源的研究做出了巨大贡献。在这本合集中，收录了亨伯格教授的第一位研究生（查尔斯·兰斯顿，1976 年博士）和最后一位研究生（赖文慧，2020 年博士）共 23 位研究生、博士后或者合作者撰写的 19 篇文章。这 19 篇文章不仅涵盖了亨伯格教授对观测地震数据的认识、对广义射线理论的创新发展、对各种尺度上的从一维到三维地震波形建模的方法、对探索更具有突破性模型空间的开放态度，还包括他在长期科学实践中留给我们的宝贵精神财富和培养教育学生的经验，读者可以从他在与研究生相处的点滴生活中感受到他启发灵感的创新精神、团结协作的协同精神、奖掖后学的奉献精神和热爱生活的乐观精神。

科技创新，贵在传承。相信每一个研究人员，尤其是年轻一代的地震学科研人员和从业人员都能从这本文集中或多或少受到一些启发，让真理的光芒照亮探索的道路。也祝愿我国和世界的地震学事业发展能够更上一个台阶，为了解地球和地震的奥秘，为防灾减灾事业做出应有的贡献！

陈运泰，我国著名地球物理学家。主要从事地震学与地球物理学研究，尤其是地震波与震源的理论与应用研究。1962 年毕业于北京大学地球物理系，1966 年研究生毕业于中国科学院地球物理研究所。1991 年当选为中国科学院学部委员（院士），1999 年当选为第三世界科学院院士。曾任中国地震局地球物理研究所所长，中国地震学会理事长，北京大学地球与空间科学院院长；现任中国地震局地球物理研究所名誉所长和北京大学地球与空间科学院名誉院长。

Preface

Thorne Lay [1] and Xiaodong Song [2]

1. Department of Earth and Planetary Sciences, University of California Santa Cruz, Santa Cruz, CA 95064, USA (Email: tlay@ucsc.edu)

2. School of Earth and Space Sciences, Peking University, Beijing 100871, China (Email: xdsong@pku.edu.cn, xiao.d.song@gmail.com)

Donald Vincent Helmberger, Ph.D. and Smits Family Professor of Geophysics Emeritus at Caltech (Figure 1), one of the primary founders of seismic waveform modeling and an extraordinary scientist, was born on 23 January 1938 and died on 13 August 2020. Don obtained his Ph.D. in 1967 at the University of California San Diego, USA. In 1970, after a two-year appointment as a research associate at MIT and one year on the faculty at Princeton University, Don moved to the Seismological Laboratory at Caltech where he was to spend the rest of his career. From 1998 to 2003 he served as the Director of the Seismo Lab, and he became emeritus in 2017. Key milestones and accomplishments during his life and career are summarized in an oral history (Cohen, 1999), a profile (Zagorski, 2006), and memorials (Caltech, 2020; Lay, 2021). Don received many honors in recognition of his contributions including selection as the first recipient of the American Geophysical Union Lehmann Medal in 1997, election for the Seismological Society of America Society Medal in 2002, and election to the U.S. National Academy of Science in 2004. This book collection, with forwards from distinguished professors Michael Gurnis and Yun-Tai Chen, is intended to provide a more personal insight into his inspirational mentorship and guidance during myriad discoveries about earthquake faulting and earth structures from crust to core from the eyes of many of the ~45 Ph.D. students and postdocs whom he advised or co-advised at the Seismo Lab over the five decades of his career.

Fig. 1   Professor Donald V. Helmberger (1938–2020). Photo courtesy of Caltech Archives

Contributors in this collection span the interval from his first graduate student (Charles Langston, Ph.D. 1976) to his last graduate student (Voon Hui Lai, Ph.D. 2020). The 19 articles are permeated by recurrent themes; Don's passion for looking at seismic data, his innovative development and extensions of Generalized Ray Theory, his enthusiasm for 1D to 3D waveform modeling of seismograms at all distance ranges, his openness to exploring wide model spaces that enabled breakthrough discoveries, his pleasure in working closely, yet loosely, with students, his care for students, and his athletic skills on the football field. The contributions sample the many topics that could be addressed as waveform modeling transformed the discipline of seismology, from upper mantle structure, to lower mantle structure to core structure to finite-source processes of earthquakes large and small. In recounting vivid experiences, the contributors also paint a picture of a master mentor whose great personal attributes inspired a stream of students and postdocs of different personalities and background and turned novices into successful researchers.

When one pauses to think how many of the thousands of papers produced in seismology on these topics directly track back to seminal theoretical advances and modeling approaches introduced by Don Helmberger, one cannot help but be stunned by his impact on the field. He was a true Master of Seismology. But one also sees the steadfast joy, kind-heartedness, and pleasure with which he made this impact with his students and postdocs. He pursued science with integrity and positivity, engendering comradery rather than competition in the effort to extract information from seismic recordings. Always smiling, always keen to chat, always encouraging; his attributes come through clearly in the articles assembled here. We hope the inspirations that many of us had the fortune to receive from him can be inspirational to new generations of students and mentors alike. We also hope the insights into this great seismologist and great man prompt all readers to embrace his philosophy of life and science.

Earthquake science is a global endeavor by nature. Don made his global impact not only by his science but also by a large number of international students including a high percentage of Chinese students who were supervised by him or by his students in their own careers. In this collection, Chinese translations are provided for all of the contributions. We hope the translations are more accessible to a vast readership in China.

The articles in this book collection were originally published in a special issue of the journal *Earthquake Science* (Lay and Song, 2022). We thank many who helped make the book possible. The authors and reviewers of the memorial articles responded in a very short time. Don's surviving spouse Annette Sellon provided most of the photos in the front pages. The Seismological Laboratory of Caltech provided a list of Ph.D. graduates who worked under Don's guidance. A group of graduate students from Peking University helped with the translations and corrections: Qiwen Zhu (Gurnis' Forward and Chapter 13), Kaixin Wu (Yun-tai Chen's Foreword and Chapter 11), Wenzhi Fan (Yun-tai Chen's Foreword), Feiyi Wang (Preface and Chapter 1), Wei Liu (Chapters 2 and 4), Zexin Wang (Chapter 3), Naidan Yun (Chapters 5 and 12), Jingnan Sun (Chapters 6 and 7), Tian Li (Chapters 8 and 14), Zeyan Zhao (Chapters 9 and 10), Weifan Lu (Chapter 15), Yuan Yao (Chapter 16), Xuezhen Zhang (Chapters 17 and 18), and Xinyu Jiang (Chapter 19). Xiaodong Song also acknowledges administrative assistances from Ms. Jing Huang and Ms. Linyue Wu.

References

Caltech (2020). Donald V. Helmberger (1938-2020). https://www.caltech.edu/about/news/donald-v-helmberger-19382020. Accessed 3 September 2020

Cohen SK (1999). Interview with Donald V. Helmberger. https://oralhistories.library.caltech.edu/155/. Accessed 3 September 2020

Lay T (2021). Donald V. Helmberger (1938-2020). Seismol Res Lett **92**(2A): 621–622.

Lay T and Song XD (2022). Preface to the special memorial issue for Professor Donald V. Helmberger. Earthq Sci **35**(1): 1−2 doi: 10.1016/j.eqs.2022.01.020

Zagorski N (2006). Profile of Don Helmberger. Proc Natl Acad Sci USA **103**(7): 2009–2011.

Thorne Lay is currently Distinguished Professor of Earth and Planetary Sciences, University of California Santa Cruz (UCSC). He completed his Ph.D. at Caltech in 1983 with Prof. Helmberger as his primary thesis advisor. He was then on the faculty at the University of Michigan for six years before joining UCSC. He is a recipient of the Lehmann Medal of the American Geophysical Union, the Reid Medal of the Seismological Society of America, the Gold Medal of the Royal Astronomical Society and is a member of the U.S. National Academy of Science. His webpage can be found at: https://websites.pmc.ucsc.edu/~seisweb/thorne_lay/.

Xiaodong Song is currently Chair Professor at School of Earth and Space Sciences, Peking University. He received his M.S. degree in 1991 and Ph.D. degree in 1994 at Caltech with Prof. Helmberger as his thesis advisor. He then joined Lamont-Doherty Earth Observatory of Columbia University as a postdoc fellow and later as Associate Research Scientist and Storke-Doherty Lecturer. He subsequently served on the faculty of Department of Geology at University of Illinois at Urbana-Champaign from 1999 to 2020 before relocating to Beijing, China. His work on the inner core differential rotation was named as a breakthrough of the year by *Science* magazine (1996). He received Doornbos Prize by the Studies of Earth Deep Interior Committee of the International Union of Geophysics and Geodesy (1996), Outstanding Overseas Young Scientist

Award by the Natural Science Foundation of China (1998), Solid Earth Distinguished Lectureship by the Asia Oceania Geosciences Society (AOGS) (2016). He currently serves as the Editor-in-Chief of *Earthquake Science*. His webpage can be found at: http://geophy.pku.edu.cn/people/songxiaodong/english/index.html.

前　言

索恩·莱[1] 和宋晓东[2]

1 美国加州大学圣克鲁兹分校地球和行星科学学院

2 北京大学地球与空间科学学院

　　唐·亨伯格博士，是加州理工学院施密茨家族地球物理学荣休教授（图 1），地震波形建模的主要创始人之一，也是卓越的科学家。他出生于 1938 年 1 月 23 日，于 2020 年 8 月 13 日去世。唐（Don）于 1967 年在美国加州大学圣迭戈分校获得博士学位。1970 年，唐（Don）在麻省理工学院担任了两年的助理研究员，并在普林斯顿大学任教一年后，转到了加州理工学院的地震实验室，他在那里度过了余下的职业生涯。从 1998 年到 2003 年，他担任地震实验室主任，并于 2017 年荣誉退休。口述历史（Cohen, 1999）、简介（Zagorski, 2006）和纪念文集（Caltech, 2020；Lay, 2021）中总结了他一生和职业生涯中的主要里程碑和成就。唐（Don）获得了许多荣誉，以表彰他的贡献，包括被选为美国地球物理联合会莱曼奖章的首位获得者（1997），美国地震学会里德奖章获得者（2002），及美国科学院院士（2004）。这本合集，以及两位著名教授迈克尔·歌尼斯和陈运泰写的序言，旨在从不同人的回忆中，走近唐（Don）在地震断层和从地壳到地核中的无数发现，了解他对后辈鼓舞人心的指导。这些回忆来自他职业生涯中在地震实验室提供指导或共同指导的约 45 名博士生和博士后中多位的亲身经历。

图 1　唐·亨伯格（1938—2020）（照片由加州理工学院档案馆提供）

本文集的撰稿人横跨了他的第一个研究生（查尔斯·兰斯顿，博士学位，1976）到最后一个研究生（赖文慧，博士学位，2020）。这19篇文章有很多高频的主题：唐（Don）对观测地震数据的热情、对广义射线理论的创新发展、对各种尺度上的地震图从一维到三维波形建模的热情、对探索更具有突破性模型空间的开放态度、与学生密切而又宽松合作的乐趣、对学生的关心，以及他在足球场上的飒爽英姿。波形建模从上地幔到下地幔、地核，再到大大小小地震的有限源过程，深刻地改变了地震学学科，这些文章涉及了许多能被波形建模解决的问题。在讲述这些生动的经历时，作者们也描绘了一位大师级导师的风采，他伟大的个人特质激励了一批批具有不同个性和背景的学生和博士后，并使他们一个个从新手逐步走上了成功学者的道路。

当有一天有人静下心来想一想在地震学领域发表的这些数以千计的论文中，有多少会直接追溯到唐·亨伯格引入的开创性理论和建模方法时，他就一定会为唐（Don）在这个领域的影响感到震惊。他是真正的地震学大师。同时，人们也看到了他在对学生和博士后产生这种影响中所获得的坚定的喜悦、善良和快乐。他鼓励合作而非竞争，以正直和积极的态度追求科学，致力于从地震记录中提取有用的信息。这些文章中清楚地体现出来了他的特质：总是面带微笑，善于与人沟通，鼓励后辈。我们希望更多的人可以有幸从他那里获得灵感，从而对新一代的学生和导师们产生启发作用。我们也希望对这位伟大的地震学家和伟人的解读，能促使更多的读者走近他的人生，了解他的科学哲学。

地震科学本质上是一项全球性的事业，唐（Don）的全球影响力不只体现在他的科学贡献上，也体现在他所指导或者他的学生在自己的职业生涯中指导的大量国际学生上，其中包括很大比例的中国学生。在这本文集中，所有章节均提供了中文翻译。我们希望这些译文可以帮助广大中国读者更容易理解唐（Don）和地震学。

这本文集中的文章最初发表在 *Earthquake Science* 杂志特刊上（Lay and Song, 2022）。我们感谢所有为这本书出版提供帮助的人。每篇文章的作者和审稿人在很短的时间内做出了回应。唐的遗孀安妮特·塞隆提供了本书前文中的大部分照片。加州理工学院地震学实验室提供了在唐的指导下毕业的博士生名单。北京大学的一批研究生为文集翻译、校正和文字整理提供了帮助：祝奇文（歌尼斯的序言和第13章）、吴恺欣（陈运泰的序言和第11章）、樊文智（陈运泰的序言）、王非翊（前言和第1章）、刘威（第2和第4章）、王泽鑫（第3章）、运乃丹（第5和第12章）、孙景南（第6和第7章）、李田（第8和第14章）、赵泽严（第9和第10章）、陆威帆（第15章）、姚圆（第16章）、张学臻（第17和第18章）和江欣余（第19章）。宋晓东还感谢黄静女士和吴琳月女士提供的行政协助。

参 考 文 献

Caltech (2020). Donald V. Helmberger (1938-2020). https://www.caltech.edu/about/news/donald-v-helmberger-19382020. Accessed 3 September 2020

Cohen SK (1999). Interview with Donald V. Helmberger. https://oralhistories.library.caltech.edu/155/. Accessed 3 September 2020

Lay T (2021). Donald V. Helmberger (1938-2020). Seismol Res Lett **92**(2A): 621–622.

Lay T and Song XD (2022). Preface to the special memorial issue for Professor Donald V. Helmberger. Earthq Sci **35**(1): 1−2 doi: 10.1016/j.eqs.2022.01.020

Zagorski N (2006). Profile of Don Helmberger. Proc Natl Acad Sci USA **103**(7): 2009−2011.

　　索恩·莱目前是加州大学圣克鲁斯分校（UCSC）地球与行星科学杰出教授。他 1983 年在加州理工学院完成了博士学位，唐·亨伯格教授是他的主要论文导师。在加入 UCSC 之前，他在密歇根大学任教了六年。他是美国地球物理学会莱曼奖章、美国地震学会里德奖章、皇家天文学会金奖章的获得者，并且是美国国家科学院院士。他的主页是 https://websites.pmc.ucsc.edu/~seisweb/thorne_lay/。

　　宋晓东现任北京大学地球与空间科学学院讲席教授，国家级人才计划专家。于 1994 年在加州理工学院获得博士学位，唐·亨伯格教授是他的论文导师。随后，他加入哥伦比亚大学拉蒙特-多尔蒂地球观测站，做博士后，后来担任副研究员和讲师。他于 1999 年加入伊利诺伊大学厄巴纳-香槟分校地质系，从助理教授到终身正教授工作 20 多年，于 2020 年全职回国。他在内核差速旋转方面的工作被《科学》杂志评为年度（1996）十大突破之一。他曾获得国际地球物理和大地测量学联合会（IUGG）地球深部内部研究委员会多恩博斯奖（1996），中国自然科学基金委海外杰出青年基金（B 类）（1998），亚洲大洋洲地球科学学会（AOGS）固体地球杰出讲座(2016)。目前担任国际英文期刊《地震科学》（英文版）主编。他的主页是：http://geophy.pku.edu.cn/people/songxiaodong/。

目　　录

Chapter 1. Donald V. Helmberger's art and science of waveforms

Charles Langston[*]

Center for Earthquake Research and Information, University of Memphis, Memphis, TN 38152, USA

[*]**Correspondence:** clangstn@memphis.edu

Citation: Langston CA (2022). Donald V. Helmberger's art and science of waveforms. Earthq Sci **35**(1): 3−5 doi: 10.1016/j.eqs.2022.01.001

I arrived at the Caltech Seismo Lab early in May 1972. The faculty and graduate students had the run of an old mansion (Donnelly Lab) that was slightly tattered around the edges but conducive to both all-night work sessions and goofing off since it still had well-kept grounds that included a tennis court. Most of the graduate students occupied the large dining room on the first floor and we hunted out our advisors, when needed, by trying their offices around the rest of the house, checking out the tennis courts, or visiting the coffee pot in the basement.

Since I arrived several months before the Fall 1972 semester, I was fortunate to be allowed to start working on graduate research. Don was assigned to be my advisor and I visited him in his second-floor office for a first encounter. He got down to business rather quickly by asking me point blank "why do you want to study geophysics?" I was totally unprepared for this question and, in fact, was probably unprepared for any other question as well. While an undergrad at Case Western Reserve, I had developed a burning hate for computer work but an intense love for geology. For some reason, I also did not like seismology, maybe because it was too esoteric, and vowed never to become a seismologist. So, I sat there stunned in front of this seismologist and finally mumbled something about wanting to study the Earth. I think Don just looked at me for a moment probably thinking that here was a guy without a whole lot of promise but that he would run me through some paces over the summer to see what would happen.

My first impression of Don was that here was a real scientist doing inscrutable things that I would really like to understand. He was very young, obviously confident and a bit stand-offish, but seemed to be a straight-ahead nice guy without a big ego. After that initial check-out question there was never a time where Don treated me (or any of his other students) other than an equal colleague. I think that this kind of behavior was what made the lab an incredible learning environment. To be treated as an equal meant that a student had to work hard to catch up with the faculty to earn that place of equality, at least in our own minds.

Don had me looking at seismograms that first summer. He had finished a short paper with an undergraduate intern on the arrival times of regional Pn and PL waves (York and Helmberger, 1973) and wanted to extend that project to determine crustal and upper mantle structure from the waveforms. Of course, I had no idea what to do but picked up some useful skills in digitizing analog seismograms that I used later in my thesis work. It would take another 7 years to complete this program of modeling Pnl waves through his work with staff member Gladys Engen (Helmberger and Engen, 1980). Even so, that open-ended dive into seismological research from Don's new perspective of using waveform shapes and amplitudes has stuck with me over my entire career. While staring at the wiggles on the paper that first summer I wondered if there were other ways of recording seismic data that would give an analyst direct knowledge of the properties of the seismic waves so they could be understood much more quickly. This question stewed for many years in my own research and has resulted in some very interesting new techniques in array seismology (e.g., Langston and Liang, 2008; Langston, 2021). I fully attribute this to the questions that Don exposed me to that first summer.

Don was too young to be considered a father figure to his students at that time. Even so, as I look back to his mentoring, it struck me that he had one characteristic that my own father displayed. That characteristic was allowing freedom. Don allowed me and his other students freedom to pursue our work wherever it led. As graduate student life settled in, Don never dictated what should be done or when it should be done, we simply (and energetically) followed the science hunt to wherever it went. This was an incredible gift which the ensuing years have validated over and over seeing how faculty at other institutions treat (or mistreat) their students.

The curriculum at the Lab was unusual in that every course was "Advanced". There was no preparation with lower-level courses that you often find in other university programs. That first year Don taught Advanced Seismology 261a and shared Advanced Seismology 261c with Dave Harkrider. There were no books, just notes which the students dutifully transcribed from the blackboard. Don's lectures were quite thorough and addressed the theory behind his cutting-edge science. During that first quarter and continuing throughout the first year, I felt something shift in terms of my appreciation for seismology. Don's lectures were pointed towards an end of developing ways to understanding the Earth by taking an almost absurdist viewpoint that every wiggle on the seismogram means something. Each feature of a waveform can say something about how seismic waves were produced by earthquakes or how they were affected by their propagation through the Earth.

As an example of how good these courses were, Don and I published a paper based on a homework problem from 261c. Working the material on using the Representation Theorem and resulting wave potentials from the Advanced Seismology course, I wanted to know what would be needed to compute synthetic seismograms from such a general source. Don was working on his seminal work on modeling teleseismic body waves from earthquakes using optic ray approximations of Cagniard-deHoop solutions for sources in plane layered media (Helmberger, 1974). However, this paper did not include the full representation of an arbitrarily oriented dislocation source but only had two out of three major source terms. I was surprised when he came to my desk in the student area and asked for my derivation. I was floored when he suggested that we write it all up in a publication (Langston and Helmberger, 1975). This was a defining moment in my graduate career since it was the first time that I had done something that would prove to be useful in Don's research and the research of many others afterward.

There is one story that I have told my students over the years on the magical wisdom of Don as a research advisor. My first project that developed into a publication involved using Don's famous computer codes to make plots of synthetic seismograms to compare to the real seismogram data (Langston and Helmberger, 1974). I spent a week of late nights at the Caltech computer center on campus running the code and generated many sheets of Calcomp pen plots of seismograms. (A Calcomp plotter was the main way to make line drawings on the IBM mainframe computer. It consisted of a roll of graph paper and computer-controlled pen to draw each graph.) I had cut each seismogram from the large plots and taped them on other sheets of paper to make record sections of the synthetics to compare with our data. I brought my opus to Don in his office. His first comment was, "can you use more tape?" Obviously, he was amazed at how I had plastered all the cut-and-paste plots with tape; the sarcasm was noted. Ten seconds later he said, "it's wrong". It was matter of fact. I tried to argue. I told him how much time I had used sitting around the computer center and that I did everything right. "Nope, it's wrong." I was frustrated but we went over the program input and showed me a parameter that was not set correctly. It was then that I learned that "experience" was a very powerful tool when dealing with complicated problems. I have been in exactly the same position with many of my own students over the years when they bring in their work having to say, "Nope, it's wrong", and then explaining why. I usually tell this story to soften the blow.

One of Don's quirks is that he might stare off into space at random times during a conversation. Some students found this unsettling but I was a bit amused by it since I sometimes do the same thing. I simply chalked it up to him trying to fit what he had just heard in the conversation with his intuition. Don was always heavily engaged in dreaming up reasons why a seismogram might look the way that it does. After a while, I came to the conclusion that Don did not do science in a "quantitative" way but did his best work with his intuition. Intuition, at least in my experience, needs some space and some time for a type of activity not too different from daydreaming. When faced with a statement, question, or observation that didn't immediately fall into line with his thinking, Don's internal intuition processor would kick in, he would turn his head to the right, and stare off for a while leaving the student to wonder what was going on.

Even though Don was at the forefront of computational seismology and had a deep grasp of the theoretical and mathematical bases of wave propagation, my view was that Don was more an artist than scientist. Perhaps more accurately, Don did excellent science by bringing his intuition to bear on the problem and then using the math to check it out. To me this was Don's gift and it deepened the way I looked at the work of other scientists as well as how I did my own work.

Don also presented a strong message of academic honesty through his actions with his students. After the first two years of work with him, I was fortunate that my own work took off and that I basically operated independently. I could find a problem, solve the problem, and then write up the results for a publication (Langston, 1976, 1977a, b, 1978; Langston and Butler, 1976; Burdick and Langston, 1977; Langston and Blum, 1977). I and my coauthors would show Don what we had accomplished, but he would not allow himself to be a coauthor on the publication because he felt that he hadn't contributed to the work. Not only did this reinforce the feeling that students were equals to the faculty, but in years after, I got many uncomprehending looks from my peers when I told them that this was standard operating procedure at the Lab. Most faculty I know would never do this even under the same situation where the student did all of the work.

Working with Don in those 5 years at the Lab was among my most significant life experiences. He was a talented guide for turning graduate students into skilled, professional scientists. There is no doubt in my mind that his approach to science and his mentoring were the primary reasons that I have had success in my own career. I am grateful that I was one of his students.

References

Burdick LJ and Langston CA (1977). Modeling crustal structure through the use of converted phases in teleseismic body-wave forms. Bull Seismol Soc Am **67**(3): 677–691.

Helmberger DV (1974). Generalized ray theory for shear dislocations. Bull Seismol Soc Am **64**(1): 45–64.

Helmberger DV and Engen GR (1980). Modeling the long-period body waves from shallow earthquakes at regional ranges. Bull Seismol Soc Am **70**(5): 1699–1714.

Langston CA and Helmberger DV (1974). Interpretation of body and Rayleigh waves from NTS to Tucson. Bull Seismol Soc Am **64**(6): 1919–1929.

Langston CA and Helmberger DV (1975). A procedure for modelling shallow dislocation sources. Geophys J Roy Astr Soc **42**(1): 117–130.

Langston CA (1976). A body wave inversion of the Koyna, India, earthquake of December 10, 1967, and some implications for body wave focal mechanisms. J Geophys Res **81**(14): 2517–2529.

Langston CA and Butler R (1976). Focal mechanism of the August 1, 1975 Oroville earthquake. Bull Seismol Soc Am **66**(4): 1111–1120.

Langston CA (1977a). Corvallis, Oregon, crustal and upper mantle receiver structure from teleseismic P and S waves. Bull Seismol Soc Am **67**(3): 713–724.

Langston CA (1977b). The effect of planar dipping structure on source and receiver responses for constant ray parameter. Bull Seismol Soc Am **67**(4): 1029–1050.

Langston CA and Blum DE (1977). The April 29, 1965, Puget Sound earthquake and the crustal and upper mantle structure of western Washington. Bull Seismol Soc Am **67**(3): 693–711.

Langston CA (1978). The February 9, 1971 San Fernando earthquake: a study of source finiteness in teleseismic body waves. Bull Seismol Soc Am **68**(1): 1–29.

Langston CA and Liang CT (2008). Gradiometry for polarized seismic waves. J Geophys Res **113**(B8): B08305.

Langston CA (2021). Phased array analysis incorporating the continuous wavelet transform. Bull Seismol Soc Am **111**(5): 2780–2798.

York JE and Helmberger DV (1973). Low-velocity zone variations in the southwestern United States. J Geophys Res **78**(11): 1883–1886.

Charles Langston is currently Professor of Geophysics, Center for Earthquake Research and Information (CERI), University of Memphis.   Serving the Center as Director since 2008, he recently stepped down to rejoin the faculty to pursue research interests in field seismology, seismo-acoustics, gradiometry, and array seismology.   He completed his M.S. and Ph.D. degrees in 1974 and 1976, respectively, with Prof. Helmberger as his primary advisor and then stayed for a year as a postdoc with Prof. Helmberger.   He subsequently served on the faculty of the Department of Geosciences at the Pennsylvania State University from 1977 to 2000 before joining CERI in 2000. He has served as President of the Seismological Society of America (1990) and Editor of the *Bulletin of the SSA* (1992-1995).   He is a Fellow of the American Geophysical Union (2003), a Dunavant Professor in the College of Arts and Sciences, University of Memphis (2008-2011), and recipient of the Jesuit Seismological Association Award of the Eastern Section of the SSA (2011).   His webpage can be found at http://www.ceri.memphis.edu/people/clangstn/.

第 1 章　唐·亨伯格的波形科学与艺术

查尔斯·兰斯顿
美国孟菲斯大学地震研究与信息中心

引用：Langston C A (2022). Donald V. Helmberger's art and science of waveforms. Earthq Sci **35**(1): 3-5 doi: 10.1016/j.eqs.2022.01.001

我于 1972 年 5 月初来到加州理工学院地震实验室。教职员工和研究生们在一座古老的大楼里（唐纳利实验室）工作。这座大楼的边角略显破烂，但方便通宵工作和偶尔偷懒，因为它仍然有一些维护完好的场地，包括一个网球场。大多数研究生们在一楼的大餐厅工作，当我们有必要找导师时，就会去他们在大楼其他地方的办公室、网球场或者地下室的咖啡壶旁边寻找。

我在 1972 年秋季学期时提前了几个月到校，很幸运地早早开始着手研究生的研究工作。我和唐（Don）的第一次见面是在他二楼的办公室，当时唐（Don）被学院安排做我的导师，我去他的办公室看望他。见面后他直截了当地问我："你为什么想研究地球物理学？"我对这个问题完全没有准备，事实上，我可能对任何其他问题也没有准备。在凯斯西储大学读本科时，我对计算机工作产生了强烈的抵触心理，但对地质学有着强烈的热爱。出于某种原因（也许是因为它太深奥了），我也不喜欢地震学，并发誓永远不会成为地震学家。所以，我坐在那里，在这位地震学家面前目瞪口呆，最后嘀咕了想要研究地球之类的话。我想唐（Don）只是看了我一会儿，可能以为这是一个没有太多希望的人，但他决定在整个夏天带我做点东西，看看会发生什么。

我对唐（Don）的第一印象是，这是一个真正的科学家，他正在做着我真正想要理解但深奥难懂的事情。他很年轻，显然很自信，甚至有点自负，但似乎是一个直率的好人，没有很大的架子。在那最初的发问之后，唐（Don）总是平等地像对同事一样对待我（或他的任何其他学生）。我认为这种做法使实验室拥有了一个良好的学习环境。因为如果被平等对待，就意味着学生必须努力工作来赶上教师，这样才能与这种平等的地位相配，至少在我们自己的心目中是这样。

第一年夏天，唐（Don）让我看了地震图。他已经和一名本科实习生一起完成了一篇关于区域 Pn 和 PL 波到达时间的短篇论文（York and Helmberger，1973）。他希望将其扩展，以从波形中确定地壳和上地幔结构。当然，我一开始并不知道该怎么做，不过我在数字化模拟地震图方面学到了一些有用的技能，这些技能对我后来的论文工作大有裨益。这之后他和同事格拉迪丝·恩金（Gladys Engen）又花了七年的时间来完成 PnL 波形建模的项目（Helmberger and Engen，1980）。即便如此，唐（Don）从使用波形形状和振幅的新视角进行的地震学的开放式深入研究，一直影响着我的整个职业生涯。第一年夏天，当我盯着纸上记录的地震波形的摆动时，我想知道是否有其他记录地震数据的方法，以便让分析人员直接地了解地震波的性质，从而更快地理解它们。这个问题在我自己的研究中酝酿了很多年，并产生了阵列地震学中一些非常有趣的新技术（例如，Langston and Liang，2008；Langston，2021）。我觉得这完全得益于唐（Don）在第一个夏天向我提出的问题。

唐（Don）当时太年轻了，对他的学生来说并没有父辈的那种形象。即便如此，当我回忆他曾经的指导时，我突然意识到他依然有一个我自己父亲才有的特征——给我自由。唐（Don）允许我和其他学生自由地从事我们的工作。随着研究生生活步入正轨，唐（Don）从未命令我们应该做什么或什么时候应该完成什么，我们只是（并且精力充沛地）朝着科学竭力而为。这是一份不可思议的礼物，特别是在随后的几年里，当我看到其他机构的教师如何对待（或虐待）他们的学生，这一点便得到了一遍又一遍的验证。

实验室的课程不同寻常，因为每门课程都是"高级"的。学生经常没有在之前的大学课程中学过对应的"初等"课程。第一年，唐（Don）教授高级地震学 261a（课程号），并与戴夫・哈克赖德（Dave Harkrider）共同教授了高级地震学 261c（课程号）。没有书，学生们只能尽职尽责地埋头从黑板上抄录笔记。唐（Don）的课讲得非常透彻，直达前沿科学背后的理论本质。从第一季度开始一直到第一年结束，我感觉到我对地震学的看法发生了一些变化。唐（Don）的讲课指向了理解地球的方法发展的终点，他假设了一种近乎"荒诞"的观点，即地震图上的每一个摆动都有其意义。波形的每个特征都可以说明地震波是如何由地震产生的，或者它们在地球上的传播是如何影响它们的。

有个例子，关于唐（Don）和我发表了一篇基于 261c（课程号）作业问题的论文，可以说明这些课程有多么棒。在使用高级地震学课程中的表示定理和推导得到的波场的势的材料时，我想知道从这样一个广义源计算合成地震图需要什么。唐（Don）正在研究他的开创性工作，即使用卡尼亚尔-德胡普（Cagniard-deHoop）方法的光学射线近似来模拟平面分层介质中的地震震源产生的远震体波（Helmberger，1974）。然而，文中没有包括任意方向位错源的完整表示，而只有包含了 3 个主要震源项中的两个。当他来到我在学生区的桌子前并要求我推导时，我感到很惊讶。当他建议我们把所有东西都写出来一起出版时（Langston and Helmberger，1975），我难掩激动，因为这是我第一次做一些对唐（Don）和后来许多其他人的研究来说有用的事情，因此，这是我研究生生涯中的一个决定性时刻。

多年来，我都会向我的学生讲述一个唐（Don）展现他作为导师的神奇智慧的故事。我的第一个工作成果发表时，使用了唐（Don）著名的计算机代码，从而绘制合成地震图，用来与真实的地震图数据进行比较（Langston and Helmberger，1974）。我整整一周都在加州理工校园内的计算机中心熬夜运行代码，并生成了许多 Calcomp 笔绘的地震图（Calcomp 绘图仪是在 IBM 大型计算机上绘制线条图的主要方式。它由一卷方格纸和计算机控制的笔组成，用于绘制每个图形）。我从大块原图上剪下了每个地震图，并将它们贴在其他纸上来制作合成数据的记录剖面，以便与我们的数据进行比较。我把我的作品带到了唐（Don）的办公室。他的第一句话是："你还能用更多的胶带吗？"显然，他对我用胶带粘贴的操作感到惊讶。我感受到了他暗含的讽刺。十秒钟后，他说："这是错误的。"这是事实，但我当时试图争辩。我告诉他我花了多少时间坐在电脑旁边，我做的都是正确的。"不，这是错误的。" 唐（Don）坚持道。我很沮丧，但他带着我检查了程序输入，并向我指出了一个设置错误的参数。就在那时，我了解到"经验"在处理复杂问题时是一个非常强大的工具。多年来，我和我的许多学生也经常处于上述这种完全相同的位置，当学生带来他们的工作时，我不得不说，"不，这是错误的"，然后解释为什么。我通常讲这个故事来减轻对他们的打击。

唐（Don）的一个怪癖是，在和别人谈话时，他随时可能会望着空气发呆。有些学生觉得这令人不安，但我觉得有点好笑，因为我有时会做同样的事情。我只是简单地把它归结为他试图用他的直觉来消化他刚刚在谈话中听到的内容。唐（Don）总是忙于构想地震图看起来是那样的原因。一段时间以后，我得出的结论是，唐（Don）没有以"定量"的方式做科学，而是用他的直觉做了他最好的工作。直觉，至少在我的经验中，是一种需要一些空间和时间来做的和白日梦没有太大区别的活动。当一个陈述、问题或观测结果并没有立即符合他的想法时，唐（Don）脑中的直觉处理器就会启动，他会把头转向右边，盯着空气看一会儿，不免会让学生好奇是怎么回事。

尽管唐（Don）处于计算地震学的最前沿，并且对波传播的理论和数学基础有深刻的了解，但我的观点是，唐（Don）更像是一个艺术家而不是科学家。也许更准确地说，唐（Don）在科学方面做得很好，他把自己的直觉和问题联系起来，然后用数学来检验它。对我来说，这是唐（Don）的天赋，这加深了我对看待其他科学家工作的方式，以及我如何做自己的工作的认识。

唐（Don）还通过他对学生们的言传身教，向他们传达了学术诚信的坚定理念。在与他一起工作的头两年之后，我很幸运，自己的工作终于迈向正轨，基本上可以独立运作。我可以独立发现问题，解决问题，然后发表结果（Langston，1976，1977a，1977b，1978；Langston and Butler，1976；Burdick and Langston，1977；Langston and Blum，1977）。我和我的合著者会向唐（Don）展示我们取得的成就，但他不允许自己成为这些成果的合著者，因为他觉得自己没有为这项工作做出贡献。这不仅强化了学生与教师平等的感觉，而且在那之后的岁月里，当我告诉他们这是地震实验室的标准操作流程时，我从同行们那里看到了许多不理解的表情。我认识的大多数教师都不会这样做，即使在学生完成所有工作的情况下也是如此。

在实验室的那五年里，与唐（Don）一起工作是我最重要的人生经历之一。他是一位才华横溢的导师，能将研究生转变为熟练的专业科学家。毫无疑问，在我看来，他的科学方法和他的指导是我在自己的职业生涯中取得成功的主要原因。我很感激我是他的学生之一。

参 考 文 献

Burdick LJ and Langston CA (1977). Modeling crustal structure through the use of converted phases in teleseismic body-wave forms. Bull Seismol Soc Am **67**(3): 677–691.

Helmberger DV (1974). Generalized ray theory for shear dislocations. Bull Seismol Soc Am **64**(1): 45–64.

Helmberger DV and Engen GR (1980). Modeling the long-period body waves from shallow earthquakes at regional ranges. Bull Seismol Soc Am **70**(5): 1699–1714.

Langston CA and Helmberger DV (1974). Interpretation of body and Rayleigh waves from NTS to Tucson. Bull Seismol Soc Am **64**(6): 1919–1929.

Langston CA and Helmberger DV (1975). A procedure for modelling shallow dislocation sources. Geophys J Roy Astr Soc **42**(1): 117–130.

Langston CA (1976). A body wave inversion of the Koyna, India, earthquake of December 10, 1967, and some implications for body wave focal mechanisms. J Geophys Res **81**(14): 2517–2529.

Langston CA and Butler R (1976). Focal mechanism of the August 1, 1975 Oroville earthquake. Bull Seismol Soc Am **66**(4): 1111–1120.

Langston CA (1977a). Corvallis, Oregon, crustal and upper mantle receiver structure from teleseismic P and S waves. Bull Seismol Soc Am **67**(3): 713–724.

Langston CA (1977b). The effect of planar dipping structure on source and receiver responses for constant ray parameter. Bull Seismol Soc Am **67**(4): 1029–1050.

Langston CA and Blum DE (1977). The April 29, 1965, Puget Sound earthquake and the crustal and upper mantle structure of western Washington. Bull Seismol Soc Am **67**(3): 693–711.

Langston CA (1978). The February 9, 1971 San Fernando earthquake: a study of source finiteness in teleseismic body waves. Bull Seismol Soc Am **68**(1): 1–29.

Langston CA and Liang CT (2008). Gradiometry for polarized seismic waves. J Geophys Res **113**(B8): B08305.

Langston CA (2021). Phased array analysis incorporating the continuous wavelet transform. Bull Seismol Soc Am **111**(5): 2780–2798.

York JE and Helmberger DV (1973). Low-velocity zone variations in the southwestern United States. J Geophys Res **78**(11): 1883–1886.

查尔斯·兰斯顿目前是孟菲斯大学地震研究与信息中心 (center for earthquake research and information, CERI) 地球物理学教授。他自 2008 年起担任该中心主任，最近卸任后重新加入教职，从事现场地震学、地震声学、梯度测量和阵列地震学的研究。主要在亨伯格 (Helmberger) 教授的指导下，他分别于 1974 年和 1976 年获得了硕士和博士学位。博士毕业后他在亨伯格教授那里做了一年的博士后。随后，他于 1977 年至 2000 年在宾夕法尼亚州立大学地球科学系任教，然后于 2000 年加入孟菲斯大学地震研究与信息中心（CERI）。他曾担任美国地震学会主席（1990 年）和 BSSA 编辑（1992~1995 年)。他是美国地球物理联合会会士（2003 年），孟菲斯大学艺术与科学学院的杜纳万特教授（2008~2011 年），以及美国地震学会东区的耶稣地震协会奖获得者（2011 年）。他的主页是http://www.ceri.memphis.edu/people/clangstn/。

Chapter 2. A graduate student experience with Professor Donald V. Helmberger

Thorne Lay[*]

Department of Earth and Planetary Sciences, University of California Santa Cruz, Santa Cruz, CA 95064, USA

[*]**Correspondence:** tlay@ucsc.edu

Citation: Lay T (2022). A graduate student experience with Professor Donald V. Helmberger. Earthq Sci **35**(1): 6−10 doi: 10.1016/j.eqs.2022.01.015

A year after the passing of Don Helmberger, it is remarkable how memories of interactions with him over my entire professional career continue to spark affection and admiration. I arrived at Caltech in the summer of 1978 having had typically little exposure to seismology as an undergraduate. One of my academic advisors during my undergraduate program in Geomechanics (a joint program between Geology and Mechanical Engineering at the University of Rochester) was Geoff Davies, who had received his Ph.D. at Caltech working in mineral physics. Perhaps two-weeks-worth of seismology was covered in a survey of geophysics class that I had taken from Geoff, so the field was pretty much unknown to me. Geoff was actually not very encouraging about me possibly going to Caltech when I applied, but I was very keen to head south from the rough Rochester winters so I ignored him. I was a graduate student at the Caltech Seismological Laboratory from 1978 to 1983, and a postdoc there for 9 months longer before leaving for a faculty position at the University of Michigan. It was, nostalgically, a golden age in the Seismo Lab, affording my classmates (Tom Hearn, Marianne C. Walck, Terry C. Wallace, Mario Vassilliou) and myself the opportunity to interact daily with Don Helmberger, Hiroo Kanamori, Don Anderson, David Harkrider, Tom Ahrens, Clarence Allen, and Bernard Minster. Figure 1 shows the Seismo Lab crew sometime in the 1978–1979 academic year. What more could a graduate student ask for than to be surrounded by these creative geophysical pioneers along with more senior graduate students while seeking your own place in the world of seismology?

Fig. 1　Photo of the faculty, research staff and graduate students in the Seismo Lab at Caltech in 1978-1979. Don Helmberger is sitting in the first row, second from the left. The author is sitting in the first row 7th from the left, yes, with no shoes on. From Caltech archives.

The immersive environment upon entry to the Seismo Lab was intoxicating; a true smorgasbord of topics was laid before us in twice daily Seismo Coffee Hour sessions (sometimes greatly exceeding the nominal 1-hour scheduled for each). Key seismological topics of the day were new applications of seismic waveform modeling to study earthquake sources and upper mantle triplication structure, modeling of long-period surface wave spectra for large earthquake faulting models, application of new frequency-dependent parameterizations of seismic attenuation, and seismic array analysis of the new digital regional seismic network (SCARLET) in Southern California. The program encouraged students to work on multiple projects with different faculty, and we were required to develop three research propositions to defend in an oral exam at the beginning of our second year. The open-door policy of the faculty enabled us to readily inquire about possible research projects (you did have to overcome the feeling that you were wasting the faculty's valuable work time), and I initiated efforts on body and surface waves from large earthquakes in the Solomon Islands with Hiroo Kanamori, lateral variation in upper mantle velocity structure and attenuation with Don Helmberger, analysis of the onset of P wave diffraction by the core using SCARLET, guided by senior students Rhett Butler and Larry Ruff, and frequency dependent reflectivity of PKiKP overseen by Don Anderson (OK, that never got published), along with a few additional aborted efforts that I barely remember.

With such different projects and advisors, it was a great opportunity to sample the diverse topics raised in coffee discussions and to feel like you were at the front edge of seismological research. Hiroo Kanamori is a tremendous teacher and patiently introduced me to his surface waves analysis codes and data processing as I undertook manual digitization of hundreds of WWSSN (World-Wide Standardized Seismograph Network; a global network of analog seismic stations deployed in the early 1960s; Peterson and Hutt, 2014) surface wave recordings for analyzing three large doublet events. Don Helmberger guided me to digitize many short-period and long-period P and SH body waveforms from deep earthquakes recorded across North American WWSSN and CSN (Canadian Seismograph Network) stations, seeking to constrain the systematic upper mantle variations in travel times and attenuation that account for the anomalous attributes of signals from nuclear tests at the Nevada Test Site (these were the days of the 1974 bilateral Threshold Test Ban Treaty which constrained underground nuclear tests by the U.S. and Soviet Union to less than 150 kt, so absolute amplitudes that are used for explosion yield estimates had to correctly account for upper mantle heterogeneity). All that digitizing (and the slow deterioration of the WWSSN analog network) made it a pleasure to work with digital data from SCARLET, but I gained an appreciation for how station gains and polarities could change even for digital recordings when sites were visited for maintenance. It was all intensely interesting and exciting to me, and these three topics were presented in my pre-oral exam (a trial-run presented to the graduate student group prior to the real oral exam before the faculty) (Figure 2). Somehow, I managed to pass my oral exam in October 1979, allowing me to continue on toward a Ph.D.

Fig. 2   Copy of the announcement posted for my pre-oral exam on September 27, 1979. Presenting to fellow grad students proved much more stressful than the subsequent exam with the faculty; I think the system was intentionally designed that way to burn-off your nervousness prior to the real exam.

While I continued to work on projects with Hiroo Kanamori, elaborating on his ideas of slip heterogeneities in large earthquakes as framed in the Asperity Model, and working on novel digital recordings for the 1980 Mt. St. Helens eruption and the 1980 Eureka (Gorda Plate) earthquake, my research focus was increasingly under the supervision of Don Helmberger. There were several reasons for this; great earthquake occurrence dropped off during the early 1980s just as I was becoming positioned to analyze their signals, while more senior students like Jeff Givens were working with Hiroo to rapidly advance efficient digital waveform analysis, so the technical side was covered. Also, I had found observational work particularly rewarding as it offered somewhat more frequent surprises; the large data set I had accumulated with Don was revealing travel time and amplitude behaviors (Lay and Helmberger, 1981, 1983a) that were not readily accounted for by the upper mantle variations that we had set out to document. One of the pleasures of looking at a *lot* of data with Don was that I realized he did not have all the answers in advance (unlike Hiroo, who seemingly always knew exactly where a project was going), and there was a sense of mutual discovery.

I began to appreciate that lower mantle structure has three-dimensional heterogeneities (Lay, 1983), only hinted at in the first-generation global tomography images that were beginning to appear, with effects that were readily apparent in the simple waveforms from deep events. Here I learned a profound lesson from Don; the Earth has myriad ways to make a seismic waveform complex (source rupture complexity, slab structure, receiver structure, instrument response, etc.), but if you observe a 'simple' waveform, it is not likely to be a fortuitous outcome of complex interference. Such simple waveforms thus indicate a clean path for which minor features can be reliably interpreted as Earth structure. This is a perspective now suppressed by automatic processing of large data sets, which is a loss. Using Don's generalized ray theory codes for 1-dimensional velocity structures, reproduction of simple waveforms by modifying radial structure had been making great progress in application to regional *Pnl* waveforms and upper mantle discontinuities. Don's one class provided deep understanding of the generalized ray theory method that he had developed based on the Cagniard-de Hoop solution. It was a great class and I sometimes sat in repeat offerings; I still teach a similar class that uses Don's lecture notes (and the nicely typed-up version from Tom Heaton's thesis).

Serendipitously, we gradually noticed that minor features in simple waveforms (Figure 3) had systematic variations with distance from the deep sources, and we sought to understand the origin of these features. This required familiarization with lots of waveforms (another profound lesson I learned from Don was to look at many waveforms carefully so that you could recognize anything unexpected), and we spent a lot of time looking at data (with Don intermittently staring out of his office windows for mysterious interludes). Through this I acquired my skill and enthusiasm for analyzing body waveforms directly from Don.

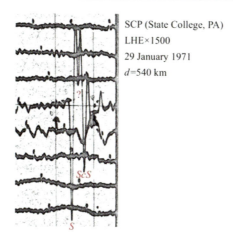

SCP (State College, PA)
LHE×1500
29 January 1971
d=540 km

Fig. 3   Segment of the recording for a deep earthquake below the Sea of Okhotsk on the EW component of the long-period WWSSN instrument (15-100 Sprengnether) at SCP, which operated with a gain of 1500 at 15 s period. The analog record was on a rotating drum that covered one hour per row, with tick marks every minute. The ground shaking shows the impulsive S and ScS arrivals, with an unexplained pulse in between that captured our attention. These signals had to be manually digitized and the horizontal components were digitally rotated to isolate the transverse (SH) component of the signal. I still have copies of several thousand seismograms like this that were used in my work with Don.

It became clear that the unexplained signals we were observing originated from the lower mantle. Don had previously worked on structure above the core-mantle boundary (CMB) when Brian Mitchell visited Caltech on sabbatical in the early 1970s. They produced an exotic model with very high shear velocity increases in a thin layer above the CMB to account for waveform differences between ScSH and ScSV (horizontally and vertically polarized reflections of *S* waves from the CMB) (Mitchell and Helmberger, 1973). Some recent array studies had proposed that a P velocity increase occurred about 170 km above the CMB based on subtle waveform interference effects (Wright and Lyons, 1980), but the prevailing perspective of the lower mantle elastic velocity structure was that it had smooth radial variations all the way down to the lowermost mantle where thermal boundary layer effects produce reduced velocity gradients and increased lateral heterogeneity in the so-called D" region overlying the CMB. I had greatly augmented the data considered by Mitchell and Helmberger (1973), and the waveform feature they had discovered was clearly supported and could be modeled as they suggested (Lay and Helmberger, 1983b), but this most likely involved anisotropic structure of D" rather thin high velocity layers, as was modeled much later (Garnero and Lay, 1997). Our focus was on the unexpected arrivals between direct S and the core reflection ScS like that in Figure 3, which are not accounted for by standard Earth models such as PREM or the JB model. Guided by Don's experience in modeling upper mantle triplications, we introduced a sharp velocity jump of 2% to 3% at the top of the D" region, about 250–300 km above the CMB, with synthetic seismograms being computed using one of his 1D generalized ray theory codes (BOUNCE) accounting for the timing and amplitude of the extra arrivals (Figure 4) as the result of triplication of the wavefront. A triplication results in three arrivals at some distances: some energy turns above the discontinuity, some reflects off it, and some turns below the discontinuity. This was the discovery of the D'' seismic shear velocity discontinuity (Lay and Helmberger, 1983c, d), and it became a focus of my Ph.D. thesis and of much work with students over the next decade. It is probably fair to say that it spurred interest in D'' structure, as related research subsequently expanded greatly. About 20 years later it was established that a phase change in $(Mg,Fe)SiO_3$ magnesium-silicate perovskite (Bridgmanite) in relatively low temperature mantle downwelling regions can plausibly account for the depth, strength and lateral variation of this seismic velocity discontinuity.

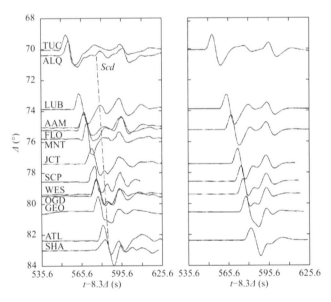

Fig. 4　Profile of digitized WWSSN SH component recordings for the 29 January 1971 event (left panel) showing the systematic move-out with increasing epicentral distance, Δ, for the extra arrival between S and ScS seen in Figure 3, which we labeled Scd. Generalized ray theory synthetics for a model with a 2.75% shear velocity discontinuity at the top of the D'' layer are shown on the right, matching the primary features of the observed signals. From Lay and Helmberger (1983d).

As an advisor, Don was very encouraging of meeting attendance, and prompted me to attend my first Air Force Research conferences, my first international meeting, which was for Mathematical Geophysics, along with other domestic meetings. He always checked to see if a meeting had been enjoyable; he particularly enjoyed international meetings with some attendant extra excursions, and I embraced that practice throughout my career. Don also sustained the Seismo Lab football games on Saturdays and he clearly enjoyed displaying his athletic skills, which outpaced most of the graduate students. These personal touches stuck with you, making you feel like a part of both the local and external scientific communities.

In the last year or two while I was a graduate student and throughout my postdoc appointment, I was a seismological consultant with Woodward Clyde Consultants, for which Don had established a Pasadena research office with funding primarily derived from the Air Force. This involved work using Don's codes ASERIES and BOUNCE to model P wave recordings for underground nuclear tests. Together with Larry Burdick, one of Don's former Ph.D. students, we developed a relative waveform equalization procedure (Intercorrelation) to estimate explosion source time functions, depths, and yields using teleseismic data (Lay et al., 1984a), and to model near-field strong motion recordings for source functions of large explosions along with absolute attenuation operators that matched the far-field observed amplitudes and waveforms (Burdick et al., 1984). Terry and I worked with Don on tectonic release from nuclear explosions using sP arrivals at regional distances and teleseismic amplitude patterns (Lay et al., 1984c). My one joint collaboration with Don and David Harkrider determined broadband source functions for the Amchitka nuclear tests using body and surface wave observations (Lay et al., 1984b); that was my last work while at Caltech.

Over the ensuing years, I had the opportunity to work with Don a bit on the 2004 Sumatra-Andaman earthquake, and in a review of the post-perovskite phase change interpretation of the D" discontinuity after he was elected to the National Academy of Sciences. I also had many visits to Caltech in which we chatted about waveforms and the impressive discoveries he was making with later generations of graduate students. His enthusiasm remained unabated and his advances in core, deep mantle, upper mantle, and earthquake source modeling were breathtaking. We also intersected at many meetings and sometimes enjoyed field trips (Figure 5), where he did his best to get some of his current and former students in trouble (with grizzly bears!). He somehow nominated me to join him in service on the Air Force Technical Applications (AFTAC) Seismic Review Panel, which advises the nuclear test monitoring operations of the government. As a result, we also met three times a year at AFTAC in Florida or in Pinedale, Wyoming, with day-long meetings in windowless rooms, after which Don was always up for a long walk on a beach or in the woods. Mostly we talked about seismic waves on those walks, as always, sharing a wonderful comaraderie born of mutual enthusiasm for the joys of extracting information from seismograms. I will always remember and miss those conversations with my mentor.

Fig. 5   A side excursion to Denali Park, after a Seismological Society of America meeting in Anchorage in 1984. Don is elevating himself above Thorne Lay and Steve Grand, while Heidi Houston relaxes. This excursion was memorable as our group left the bus into the park (illegally) so we could walk across the tundra to see Denali better. Of course, there were grizzly bears, and Don just had to try to get their attention. Photo by John Vidale.

References

Burdick LJ, Wallace TC and Lay T (1984). Modeling near-field and teleseismic observations from the Amchitka test site. J Geophy Res: Solid Earth **89**(B6): 4373–4388.

Garnero EJ and Lay T (1997). Lateral variations in lowermost mantle shear wave anisotropy beneath the north Pacific and Alaska. J Geophy Res: Solid Earth **102**(B4): 8121–8135.

Lay T (1983). Localized velocity anomalies in the lower mantle. Geophys J Int **72**(2): 483–516.

Lay T and Helmberger DV (1981). Body wave amplitude patterns and upper mantle attenuation variations across North America. Geophys J Int **66**(3): 691–726.

Lay T and Helmberger DV (1983a). Body-wave amplitude and travel-time correlations across North America. Bull Seismol Soc Am **73**(4): 1063–1076.

Lay T and Helmberger DV (1983b). The shear-wave velocity gradient at the base of the mantle. J Geophys Res: Solid Earth **88**(B10): 8160– 8170.

Lay T and Helmberger DV (1983c). A shear velocity discontinuity in the lower mantle. Geophys Res Lett **10**(1): 63–66.

Lay T and Helmberger DV (1983d). A lower mantle *S*-wave triplication and the shear velocity structure of D". Geophys J Int **75**(3): 799–838.

Lay T, Burdick LJ and Helmberger DV (1984a). Estimating the yields of the Amchitka tests by waveform intercorrelation. Geophys J Int **78**(1): 181–207.

Lay T, Helmberger DV and Harkrider DG (1984b). Source models and yield-scaling relations for underground nuclear explosions at Amchitka Island. Bull Seismol Soc Am **74**(3): 843–862.

Lay T, Wallace TC and Helmberger DV (1984c). The effects of tectonic release on short-period P waves from NTS explosions. Bull Seismol Soc Am **74**(3): 819–842.

Mitchell BJ and Helmberger DV (1973). Shear velocities at the base of the mantle from observations of *S* and *ScS*. J Geophys Res **78**(26): 6009–6020.

Peterson J and Hutt CR (2014). World-wide standardized seismograph network: A data users guide. U. S. Geological Survey, Reston, pp 74

Wright C and Lyons JA (1980). Further evidence for radial velocity anomalies in the lower mantle. Pure Appl Geophys **119**(1): 137–162.

Thorne Lay is currently Distinguished Professor of Earth and Planetary Sciences, University of California Santa Cruz (UCSC). He completed his Ph.D. at Caltech in 1983 with Prof. Helmberger as his primary thesis advisor. He was then on the faculty at the University of Michigan for six years before joining UCSC.   He is a recipient of the Lehmann Medal of the American Geophysical Union, the Reid Medal of the Seismological Society of America, the Gold Medal of the Royal Astronomical Society and is a member of the U.S. National Academy of Science. His webpage can be found at: https://wcbsites.pmc.ucsc.edu/~seisweb/thorne_lay/.

第 2 章　一段同唐·亨伯格教授的研究生经历

索恩·莱
美国加州大学圣克鲁斯分校地球与行星科学系

引用：Lay T (2022). A graduate student experience with Professor Donald V. Helmberger. Earthq Sci **35**(1): 6–10 doi: 10.1016/j.eqs.2022.01.015

　　尽管唐·亨伯格（Don Helmberger）故去已经有一年多了，但时至此刻我整个职业生涯中与他交流的点滴仍然激发着我对他的思念与崇敬。1978 年夏天，我来到了加州理工学院，彼时的我还只是个对地震学知之甚少的本科毕业生；杰夫·戴维斯（Geoff Davies）是我本科阶段地质力学项目（罗切斯特大学的一个地质学和机械工程联合项目）的指导教师之一，他在加州理工取得了矿物物理学博士学位。我在杰夫（Geoff）教授的地球物理学课上学了大概两周的地震学概论，因此我对这个研究领域十分陌生。实际上，在我申请阶段得知我可能想去加州理工时，杰夫（Geoff）本人也并不是很鼓励我。但是当时我十分渴望远离罗切斯特的寒冬并南下，因此我忽视了他的建议。1978 年到 1983 年，我开启了在加州理工学院地震实验室学习的研究生生涯，并在那里做了九个月的博士后，然后离开前往密歇根大学任教。在地震实验室的时光是一段值得怀念的黄金岁月，在那里，我和我的同学们［汤姆·赫恩（Tom Hearn）、玛丽·安娜·瓦尔克（Marianne C. Walck）、特里·华莱士（Terry C. Wallace）、马里奥·瓦西克乌（Mario Vassilliou）］得以和唐·亨伯格（Don Helmberger）、金森博雄（Hiroo Kanamori）、唐·安德森（Don Anderson）、戴维·哈克赖德（David Harkrider）、汤姆·阿伦斯（Tom Ahrens）、克拉伦斯·艾伦（Clarence Allen），以及伯纳德·明斯特（Bernard Minster）各位前辈进行日常交流互动。图 1 是 1978~1979 学年某天拍摄的地震学实验室全体人员合影。作为一个要在地震学世界中找寻一席之地的研究生，所能要求的难道还能比身边环绕着一群富有创造性的地球物理学先驱以及高年级研究生更多吗？

　　地震实验室的沉浸式环境令人陶醉。在每天两次的地震学咖啡时间上（有时大大超过了我们预定的每次 1 小时的期限），我们总是讨论各种大杂烩式的话题。其中关键的地震学话题有关于震源和上地幔三重结构研究中地震波新模型的运用，大地震断层模型的长周期面波频谱建模，地震衰减新的频率参数化方法的应用以及南加州最新的数字区域地震台网（SCARLET）的地震阵列分析。地震实验室鼓励学生和不同的老师一起从事多个领域的研究，而在第二学年年初的口试中我们被要求准备三个研究课题进行答辩。这种开放的政策使得我们能够随时询问探讨潜在的研究课题（你必须克服那种你在浪费老师们宝贵的工作时间的负罪感），而我因此开始和金森博雄（Hiroo Kanamori）合作关于所罗门群岛大地震的体波和面波工作，和唐·亨伯格（Don Helmberger）一起研究了上地幔速度结构和衰减的横向变化，在高年级研究生雷特·巴特勒（Rhett Butler）和拉里·拉夫（Larry Ruff）帮助下，用 SCARLET 分析地核影响的 P 波衍射起始，以及在唐·安德森（Don Anderson）指导下研究 PKiKP 波反射率的频率依赖关系（好吧，这个工作没能够发表），此外还有一些我记不起来了的失败尝试。

图 1　1978~1979 年加州理工地震学实验室教职工、研究员和研究生全体合影。唐·亨伯格（Don Helmberger）位于第一排左起第二位。作者本人位于第一排左起第七位（是的，没有穿鞋）。图源加州理工学院档案。

有着这样的不同项目和导师，并可以在咖啡时间中接触五花八门的话题，这使得我仿佛身处于地震学研究的前沿之中。金森博雄（Hiroo Kanamori）是一位极好的老师，他耐心地向我介绍了他的面波分析代码和数据处理流程，而当时我正在从事手动数字化数百个 WWSSN（World-Wide Standardized Seismograph Network，全球标准化地震网络；20 世纪 60 年代部署的全球模拟地震台站网络；Peterson and Hutt, 2014)台站的面波记录，用于分析三个大的双震事件。唐·亨伯格（Don Helmberger）指导我将北美的 WWSSN 和 CSN（Canadian Seismograph Network，加拿大地震台网）台站的深震记录的短周期与长周期 P 波和 SH 波数字化，寻求约束上地幔到时和衰减的系统性变化，用以解释内华达实验场核试验中接收信号的异常（那时正处于 1974 年双边禁止核试验协定内，协定限制了美国和苏联的地下核试验当量须小于 150kt，所以用以估计爆炸当量的绝对振幅必须正确地考虑上地幔的不均一性）。所有的这些数字化工作（以及 WWSSN 模拟台网逐渐退出使用）让我享受使用 SCARLET 的数字记录的愉悦，使我对台站的增益和极性是如何变化的，甚至是数字记录在站点维护时的变化，有了更深的体会。这一切对我来说都是极其有趣和令人激动的，这三个话题也在我的预答辩（先于教师面前的正式口试答辩的在研究组中的预演展示）中都被呈现出来了（图 2）。最终，我在 1979 年 10 月成功通过了口试，得以继续攻读博士学位。

图 2　我的博士资格预口试通知的复印件，预口试于 1979 年 9 月 27 日举行。事实证明，给研究组同学做报告远比随后的在老师面前的正式口试压力大。我觉得这个程序是被故意设计的，用以缓解你正式考试前的紧张情绪。

尽管我仍然在与金森博雄（Hiroo Kanamori）合作课题，详细地阐述他以凹凸体模型为框架下的大地震中滑动不均一性观点，以及处理 1980 年圣海伦斯火山喷发和 1980 年尤里卡（戈尔达板块）地震最新的数字记录，我的研究重点却逐渐更多地在唐·亨伯格（Don Helmberger）指导下进行。这其中有好几个原因：在整个 20 世纪 80 年代初期，正当我准备分析大地震信号时，它的发生次数减少了，而像杰夫·吉文斯（Jeff Givens）这样的高年级研究生正与博雄（Hiroo）一起快速推进高效的数字信号波形分析，所以技术层面上它被涵盖了。此外，我发现观测工作也是十分有益的，因为它似乎能带来更频繁的惊喜。我和唐（Don）一起积累的大量数据集揭示了到时和振幅的异常行为，他们并不能够被我们已经记录到的上地幔结构变化所解释（Lay and Helmberger, 1981, 1983a）。和唐（Don）一起挖掘海量数据的乐趣之一是我意识到他并非提前知道了所有答案[不像博雄（Hiroo），他似乎总是了解项目的具体走向]，这是一种逐步发现的感觉。

我开始意识到下地幔三维结构具有不均一性（Lay，1983），这一情况只在开始出现的第一代全球层析成像结果中有线索，其影响很容易在深震事件中的简单波形中看到。我从唐（Don）那里学到了一个深刻教训，地球有无数种方法让地震波形变得复杂（震源破裂复杂性、板片结构、接收介质结构和仪器响应等等），但如果你观察到一个简单波形的话，它不太可能只是复杂干扰的偶然结果。因此这种简单的波形指示了一条清晰的路径，路径上微小的特征可以可靠地解释为地球结构。然而这种观点如今正被大型数据集的自动处理所湮没，这是一种损失。利用唐（Don）的一维速度结构的广义射线理论代码，通过修正径向结构再现简单波形，并将其应用于区域 Pnl 波形和上地幔不间断面的研究，我们取得了很大的突破。唐（Don）的一门课程可以让我们深刻理解广义射线理论，那是他基于卡尼亚尔-德胡普（Cagniard-de Hoop）法发展的一套方法。那是一门很棒的课程，我有时会去重复温习其中精髓。现在我依然用着唐（Don）的课堂笔记[以及用打字机打的工整打印版的汤姆·希顿（Tom Heaton）博士论文]讲授相似的课程。

机缘巧合下，我们逐渐意识到来自深震的简单波形中的微小特征（图 3）随着震源距离有系统性的变化，于是我们试图理解这些特征的根源。这需要熟悉大量的波形[另一个我从唐（Don）那学到的深刻教训就是仔细地观察大量的波形，以便你从中识别出任何意想不到的发现]，因此我们花了大量的时间观察数据[作为期间神秘的插曲,唐（Don）会间歇性地望向办公室的窗户]。通过这些我直接从唐（Don）那里收获了分析体波数据的技巧与热情。

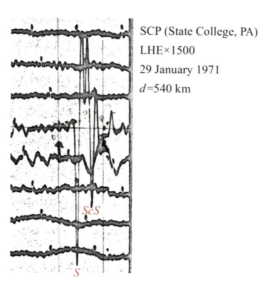

图 3　一段来自 SCP 台站的 WWSSN 仪器记录到的鄂霍茨克海下深震长周期 EW 分量的地震图，仪器增益为 1500，主频周期为 15s。模拟记录位于一个旋转的鼓上，每一行为记录一小时，其中一分钟一个刻度。地面震动表明 S 和 ScS 脉冲信号到达，但其中一个没有解释的脉冲引起了我们的注意。这些信号需要进行手动数字化，并将水平分量数字化旋转分离出信号的切向（SH）分量。我还有几千个这样的地震图的副本，这些都是我和唐（Don）在研究中使用的。

很明显，我们观察到的没有解释的信号来自下地幔。19 世纪 70 年代初，布莱恩·米切尔（Brian Mitchell）曾在休假期间访问了加州理工，唐（Don）同他一道研究了核幔边界结构。他们提出了一个独特的模型，认为在核幔边界上方的薄层中有非常高的剪切波速度增加，用以解释 ScSH 和 ScSV（来自核幔边界的 S 波的水平和垂直偏振反射）之间的波形差异（Mitchell and Helmberger, 1973）。一些台阵研究表明，基于微小的波形干涉效应，在核幔边界 170km 上方处出现了 P 波速度突然上升(Wright and Lyons, 1980)，但是普遍观点认为下地幔弹性速度结构一直延伸到下地幔底部的径向的速度变化是平滑的。而在下地幔底部，热边界层效应降低了速度梯度，并且增加了覆盖核幔边界的所谓D″层的横向非均匀性。我极大地拓展了 Mitchell and Helmberger （1973）所使用的数据，证明他们发现的波形特征能够很好地被他们的观点所支持和模拟(Lay and Helmberger, 1983b)，但是这很可能涉及D″层的各向异性结构，而不只是高速薄层，正如之后所建立的模型那样（Garnero and Lay, 1997）。我们的关注点在于图 3 所示的 S 波和地核反射波 ScS 波之间预料之外的信号，它无法被一些标准地球模型如 PREM 和 JB 模型所解释。基于唐（Don）对上地幔三叉震相的经验的指导，我们在D″层顶部引入了一个 2%～3%的速度急剧跳跃，大概位于核幔边界上部 250~300km 处，并使用唐（Don）的一维广义射线理论代码（BOUNCE）计算合成地震图，通过波前的三叉震相解释了额外信号的到时与振幅(图 4)。三叉震相导致了在某些震中距上的波的三次到达：一些能量在不连续面上方折射，一些在界面被反射，一些在不连续面下方折射。此即为 D″层地震剪切波速度不连续的发现(Lay et al., 1983c,d)，这也成为了我博士论文的焦点，以及接下来 10 年中和学生工作的重点。可以这么说，它激发了人们对 D″层结构的兴趣，随后与之相关的研究得到了大大扩展。大约 20 年后，在相对低温的地幔沉降界面上,(Mg,Fe)SiO₃镁硅酸盐钙钛矿(布里奇曼石)相变的确立，合理地解释了这种地震速度不连续面的深度、强度和横向变化。

作为一名导师，唐（Don）非常鼓励我参加会议，并促使我第一次参加了空军研究会议，第一次参加关于数学地球物理学的国际会议，以及参加一些其他国内会议。他总是会审视会议是否令人愉快，他尤爱参与国际会议，以及其中穿插的短途旅行，我在整个职业生涯中借鉴了这种做法。唐（Don）还会在周六参加地震实验室的橄榄球比赛，他显然很享受展示自己的运动技能，这一点超过了大多数研究生。这些同你的私人接触一直保持着，使得你在当地和外面的科学圈子中都很有归属感。

在研究生生涯的最后一两年以及整个博士后阶段，我担任伍德沃德咨询公司（Woodward Clyde Consultants）的地震顾问，唐（Don）依靠来自空军的资金为该公司建立了帕萨迪纳（Pasadena）研究所。在这的工作包括使用唐（Don）的代码包 ASERIES 和 BOUNCE 来模拟地下核试验的 P 波记录。我与唐（Don）之前的一个博士生拉里·伯迪克（Larry Burdick）一起开发了一个相对波形均衡程序（相关关系），利用远震数据估计爆炸源的震源时间函数、震源深度和当量（Lay et al., 1984a），以及使用匹配远场观测振幅和波形的绝对衰减算子模拟大爆炸震源时间函数的近场强地面运动记录(Burdick et al., 1984)。特里（Terry）和我一道同唐（Don）利用区域距离的 sP 到时和远震振幅花样研究核爆的构造释放（Lay et al., 1984c）。我和唐（Don）还有戴维·哈克赖德（David Harkrider）的一次联合工作利用体波和面波观测得到了阿姆奇特卡（Amchitka）核试验的宽频带震源时间函数（Lay et al., 1984b）。这是我在加州理工期间的最后一项工作。

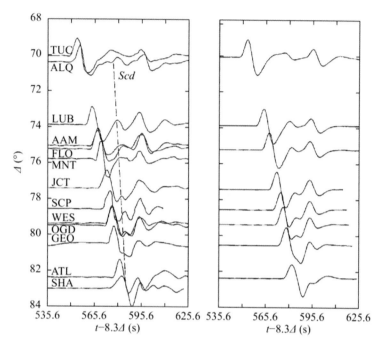

图 4 1971 年 1 月 29 日地震在 WWSSN 台站记录的 SH 分量数字化剖面图（左图），它展现了图 3 中所见的 S 和 ScS 波之间的额外震相随着震中距Δ的系统偏移，我们把它标记为 Scd。右边是给定在D″层顶部有一个 2.75%剪切波速间断面模型下，基于广义射线理论生成理论地震对比图，这与观测信号的主要特征相匹配。图源自 Lay 和 Helmberger (1983d)。

在随后的年月里，我有机会与唐（Don）一起研究了 2004 年苏门答腊地震，并在他当选为国家科学院院士后，总结了关于后钙钛矿相变导致 D″层不连续性的解释。我也曾多次访问加州理工，在那与他谈论有关波形的问题以及他之后的几届研究生的令人印象深刻的研究成果。他的学术热情丝毫未减，在地核、深地幔、上地幔和震源模型方面取得的研究进展无不令人惊叹。我们一道参加了许多会议，有时还一起享受野外旅行（图5），他总是在那种场合让他的曾经和现在的学生陷入"麻烦"（与灰熊！）。他以某种方式提名我同他一道为空军技术应用（AFTAC）地震审查委员会服务，该委员会为政府的核试验检测操作建言献策。因此，我们每年还会在佛罗里达或者怀俄明州的派恩戴尔的委员会机构碰面三次，在没有窗户的房间里开一整天的会，之后唐（Don）总是会在海滩或者树林里长时间散步。和往常一样，在这个过程的大部分时间里我们都在谈论地震波，分享奇妙的同志般的情谊，这种关系源于对从地震图中提取信息的乐趣和共同热情。我将铭记并怀念与我的导师的那些对话。

图 5.在 1984 安克雷奇美国地震学年会后德纳里公园的一次顺路观光。唐（Don）在索恩·莱（Thorne Lay）和史蒂夫·格兰德（Steve Grand）肩上撑起自己，而海迪·休斯敦（Heidi Houston）在一旁放松。这次旅途十分难忘。为了步行穿过苔原近距离接触德纳里峰，我们一行离开了巴士独自进入公园（非法地）。当然，那里有灰熊，唐（Don）非得设法引起它们的注意……由约翰·维达莱（John Vidale）拍摄。

参 考 文 献

Burdick LJ, Wallace TC and Lay T (1984). Modeling near-field and teleseismic observations from the Amchitka test site. J Geophy Res: Solid Earth **89**(B6): 4373–4388.

Garnero EJ and Lay T (1997). Lateral variations in lowermost mantle shear wave anisotropy beneath the north Pacific and Alaska. J Geophy Res: Solid Earth **102**(B4): 8121–8135.

Lay T (1983). Localized velocity anomalies in the lower mantle. Geophys J Int **72**(2): 483–516.

Lay T and Helmberger DV (1981). Body wave amplitude patterns and upper mantle attenuation variations across North America. Geophys J Int **66**(3): 691–726.

Lay T and Helmberger DV (1983a). Body-wave amplitude and travel-time correlations across North America. Bull Seismol Soc Am **73**(4): 1063–1076.

Lay T and Helmberger DV (1983b). The shear-wave velocity gradient at the base of the mantle. J Geophys Res: Solid Earth **88**(B10): 8160– 8170.

Lay T and Helmberger DV (1983c). A shear velocity discontinuity in the lower mantle. Geophys Res Lett **10**(1): 63–66.

Lay T and Helmberger DV (1983d). A lower mantle *S*-wave triplication and the shear velocity structure of D". Geophys J Int **75**(3): 799–838.

Lay T, Burdick LJ and Helmberger DV (1984a). Estimating the yields of the Amchitka tests by waveform intercorrelation. Geophys J Int **78**(1): 181–207.

Lay T, Helmberger DV and Harkrider DG (1984b). Source models and yield-scaling relations for underground nuclear explosions at Amchitka Island. Bull Seismol Soc Am **74**(3): 843–862.

Lay T, Wallace TC and Helmberger DV (1984c). The effects of tectonic release on short-period P waves from

NTS explosions. Bull Seismol Soc Am **74**(3): 819–842.

Mitchell BJ and Helmberger DV (1973). Shear velocities at the base of the mantle from observations of *S* and *ScS*. J Geophys Res **78**(26): 6009–6020.

Peterson J and Hutt CR (2014). World-wide standardized seismograph network: A data users guide. U. S. Geological Survey, Reston, pp 74

Wright C and Lyons JA (1980). Further evidence for radial velocity anomalies in the lower mantle. Pure Appl Geophys **119**(1): 137–162.

　　索恩·莱目前是加州大学圣克鲁斯分校 (UCSC) 地球与行星科学杰出教授。他 1983 年在加州理工学院完成了博士学位，亨伯格教授是他的主要论文导师。在加入 UCSC 之前，他在密歇根大学任教了六年。他是美国地球物理学会莱曼奖章、美国地震学会里德奖章、皇家天文学会金奖章的获得者，并且是美国国家科学院院士。他的主页是 https://websites.pmc. ucsc.edu/~seisweb/thorne_lay/。

Chapter 3. A strange symbiosis: Seismic ray theory and Saturday touch football — Donald V. Helmberger as a graduate advisor

Terry Wallace [*]

Director Emeritus, Los Alamos National Laboratory, Los Alamos, NM 87544, USA

[*]**Correspondence:** wallace.terrycjr@gmail.com

Citation: Wallace TC (2022). A strange symbiosis: Seismic ray theory and saturday touch football — Donald V. Helmberger as a graduate advisor. Earthq Sci **35**(1): 11−13 doi: 10.1016/j.eqs.2022.01.017

At the end of December of 1978，I was sitting in the office of Caltech Professor Don Helmberger, and he was peering out his window towards the San Gabriel Mountains, silent and I supposed, deep in thought about some mystery of seismology. When he finally spoke, he said "Chuck Foreman's days as a great running back are over". The previous day the Los Angeles Rams had eliminated the Minnesota Vikings (despite Fran Tarkington's best efforts) from the NFL playoffs. Don grew up in Minnesota, and was a Vikings fan – something he and I shared. We then had a brief discussion about the Vikings, and finally Don returned to peering out the window. When he next spoke ，it was to ask about the status of my digitizing LRSM seismic records for a series of large yield nuclear explosions that had been detonated at the Nevada Test Site in the 1960s. He never talked about the Vikings again in his office: however, he always asked me what I thought about them every Saturday when we played a rousing game of touch football on the Caltech field across from the South Mudd building. Don was a deeply passionate man — his curiosity for seismology was profound, but he also loved life in a way that made him a remarkable graduate advisor. In my thesis I had a simple acknowledgement: "I have particularly benefited from the support of, and interaction with my thesis advisor Don Helmberger. Don, besides being a Minnesota Vikings fan, has deluged me with ideas, good and bad!"

In the fall of 1973, I had every intention of attending Caltech after I graduated from Los Alamos High School the following May. However, it was not to be, and I would not arrive in Pasadena until the summer of 1978 when I matriculated in the PhD program after getting my undergraduate degrees at New Mexico Institute of Mining and Technology. On reflection, this delay in arriving at Caltech was one of the best things that ever happened to me; I arrived in what others have coined "the golden age of seismology" and the Seismo Lab was unlike any place else in the world. Only a decade earlier Oliver, Isacks and Sykes had published "Seismology and the New Global Tectonics", and for a brief period of time Earth physics was the hottest science topic around. Seismo Lab professors, graduate students, and a steady stream of visitors from around the globe created an incredible environment of discovery. Daily coffee breaks — with attendance from nearly everyone – always produce lively (and often heated) discussion on topics ranging from the nature of the core to the predictability of earthquakes. I have seen many attempts at creating a similar environment in the nearly 40 years since I left Caltech, but nothing has come close.

Arriving into such a remarkable place was both exciting and extraordinarily intimidating. All the incoming students had to choose three research topics (with different professors) that would be defended in a qualifying exam that felt like the star chamber trials of 16th century England. In retrospect, the pressure to succeed in the qualifying exam was mostly peer pressure; a chance to show your fellow students that "you belonged, intellectually and creatively". In August of 1978 a moderate sized earthquake occurred near Santa Barbara (and earthquakes seemed to be quite rare in California after the 1971 San Fernando earthquake) that produced some interesting strong motion recordings. This provided the opportunity for one of my research topics, and how I first came to work directly with Don Helmberger. One of Don's first students, Tom Heaton, had used Don's work on computing synthetic seismograms with generalized ray theory to model the San Fernando earthquake and showed that the rupture of fault was rough; there were areas, or patches, of large and small displacement, not a smooth rupture from one end of the fault to the other. Using Heaton's work as a guide I produced my first paper at Caltech, Wallace, Helmberger and Ebel (1981a). When I went to see Don about my proposal for working on the strong motion records, he asked me if I played football, and invited me (or, from my perspective, strongly suggested) to play in the Saturday touch game. I rarely missed a game for the next 4.5 years, and I can say today whenever I smell the pungent aroma of ozone, I get happy tears in my eyes. The LA basin was pretty polluted in the late 1970s, and ozone was one of the most obvious irritants created by 10 million automobiles driving on the freeways. I remember with great fondness the burning eyes and lungs created by chasing down (or at least trying to) Don on a field marked with scattered tee shirts before he could score a touchdown.

The introduction to modeling an earthquake made it obvious to me that I was far more interested in the mathematics of the simulation methods than actually understanding the earthquake. Fortunately, Don was very supportive of exploring improvements to his Cagniard-de Hoop formulization of ray theory. Don suggested I should work on regional distance seismograms. These seismograms, recorded at regional distances (2°–12°), are quite "messy" and complicated due to the waveguide nature of the crust. The body wave trains are essentially crustal reverberations. If these complicated waveforms are modeled with synthetic seismograms then significant information can be learned about the seismic source and the structure along the travel path. With certain restrictions, the long-period regional body waves (Pnl) from shallow, continental earthquakes can be modeled with layers (crust) over a half-space (mantle). Generalized ray theory and the Cagniard-de Hoop technique can be streamlined for computing a synthetic seismogram in such a structure. We developed an approximation to the travel-time equation, which results in an analytic inversion for the de Hoop contour. The simplicity of the individual rays required that the displacement potential need only be evaluated at a small number of time points; small changes in structure are, to first order, expressed in terms of the timing of different arrivals. It is possible to "stretch" or "squeeze" the synthetic to simulate a change in structure. Therefore, a single Green's function can be used to investigate a whole suite of structural models.

This mathematical work meant that I had the "opportunity" to rewrite a version of Don's generalized ray theory computer code, ASERIES. In the late 1970s that meant Fortran coding on punched cards. My new computer code, named DeHoopster, required 3 full boxes of punched cards (with inputs) that I would have to haul across the Caltech campus to submit to an operator sitting behind a high wall at the computer center. It was not simple converting the Helmberger code to DeHoopster because Don was quite fond of "picket" do-loops that he would simply insert an instruction to skip hundreds of cards in his computer stack. Finding these programing treasures always meant days of making sure the modified code could be verified. After the code was done it opened up a plethora of modeling opportunities. I wrote a half dozen papers on modeling regional distance seismograms for seismic source, crustal and upper mantle structure, and the forensic analysis of underground nuclear explosions (these papers are included in the references: Wallace et al., 1981b; Wallace and Helmberger, 1982; Wallace et al., 1983, 1985, 1986, Burdick et al., 1984, and Lay et al., 1984).

One of the forgotten aspects of the late 1970s and early 1980s is that the primary funder of seismic research in the US was not the National Science Foundation, but rather it was the Department of Defense through ARPA and DTRA. In the late 1950s there was an intense debate about the viability of monitoring a complete prohibition of nuclear testing. The US decided to conduct a nuclear test that was underground, and fully contained (meaning no release of materials and debris from the explosion). This test, code named RAINIER, was quite modest having a yield of 1.7 kt (less than 8 percent of the size of the first nuclear explosion, TRINITY, which had a nuclear yield of approximately 25 kt). The seismic waves created by RAINIER were quite unexpected; it was detected at least 1000 km from the Nevada Test Site, and there were very "earthquake like looking" S waves. This prompted a US group of experts chaired by Lloyd Berkner to exam the needs of the country to monitor a comprehensive test ban. The so-called Berkner Report was breathtaking in its recommendations: a funded international seismic network, improvements in seismic instrumentation, and perhaps most importantly, a massive program in basic seismology research (not just focused on nuclear explosions). This program came into existence, and ultimately funded the education and research of a generation of seismologists. I am one of those, and Don Helmberger had dozens of research grants that can be traced back to the RAINIER nuclear test.

I wrote several dozen reports and papers on various aspects of what is now called "forensic seismology" trying to understand what seismic and other geophysical signals could tell us about a nuclear weapon explosion (for a few of these papers see the last five references in the bibliography). My early focus with Don's guidance was to understand the complexity of the body waves, exploring why S waves could be so strong for a purely compressional source. Figure 1 shows how a large explosion at NTS, COLBY, could be used to simulate another large explosion, BOXCAR by the addition of a simulated earthquake. This simulated earthquake-type source became known as tectonic release and is thought to represent the explosively driven fracturing of rock around the explosion source.

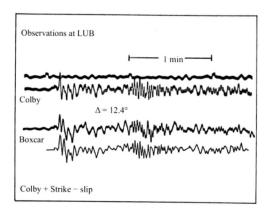

Fig. 1   A comparison of the P and PL waveforms for BOXCARand COLBY at WWSN station LUB. Shown below is the COLBY waveform summed with a synthetic seismogram to simulate the tectonic release. The synthetic is created with a pure strike slip orientation and a moment of 5×10^{24} dyne·cm (From Wallace et al., 1983).

Every year the results of the research funded by the DOD were presented at a meeting which became known as the Seismic Research Symposium. Thorne Lay (my classmate) and I would attend these meetings with Don, which indirectly led my career path back to my hometown of Los Alamos, and I eventually became the 11th director of the birthplace of the atomic bomb. At the Research Symposium we would present our results — in those days the preferred presentation media was transparencies projected on an always too small screen in front of an audience of a hundred scientists and officials from the funding agencies. Don would always ask to "help" by placing and changing the transparencies during the course of the talk. This was a major challenge because Don would become interested in some aspect of the talk and would decide to skip whole sections of the presentation to get to the material he was thinking about. The first time Don did this it was quite unnerving; by the fifth meeting I actually looked forward to the improvisation I would be forced into with Don's whim (or guidance).

Don Helmberger was an extraordinary advisor. It is easy to point to his brilliant insight on the nature of wiggles on a seismogram as his greatest talent. However, in the hindsight of a career, it is obvious Don's contributions were far, far greater. His insatiable curiosity, passion for understanding, and his hidden playfulness exposed mostly on the gridiron, taught us how to be a scientist, how to be a critical thinker. I am sure that Don Helmberger's thousand papers will be cited as his legacy, but his biggest contribution was actually molding a generation of scientists.

References

Burdick LJ, Wallace T and Lay T (1984). Modeling near-field and teleseismic observations from the Amchitka test site. J Geophys Res: Solid Earth **89**(B6): 4373–4388.

Lay T, Wallace TC and Helmberger DV (1984). The effects of tectonic release on short-period P waves from NTS explosions. Bull Seismol Soc Am **74**(3): 819–841.

Wallace TC, Helmberger DV and Ebel JE (1981a). A broadband study of the 13 August 1978 Santa Barbara earthquake. Bull Seismol Soc Am **71**(6): 1701–1718.

Wallace TC, Helmberger DV and Mellman GR (1981b). A technique for the inversion of regional data in source parameter studies. J Geophys Res **86**(B3): 1679–1685.

Wallace TC and Helmberger DV (1982). Determining source parameters of moderate-size earthquakes from regional waveforms. Phys Earth Planet Int **30**(2-3): 185–196.

Wallace TC, Helmberger DV and Engen GR (1983). Evidence of tectonic release from underground nuclear explosions in long-period P waves. Bull Seismol Soc Am **73**(2): 593–613.

Wallace TC, Helmberger DV and Engen GR (1985). Evidence of tectonic release from underground nuclear explosions in long-period S waves. Bull Seismol Soc Am **75**(1): 157–174.

Wallace TC, Helmberger DV and Lay T (1986). Reply to comments by A. Douglas, J. B. Young, and N. S. Lyman and a note on the revised moments for Pahute Mesa tectonic release. Bull Seismol Soc Am **76**(1): 313–318.

Terry Wallace is Director Emeritus at Los Alamos National Laboratory. He was the 11th Director of the Laboratory; previously he was the Principal Associate Director for Global Security and the Senior Intelligence Officer. Terry received his PhD at Caltech in 1983 with Don Helmberger as his primary thesis advisor. After leaving Caltech he was on the faculty at the University of Arizona for 20 years. He was a member of both the Geosciences and Applied Mathematics programs. While an academic Terry was the recipient of the Macelwane Medal from the AGU, served as the President of the Seismological Society of America, and was awarded the Carnegie Mineralogical Medal. In 2018 he was awarded the National Nuclear Security Administrations gold medal for service.

第 3 章　地震射线理论与周六触身式橄榄球的奇异结合——作为研究生导师的唐·亨伯格

特里·华莱士

美国洛斯阿拉莫斯国家实验室名誉主任，美国洛斯阿拉莫斯，新墨西哥州

引用：Wallace TC (2022). A strange symbiosis: Seismic ray theory and saturday touch football — Donald V. Helmberger as a graduate advisor. Earthq Sci **35**(1): 11–13 doi: 10.1016/j.eqs.2022.01.017

　　1978 年 12 月底，我坐在加州理工学院教授唐·亨伯格（Don Helmberger）的办公室里；他向窗外的圣盖博山望去，一言不发，我想，他在思考地震学的某些奥秘。当他终于开口时，他说：“查克·福尔曼作为一个伟大的跑卫的日子已经结束了”。前一天，洛杉矶公羊队在 NFL 季后赛中淘汰了明尼苏达维京人队（尽管弗兰·塔金顿已经尽力了）。唐（Don）在明尼苏达州长大，是维京人队的球迷——这是他和我的共同点。我们随后就维京人队进行了简短的讨论，最后唐（Don）回到了窗边继续望向窗外。当他下一次说话时，是询问我对 60 年代在内华达试验场引爆的一系列大当量核爆炸的 LRSM 地震记录的数字化情况。他在办公室里再也没有谈论过维京人队。然而，每个星期六，当我们在南马德楼对面的加州理工学院球场上进行一场激情的触身式橄榄球①比赛时，他总是询问我对他们的看法。唐（Don）是一个充满激情的人——他对地震学的好奇心很强，但他也热爱生活，这使他成为一个出色的研究生导师。在我的毕业论文中只有一个简短的致谢：“我特别受益于我的论文导师唐·亨伯格（Don Helmberger）的支持，以及与他的互动。唐（Don），除了是一个明尼苏达维京人队的球迷，也是为我提供了大量的想法的人，无论是好的还是坏的！”①

　　1973 年秋天，我一心想在次年 5 月从洛斯阿拉莫斯高中毕业后去加州理工学院学习。然而，事与愿违，我直到 1978 年夏天才到达帕萨迪纳，当时我在新墨西哥矿业和技术学院获得本科学位后开始博士的课程学习。仔细想想，这次在加州理工学院的“迟到”是我所遇到的最棒的事情之一；我赶上了由他人开创的 “地震学的黄金时代”，地震学实验室与世界上任何其他地方都不同。十年前，欧理渥（Oliver）、艾萨克（Isacks）和赛克斯（Sykes）出版了《地震学和新全球构造》，地球物理学一度是当时最热门的科学话题。地震学实验室的教授、研究生和来自全球各地源源不断的访问学者创造了一个令人难以置信的探索的环境。每天的咖啡时间——几乎每个人都会参加——总是会产生热烈的（而且常常是激烈的）讨论，讨论的主题包括从地核的性质到地震的可预测性。在我

---

　　① 译者注：触身式橄榄球（touch football），以单手或双手碰触（touch）对方持球人身体取代擒抱（tackle）和摔倒动作的变种橄榄球运动，因其更加温和、受伤风险更小，不需要佩戴厚重的护具，因而在大部分学校的普通爱好者中更为流行。

离开加州理工学院后的近 40 年里，我看到了许多地方尝试创造类似的环境，但其中没有任何一个能与之媲美。

来到这样一个了不起的地方，既让人兴奋，又让人异常恐惧。所有新生必须选择三个研究课题（由不同的教授负责），在资格考试中进行答辩，感觉就像 16 世纪英国的星室审判[①]。现在回想起来，在资格考试中取得成功的压力主要来自同伴，这是一个向你的同学展示 "你的智力和创造力配得上这里" 的机会。1978 年 8 月，圣塔巴巴拉附近发生了一个中等规模的地震（1971 年圣费尔南多地震后，加州的地震似乎相当罕见），产生了一些有趣的强地面运动记录。这为我的一个研究课题提供了机会，也是我第一次直接与唐·亨伯格（Don Helmberger）合作的原因。唐（Don）的第一个学生汤姆·希顿（Tom Heaton）利用唐（Don）的工作，用广义射线理论计算合成地震图来模拟圣费尔南多地震，结果表明，断层的破裂是粗糙的；一些区域（或斑块）的位移大，另一些的位移小，而不是从断层的一端到另一端的平滑破裂。以希顿（Heaton）的工作为指导，我在加州理工学院发表了我的第一篇论文（Wallace, et al., 1981a）。当我去见唐（Don）以寻求对我的强地面运动记录的工作的建议时，他问我是否打橄榄球，并邀请我（或者从我的角度看，强烈建议我）参加星期六的触身式比赛。在接下来的 4 年半时间里，我很少错过比赛，可以说每当我闻到臭氧的刺鼻香味时，我的眼睛里就会有幸福的泪水。在 20 世纪 70 年代末，洛杉矶盆地的空气污染相当严重，而臭氧是 1000 万辆汽车在高速公路上行驶时产生的最明显的刺激物之一。我深深地记得每次在散落 T 恤的场地上追逐（或者说至少试图追上）带球得分的唐（Don）时我眼睛和肺灼烧的感觉。

接触到地震模拟的工作后，我清楚地认识到，我对模拟方法的数学知识的兴趣远远超过对了解地震的兴趣。幸运的是，唐（Don）非常支持我对他射线理论中卡尼亚尔-德胡普（Cagniard-de Hoop）公式进行改进。唐（Don）建议我从事区域尺度的地震图的研究。因为地壳存在波导性质，这些在区域距离（2°~12°）记录的地震图相当 "混乱" 和复杂。体波波列基本上就是地壳的混响。如果用理论地震图对这些复杂的波形进行分析，就可以了解震源和传播路径上结构的重要信息。在某些条件下，来自浅部大陆地震的长周期区域体波（Pnl）可以用半空间（地幔）上的分层（地壳）模型来计算。广义射线理论和卡尼亚尔-德胡普（Cagniard-de Hoop）技术可以在这样的结构中简化计算理论地震图。我们推导了一个走时方程的近似，得到了一个求解德胡普（de Hoop）回路的解析方法。单个射线只需要在少数几个时间点计算位移势；在一级近似下，结构的微小变化可用不同的到时表达，从而可以通过 "拉伸" 或 "压缩" 理论地震图来模拟结构的变化。也就是说，一个格林函数可以用来研究一整套结构模型。

这项数学工作使我有"机会"重写唐（Don）的广义射线理论的计算机代码 ASERIES。在 20 世纪 70 年代末，这意味着在打孔卡片上进行 Fortran 编码。我的新计算机代码被命

---

① 译者注：星法院，star chamber，又称 court of the star chamber。在威斯敏斯特宫的星室（star chamber）里开庭而得名。早期英格兰国王的谘议会在星室处理政务。亨利七世和亨利八世时期，重组了这一机构，授予其司法管辖权，并规定了法官的组成人选。星室法庭在审理时，不采用陪审团。这种审判不经一般的司法审判辩护程序而是秘密进行的。为使罪犯招供，可以运用各种酷刑。在斯图亚特王朝时期，星室法庭被用作镇压清教徒的工具，因其独断行使权力和非法扩权而极不受欢迎，1641 年被撤销。此后，星室法庭成为专断司法的同义语。

名为DeHoopster，需要3整箱的打孔卡（包括输入），我必须搬着它们穿过加州理工学院的校园，提交给坐在计算机中心高墙后面的操作员。将 Helmberger 代码转换为 DeHoopster 并不简单，因为唐（Don）常用"选择的"do 循环，插入一条指令跳过数百张指令卡片。找到他的这些程序指令总是意味着要花好几天时间来验证修改后的代码。完成后的新代码为我带来了大量的建模应用。我写了半打论文，内容是模拟震源、地壳、上地幔结构以及地下核爆炸的区域地震图（这些论文包括在参考文献中。Wallace et al., 1981b; Wallace and Helmberger, 1982; Wallace et al., 1983, 1985, 1986; Burdick et al., 1984; Lay et al., 1984）。

　　20 世纪 70 年代末和 80 年代初常被人遗忘的一个方面是，美国地震研究的主要资助者不是国家科学基金会，而是国防部的高级研究计划局和国防威胁降低局。在 20 世纪 50 年代末，人们对监测全面禁止核试验的可行性进行了激烈的辩论。美国决定进行一次地下的核试验，而且是完全封闭的（意味着爆炸后不会释放材料和碎片）。这次代号为 RAINIER 的试验相当温和，其当量为 1.7 千吨（不到第一次核爆炸 TRINITY 的 8%，其当量约为 25 千吨）。RAINIER 所产生的地震波是相当出乎意料的：它在距离内华达试验场至少 1000km 的地方被探测到，而且有非常 "像地震一样 "的 S 波。这促成了一个为国家监测禁止核试验的由劳埃德·伯克纳主持的美国专家组。所谓的《伯克纳报告》的建议令人叹为观止：一个受资助的国际地震网络，需要地震仪器的改进，以及也许最重要的是，需要一个大规模的地震学基础研究项目（不只是关注核爆炸）。这个计划的出现，最终资助了一代地震学家的教育和研究。我是其中之一，而唐·亨伯格（Don Helmberger）有几十项研究资助可以追溯到 RAINIER 核试验。

　　我写了几十份报告和论文，涉及现在被称为 "法医地震学 "的各个方面，试图了解地震和其他地球物理信号可以告诉我们哪些是关于核武器爆炸的情况（其中几篇论文见本章中的最后五个参考文献）。在唐（Don）的指导下，我早期的研究重点是了解体波的复杂性，探索对于一个纯粹的压缩源来说为什么 S 波会如此强烈。图 1 显示了如何通过添加模拟地震，利用在 NTS 的一次大型爆炸 COLBY 来模拟另一次大型爆炸 BOXCAR。这种模拟地震类型的震源后来被称为构造能量释放，代表了爆炸源周围岩石的爆炸驱动断裂。

　　由国防部资助的研究成果每年都会在一个被称为地震研究研讨会的会议上展示。索恩·莱（Thorne Lay）（我的同学）和我都会和唐（Don）一起参加这些会议，这间接地把我的职业道路引回到我的家乡洛斯阿拉莫斯，我最终成为原子弹诞生地的第 11 任主任。在研究研讨会上，我们会展示我们的成果——在那些日子里，首选的方法是把胶片投影到一个总是太小的屏幕上展示给一百名科学家和来自资助机构的官员。在演讲过程中，唐（Don）总是要求我们 "帮忙"放置和更换透明胶片。这是一个重大的挑战，因为唐（Don）会对演讲的某些方面感兴趣，并决定跳过整个演讲的部分，而进入他正在思考的部分。唐（Don）第一次这样做时，我感到很不安；到了第五次会议时，我实际上期待着在唐（Don）的突发奇想（或指导）下的即兴发挥。

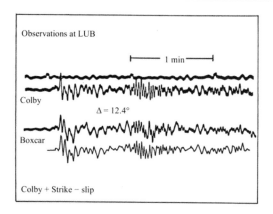

图 1 世界范围地震台网(WWSN)LUB 台站记录到的 BOXCAR 和 COLBY 事件的 P 和 PL 波形比较。下面显示的是用 COLBY 的地震图和模拟构造能量释放的理论地震图叠加以得到的波形,该理论地震图是以纯走滑方向和 5×10^{24} 达因·厘米的力矩生成的。来自 Wallace 等（1983）。

　　唐·亨伯格（Don Helmberger）是一位非凡的导师。人们很容易把他对地震图上波动的本质的卓越洞察力视为他最大的才能。然而，在事后看来，唐（Don）的贡献显然要比这大得多。他永不满足的好奇心，对理解世界的热情，以及他主要在球场上流露出来的隐秘的玩心，教会了我们如何成为一个科学家，如何成为一个批判性的思想家。我确信，唐·亨伯格（Don Helmberger）的一千多篇论文将被作为他的遗产来引用，但他最大的贡献实际上是塑造了一代科学家。

参 考 文 献

Burdick LJ, Wallace T and Lay T (1984). Modeling near-field and teleseismic observations from the Amchitka test site. J Geophys Res: Solid Earth **89**(B6): 4373–4388.

Lay T, Wallace TC and Helmberger DV (1984). The effects of tectonic release on short-period P waves from NTS explosions. Bull Seismol Soc Am **74**(3): 819–841.

Wallace TC, Helmberger DV and Ebel JE (1981a). A broadband study of the 13 August 1978 Santa Barbara earthquake. Bull Seismol Soc Am **71**(6): 1701–1718.

Wallace TC, Helmberger DV and Mellman GR (1981b). A technique for the inversion of regional data in source parameter studies. J Geophys Res **86**(B3): 1679–1685.

Wallace TC and Helmberger DV (1982). Determining source parameters of moderate-size earthquakes from regional waveforms. Phys Earth Planet Int **30**(2-3): 185–196.

Wallace TC, Helmberger DV and Engen GR (1983). Evidence of tectonic release from underground nuclear explosions in long-period P waves. Bull Seismol Soc Am **73**(2): 593–613.

Wallace TC, Helmberger DV and Engen GR (1985). Evidence of tectonic release from underground nuclear explosions in long-period S waves. Bull Seismol Soc Am **75**(1): 157–174.

Wallace TC, Helmberger DV and Lay T (1986). Reply to comments by A. Douglas, J. B. Young, and N. S. Lyman and a note on the revised moments for Pahute Mesa tectonic release. Bull Seismol Soc Am **76**(1): 313–318.

　　特里·华莱士，洛斯阿拉莫斯国家实验室名誉主任，是该实验室的第 11 任主任；此前为负责全球安全的首席副主任和高级情报官。于 1983 年在加州理工学院获得博士学位，唐·亨伯格教授是他的主要论文导师。离开加州理工学院后，在亚利桑那大学任教 20 年，是地球科学系和应用数学系的成员。曾获美国地球物理联合会麦凯尔温奖，曾担任美国地震学会主席，并被授予卡内基矿物学奖章。2018 年被授予国家核安全管理局服务金质奖章。

Chapter 4. Recollections of my mentor, Donald V. Helmberger

Stephen Grand [*]

Department of Geological Sciences, Jackson School of Geosciences, University of Texas at Austin, TX 78712, USA

[*]**Correspondence:** steveg@jsg.utexas.edu

Citation: Grand SP (2022). Recollections of my mentor, Donald V. Helmberger. Earthq Sci **35**(1): 14−16 doi: 10.1016/j.eqs.2022.01.013

I arrived at Caltech as a graduate student in the summer of 1979. With a BSc degree in physics, I knew little to nothing about seismology or geophysics. The Seismo Lab encouraged new students to immediately start some research with a great latitude on what to work on. That summer I started projects relocating aftershocks of the 1978 Oaxaca earthquake with Karen McNally, learning a normal mode code with Bernard Minster, and investigating the source mechanism of the 1979 St. Elias earthquake with Hiroo Kanamori. I didn't feel particularly excited by my early projects, probably due to my ignorance, so I was still open to some new direction. Senior students suggested I should ask Don if he had any possible projects. After a brief discussion with Don, he called me to his office. On a large table in his office he had laid out paper copies of the north-south component seismograms from stations in eastern Canada. These showed tangential motions produced by the 1966 El Golfo earthquake that occurred in the Gulf of California. Don was excited and pointed out two peaks in the recordings at WES and SFA (marked in Figure 1) that seemed to coalesce to a single large peak at SCH. He thought they might be reflections from the discontinuities at 410 km and 660 km depth and suggested I model them. The arrivals were well after the S waves (they were SS waves) and given the computational resources available at the time it was not clear how to model them, so Don suggested looking into a new synthetic seismogram approach that he called "chapstick" (Chapman, 1978). Of course I had no idea what modeling entailed, nor could I understand what was in the seismograms. But Don was encouraging and optimistic so I went off and learned the theory behind WKBJ synthetics and wrote a simple code to compute synthetic seismograms. At that point Don said "now for the fun part" and I began to make synthetics to compare to the data. Don was right, it was fun and I was hooked on modeling seismograms, like so many of his other students over the years.

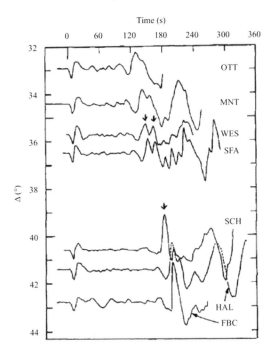

Fig. 1   Tangential component seismograms produced by the El Golfo earthquake recorded in eastern Canada (Grand and Helmberger, 1984a). S waves are aligned at zero time and the seismograms are normalized by the S wave amplitudes. Arrows above station WES indicate two peaks in the waveforms that appear to coalesce to one large peak at SCH.

Through trial and error, I was able to find a shear wave velocity model that fit the El Golfo seismograms, and to understand what paths waves took to produce the peaks in the seismograms. It turned out the first peak was a wave that turned near 200 km depth and the second from the discontinuity near 410 km depth. Don was happy with the results and wrote a short (10 pages) NSF proposal to fund me going forward. The model we developed was one-dimensional, and unfortunately there was clear evidence that mantle shear velocities beneath the western United States and eastern Canada were different. That led us to search for data similar to the El Golfo earthquake data that sampled homogenous tectonic provinces. Modeling these data resulted in upper mantle shear velocity models for the East Pacific Rise-western United States, Canadian Shield, and the northwestern Atlantic Ocean (Grand and Helmberger, 1984a, 1984b). Realizing the potential of using the waveforms of multiple bounce P and S waves to investigate the upper mantle, Don encouraged a number of studies sampling the mantle on a global scale (Rial et al., 1984; Grand and Helmberger, 1985; Graves and Helmberger, 1988; Lefevre and Helmberger, 1989) and made efforts to model data in 2D structures (Helmberger et al., 1985a, 1985b) . Ultimately, using the ability to identify the mantle paths that produced individual pulses in complicated seismograms led to efforts to develop fully 3D mantle models using tomography methods that my classmate, Gene Humphreys, taught me (Grand, 1987).

Over the years I have been amazed at the many discoveries made by Don and his students. We would have a dinner at most AGU fall meetings and he would always be excited by the most recent results that one of his students had found that year. Don looked at structures spanning from the inner core (Song XD and Helmberger, 1992) to the surface of the Earth (Helmberger and Vidale, 1988) . In most of these studies Don used three skills that I think he was uniquely supreme in. First, he loved looking at seismic data and had the ability to notice significant features in seismograms that could be used to discover something about the Earth. I doubt if any other seismologist would have noticed anything unusual in the waveforms preceding the Love wave that led me to a career studying the mantle. His second skill was to understand what structural feature could cause an observed anomaly in a seismic waveform. He had an incredible intuition about seismic wave propagation. I was particularly impressed with his intuition when he started looking at 3D structures, for example multi-pathing of waves sampling the edges of the large low shear velocity provinces (Ni SD et al., 2005). His third strength was the ability to develop synthetic seismogram codes that were practical to use for solving Earth problems and to apply them. Starting in his graduate student days, he developed the Cagniard de Hoop method for computing synthetic seismograms (Helmberger, 1968) and used the approach to model observed seismograms. I believe he was the first to really try to match higher frequency waveforms with synthetics, ultimately leading to many discoveries. Over the years he modified synthetic methods applicable to more complex structures, but always based on a generalized ray approach. Even though he embraced numerical methods as they became more feasible to apply, his ray-based approach was productive due to the intuitive nature of the method and his ability to both interpret synthetics and data.

As an advisor, Don did not push his ideas hard but showed confidence and trust in his students to explore on their own. I remember early in my career asking him what to do next and he responded "whose project is this?". I needed that comment to become more independent in my research and appreciated it a lot as I moved forward in my career. Don was very accepting of all the different personalities of his students and I think he was often amused by their different quirks. The only times I saw an indication of competitiveness in him was during the Saturday morning football games that he always participated in with students and other faculty. Aside from his great knowledge of seismic waveforms, I think Don's greatest strength as an advisor was his infectious enthusiasm and joy when explaining seismic waveforms.

Donald V. Helmberger was a great, unique scientist and advisor of students. I owe him more than I can express and miss him dearly.

References

Chapman CH (1978). A new method for computing synthetic seismograms. Geophys J R Astr Soc 54(3): 481–518.

Grand SP and Helmberger DV (1984a). Upper mantle shear structure of North America. Geophys J Int 76(2): 399–438.

Grand SP and Helmberger DV (1984b). Upper mantle shear structure beneath the northwest Atlantic Ocean. J Geophys Res: Solid Earth 89(B13): 11465–11475.

Grand SP and Helmberger DV (1985). Upper mantle shear structure beneath Asia from multi-bounce S waves. Phys Earth Planet Inter 41(2-3): 154–169.

Grand SP (1987). Tomographic inversion for shear velocity beneath the North American plate. J Geophys Res: Solid Earth 92(B13): 14065–14090.

Graves RW and Helmberger DV (1988). Upper mantle cross section from Tonga to Newfoundland. J Geophys Res: Solid Earth 93(B5): 4701–4711.

Helmberger DV (1968). The crust-mantle transition in the Bering Sea. Bull Seismol Soc Am 58(1): 179–214.

Helmberger DV, Engen GR and Grand SP (1985a). Notes on wave propagation in laterally varying structure. J Geophys 58(1): 82–91.

Helmberger DV, Engen GR and Grand SP (1985b). Upper-mantle cross-section from California to Greenland. J Geophys 58(1): 92–100.

Helmberger DV and Vidale JE (1988). Modeling strong motions produced by earthquakes with two-dimensional numerical codes. Bull Seismol Soc Am 78(1): 109–121.

Lefevre LV and Helmberger DV (1989). Upper mantle P velocity structure of the Canadian Shield. J Geophys Res: Solid Earth 94(B12): 17749–17765.

Ni SD, Helmberger DV and Tromp J (2005). Three-dimensional structure of the African superplume from waveform modelling. Geophys J Int 161(2): 283–294.

Rial JA, Grand SP and Helmberger DV (1984). A note on lateral variation in upper mantle shear-wave velocity across the Alpine front. Geophys J Int 77(3): 639–654.

Song XD and Helmberger DV (1992). Velocity structure near the inner core boundary from waveform modeling. J Geophys Res: Solid Earth 97(5): 6573–6586.

Stephen Grand is currently the Shell Chair in Geophysics in the Department of Geological Sciences, University of Texas at Austin. He completed his Ph.D. at Caltech in 1986 with Prof Helmberger as his thesis advisor. He was then on the faculty at the University of Illinois for two years before joining the University of Texas at Austin. He is an AGU Fellow and a recipient of the Inge Lehmann Medal of the AGU. His webpage can be found at: https://www.jsg.utexas.edu/researcher/stephen_grand/.

第4章　回忆我的导师：唐·亨伯格

史蒂夫·格兰德
美国得克萨斯大学奥斯汀分校地质科学系杰克逊地球科学学院

引用：Grand SP (2022). Recollections of my mentor, Donald V. Helmberger. Earthq Sci 35(1): 14−16 doi: 10.1016/j.eqs.2022.01.013

　　1979 年夏天我来到加州理工学院攻读研究生。虽然我已经获得了物理学学士学位，但我对地震学或者说地球物理学知识几乎一无所知。地震实验室鼓励新学生立刻开始一些研究，而在研究内容方面自由度很大。从那年夏天开始，我与卡伦·麦克纳利（Karen McNally）进行了 1978 年瓦哈卡（Oaxaca）地震余震的重定位研究，学习了伯纳德·明斯特（Bernard Minster）自由震荡代码，还和金森博雄（Hiroo Kanamori）一起研究了 1979 圣伊莱亚斯（St.Elias）地震的震源机制。我对我早期的研究课题并不感冒，这可能是因为我的无知，所以我对新的研究方向始终保持开放的态度。高年级学生建议我咨询一下唐·亨伯格（Don Helmberger）是否有新的研究课题。一番简短的讨论之后，他把我叫到了他的办公室。在他办公室的大桌子上摆放了一张来自加拿大东部地震台的南北分量地震图的纸质副本。这些图像展现了 1966 年加利福尼亚湾 El Golfo 地震引起的切向运动。唐（Don）十分激动，并指着 WES 和 SFA 两个台站记录的两个峰值（图 1 标注位置），在 SCH 台站上这两个峰值似乎合并成了一个。他认为它们可能是 410km 和 660km 不连续面的反射信号，并建议我对其进行模拟。它们到时远远晚于 S 波（SS 波），考虑到当时可用的计算资源，难以清楚地知道如何模拟它们，因此唐（Don）建议研究一种新的合成地震图方法，他称之为"唇膏"。当然我当时并不知道建模意味着什么，也无法理解地震记录中有什么。但唐（Don）看上去是十分令人鼓舞以及乐观的，所以我离开后开始学习 WKBJ 合成图背后的理论并且写了一个简单的代码用于计算理论地震图。这时唐（Don）说"现在到了有趣的部分了"，我开始生成理论波形并与实际数据相比较。事实证明唐（Don）是对的，这过程很有趣而我也迷上了模拟地震图，就像多年来他的其他学生一样。

　　经过反复尝试后，我成功找到了符合 El Golfo 地震记录的剪切波速度模型，并理解了地震图中导致峰值形成的射线路径。结果表明第一个峰是由在 200km 深度左右出现的波导致，而第二个是由 410km 不连续面导致的。唐（Don）对结果十分满意并写了一份简短的（10 页）NSF 项目申请书来资助我继续探索。我们发展了一个一维模型，但不幸的是现有的明确证据表明美国西部和加拿大东部的地幔剪切波速度是不同的。这促使我们寻找类似于 El Golfo 地震的数据，这些数据采样了相同地质构造区域。我们对这些数据进行模拟，最终得到了东太平洋隆起-美国西部、加拿大地盾和大西洋西北部的上地幔剪切波速度模型（Grand and Helmberger, 1984a, 1984b）。唐（Don）意识到利用 P 波和 S 波的多次反射波研究上地幔的潜力，他鼓励我进行一系列的采样研究全球尺度的地幔结构（Rial et al., 1984; Grand and Helmberger, 1985; Graves and Helmberger, 1988; Lefevre and Helmberger, 1989），并努力建立二维结构模型（Helmberger et al., 1985a, 1985b）。最终，通过识别由地幔中射线路径传播产生的地震图上的单个脉冲信号，并利用我同学基恩·汉弗莱斯（Gene Humphreys）教我的成像方法，我建构了三维全地幔模型（Grand, 1987）。

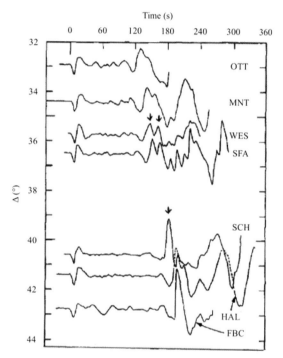

图 1　加拿大东部台站记录的 El Golfo 地震切向分量地震图。S 波在零时刻对齐，并用 S 波振幅对地震图归一化。WES 台站上的箭头指示了波形的两个峰，在 SCH 记录上似乎合并成了一个振幅更大的峰。

　　这些年来我一直惊叹于唐（Don）和他的学生所取得的成就。我们会在大多数美国地球物理学会（American Geophysical Union，AGU）会议期间共进晚餐，他总是为这一年间他学生的最新发现感到兴奋。唐（Don）的研究覆盖了从地球内核（Song XD and Helmberger, 1992）到地球表面的结构（Helmberger and Vidale, 1988）。在大部分研究中，唐（Don）使用了三种我认为是他最具特色的能力。首先，他尤其喜欢挖掘地震数据，并且总能从中窥探到有关地球的奥妙。我怀疑是否有其他地震学家能注意到勒夫波到达之前的波形的异常，而正是这使我走上了研究地幔之路。他的第二个技能是能够察觉到怎样的结构特征会导致观察到的地震波波形异常。他对地震波的传播有着惊人的直觉。我对此印象尤深的是他开始研究三维结构时，比如在低剪切波速区域边缘的波的多路径采样（Ni SD et al., 2005）。他的第三个强项是能开发实用的生成理论地震图的代码，能够解决实际地球问题并加以应用。从他的研究生时代开始，他发展了卡尼亚尔·德胡普（Cagniard de Hoop）理论用来计算生成理论地震图（Helmberger, 1968），并用它来模拟实际观测的地震图。我相信他是首位真正尝试用合成理论地震图匹配更高频波形的人，这最终引导了很多结果的发现。多年来，他改进了他的合成方法，使之能应用于更复杂的结构，但这一方法始终基于广义射线理论。尽管因为应用可行性的提高，他接受了数值方法，但他基于射线路径的方法仍然是富有成效的，这源于这一理论的直觉性以及他解释理论地震图和实际数据的能力。

作为一名导师，唐（Don）并没有过分强调自己的想法，而是对学生自我探索充满信心和信任。记得在我的职业生涯早期，我询问他下一步怎么做时，他反问我："这是谁的项目？"不得不承认的是这使我在我自己的研究中变得更独立，在我的职业生涯中我非常感激这一点。唐（Don）能够接受多元化性格的学生，我想他经常会被他们不同的怪癖逗乐吧。我唯一能看到他充满求胜欲的时刻是在周六早上的橄榄球比赛中，他总是同学生还有其他教师一起参与比赛。除去他对地震波形的渊博知识外，我认为唐（Don）作为一名导师的最大优点是在解释地震波形时那种富有感染力的热情和喜悦。

唐·亨伯格（Don Helmberger）是一位伟大而独特的科学家和导师。我对他的崇敬之情无以言表，仅在此表达我对他的深情思念。

参 考 文 献

Chapman CH (1978). A new method for computing synthetic seismograms. Geophys J R Astr Soc 54(3): 481–518.

Grand SP and Helmberger DV (1984a). Upper mantle shear structure of North America. Geophys J Int 76(2): 399–438.

Grand SP and Helmberger DV (1984b). Upper mantle shear structure beneath the northwest Atlantic Ocean. J Geophys Res: Solid Earth 89(B13): 11465–11475.

Grand SP and Helmberger DV (1985). Upper mantle shear structure beneath Asia from multi-bounce S waves. Phys Earth Planet Inter 41(2-3): 154–169.

Grand SP (1987). Tomographic inversion for shear velocity beneath the North American plate. J Geophys Res: Solid Earth 92(B13): 14065–14090.

Graves RW and Helmberger DV (1988). Upper mantle cross section from Tonga to Newfoundland. J Geophys Res: Solid Earth 93(B5): 4701–4711.

Helmberger DV (1968). The crust-mantle transition in the Bering Sea. Bull Seismol Soc Am 58(1): 179–214.

Helmberger DV, Engen GR and Grand SP (1985a). Notes on wave propagation in laterally varying structure. J Geophys 58(1): 82–91.

Helmberger DV, Engen GR and Grand SP (1985b). Upper-mantle cross-section from California to Greenland. J Geophys 58(1): 92–100.

Helmberger DV and Vidale JE (1988). Modeling strong motions produced by earthquakes with two-dimensional numerical codes. Bull Seismol Soc Am 78(1): 109–121.

Lefevre LV and Helmberger DV (1989). Upper mantle P velocity structure of the Canadian Shield. J Geophys Res: Solid Earth 94(B12): 17749–17765.

Ni SD, Helmberger DV and Tromp J (2005). Three-dimensional structure of the African superplume from waveform modelling. Geophys J Int 161(2): 283–294.

Rial JA, Grand SP and Helmberger DV (1984). A note on lateral variation in upper mantle shear-wave velocity across the Alpine front. Geophys J Int 77(3): 639–654.

Song XD and Helmberger DV (1992). Velocity structure near the inner core boundary from waveform modeling. J Geophys Res: Solid Earth 97(5): 6573–6586.

　　史蒂芬•格兰德，现得克萨斯大学奥斯汀分校地质科学系地球物理学教授。1986 年于加州理工学院获得博士学位，论文导师为亨伯格教授。曾于伊利诺伊大学工作两年，后加入得克萨斯大学奥斯汀分校并工作至今。他是美国地球物理联合会会士和莱曼奖章获得者。他的主页是 https://www.jsg.utexas.edu/researcher/stephen_grand/。

Chapter 5. Graduate studies with Donald V. Helmberger

John Vidale[*]

Department of Earth Sciences, University of Southern California, CA 90089, USA

[*]**Correspondence:** seismoguy@mac.com

Citation: Vidale JE (2022). Graduate studies with Donald V. Helmberger. Earthq Sci **35**(1): 17–18 doi: 10.1016/j.eqs.2022.01.009

Arriving at the Seismo Lab in 1981, I first worked with Hiroo Kanamori on the seismotectonics of the New Hebrides (Vidale and Kanamori, 1983) (I don't remember why). Then with Rob Clayton I worked on finite-difference methods of modeling seismic waves, specifically how to bump second-order methods to fourth-order and encode the inner loop in assembly language to make it run twice as fast (Vidale, 1990). My studies progressed to wandering the third-floor hall in search of chatty mentors who would have insight into the random real and synthetic seismograms I carried, which increasingly meant Don, although Rob and Hiroo also were often interrupted. By graduation at the end of 1986, I'd concocted some numerical methods (Vidale, 1986, 1988, 1990; Vidale et al., 1985) and explored LA basin resonance (Vidale and Helmberger, 1988; Helmberger and Vidale, 1988), subducting slab structure (Vidale, 1987), nuclear-explosion-powered near-field Rayleigh waves in the Aleutians (Vidale and Helmberger, 1987), and abandoned numerous less successful forays.

It's remarkable, at least in my memory, that Don gave few imperatives or barriers to my aimless progress. Fortunately, Heidi Houston was more incisive. Perhaps due to fellowships, I was left free to dabble with faint reflections of mantle discontinuities–at least until Terry Wallace asked the obvious question how minuscule would they be compared to the overwhelming noise level. I was searching for subtle waveform distortions of subducting slabs (Vidale, 1987), until we realized some early MIT slab anomaly models were erroneously strong. There was something unresolved about stresses in slabs (I warned my qualifying exam committee not to ask about my vaporware third proposition), so I tried refining mantle discontinuity triplications with numerical magic until I learned one cannot get something from nothing. I still don't know why I tried to re-code the Zoeppritz equations or make a grid-based travel time calculator (Vidale, 1988) and a complex polarization filter (Vidale, 1986). Don was a gentle guide, as were Rob and Hiroo.

Don was generous. He overlooked the homework I didn't do for his and Dave Harkrider's classes, settling for having me work as TA (teaching assistant) for both classes the next year, with re-adjustment of the grade (unlike my equally-earned and more permanent D in Brad Hager's geodynamics) and added the TA pay to my fellowship. He hired me with double salary as a post-doc for a month or two when I defended my thesis sooner than I'd projected.

But mostly Don trained immersion in the data until the wiggles could be plausibly explained by synthetics. We first laid out the figures, then I filled in the rest of the paper. The seismograms, and the cartoons explaining how they were derived, and the models they required to be true are the core; the words are secondary. If the story is not convincing, we will go back to get more data and calculate more and better synthetics. Entertain as many ideas as one could, but don't get too attached, and the geology was much less interesting to us than the seismic velocity structure. He was adept, as he knew the influence of many levels and scales of structure, as well as the peculiarities of earthquakes and foibles of data and synthetics, and places to find more data. I've striven to follow his path for better and worse.

Many of the stories of Don have documented his contributions to understanding the crust, mantle, core, earthquakes, and explosions. One prescient paper that he never mentioned to me struck me as potentially seminal and underappreciated. So I'll offer an interpretation. The 1973 paper (Allen and Helmberger, 1973) in a Stanford volume with Clarence Allen cleanly showed no changes of the sort that would match highly publicized claims about the temporal velocity changes associated with the "Palmdale Bulge." A several-inch-high bulge across the Mojave Desert was claimed to be a symptom of dilatancy-diffusion along the San Andreas fault. This was a fashionable theory of the time that suggested earthquakes would soon be predictable, and that Los Angeles in particular had reason to be alarmed (therefore seismologists needed a funding boost, which showed up as the National Earthquake Hazards Reduction Program in 1976). The geodetic bump turned out a few years later to probably be optical leveling survey errors, not a real bulge. Don cleanly demonstrated there were no resolvable velocity changes to be seen and moved on, although it took several years for many prominent seismologists, some down the hall, to follow. Don understood data.

One of my more oblique interactions with Don came through his proposals. Any cutting edge seismologist recognized Don's wide ranging contributions, despite an inexplicable rivalry between those using Don's approximations and purists, usually in San Diego or on the East Coast, who denigrated less than an exact analytic solution with formal error bars. But Don's proposals were famously quirky. More than once, I found myself on a proposal review panel mulling in puzzlement at Don's verbiage. Don had plenty of accomplishments from past funding, but the proposed plan was inscrutable to any but his former students, who were fortunately legion. Upon translation into English and straightforward thought patterns, the proposals were impressive, but translation was often required.

A last anecdote: Don featured prominently in an encounter with grizzlies in Denali

National Park in 1984. Grad students Steve Grand, Heidi Houston, and I, plus Don and recently-graduated Thorne Lay, unwisely chose to hike across the tundra, and noticed increasingly fresh bear tracks as we walked. After a while, we spotted a mother grizzly with her two cubs on a hillside about 100 m away. Don must have been bored — he loudly clanked a rock against a culvert pipe, proclaiming "If the bear comes this way, I don't have to be the fastest, just not the slowest to climb into the culvert." The bear abruptly turned and stared, but fortunately was not hungry. Despite their claim to be full, we forced our way onto the next bus that went down the road.

　　With Don, one usually found a path to the next adventure.

References

Allen CR and Helmberger DV (1973). Search for temporal changes in seismic velocities using large explosions in southern California. In: Proceedings of Conference on Tectonic Problems of the San Andreas Fault System. Stanford University, Palo Alto, pp 436–445.

Helmberger DV and Vidale JE (1988). Modeling strong motions produced by earthquakes with two-dimensional numerical codes. Bull Seismol Soc Am **78**(1): 109–121.

Vidale JE and Kanamori H (1983). The October 1980 earthquake sequence near the new hebrides. Geophys Res Lett **10**(12): 1137–1140.

Vidale JE, Helmberger DV and Clayton RW (1985). Finite-difference seismograms for SH waves. Bull Seismol Soc Am **75**(6): 1765–1782.

Vidale JE (1988). Finite-difference calculation of travel times. Bull Seismol Soc Am **78**(6): 2062–2076.

Vidale JE (1986). Complex polarization analysis of particle motion. Bull Seismol Soc Am **76**(5): 1393–1405.

Vidale JE (1987). Waveform effects of a high-velocity, subducted slab. Geophys Res Lett **14**(5): 542–545.

Vidale JE and Helmberger DV (1987). Path effects in strong motion seismology. In: Bolt BA ed. Seismic Strong Motion Synthetics. Elsevier, Amsterdam, pp 267–319.

Vidale JE and Helmberger DV (1988). Elastic finite-difference modeling of the 1971 San Fernando, California earthquake. Bull Seismol Soc Am **78**(1): 122–141.

Vidale JE (1990). Comment on "a comparison of finite-difference and fourier method calculations of synthetic seismograms". Bull Seismol Soc Am **80**(2): 493–495.

John Vidale is currently professor and dean's chair at the University of Southern California. After majoring in physics and geology at Yale, he completed his Ph.D. at Caltech in 1986 with Profs. Helmberger and Clayton as advisors. Next, he became a research scientist at UC Santa Cruz and then the US Geological Survey. He subsequently spent a decade each at UCLA and the University of Washington, running the Institute of Geophysics and Planetary Physics and the Pacific Northwest Seismic Network. At USC, he ran the Southern California Earthquake Center for a very short while. He is a recipient of the Macelwane Medal of the American Geophysical Union, and is a member of the U.S. National Academy of Science. His webpage can be found at: https://dornsife.usc.edu/profile/john-vidale/.

第 5 章　跟随唐·亨伯格的研究生学习

约翰·维达莱
美国南加州大学

引用：Vidale JE (2022). Graduate studies with Donald V. Helmberger. Earthq Sci **35**(1): 17–18 doi: 10.1016/j.eqs.2022.01.009

　　1981 年来到加州理工学院地震实验室，我首先与金森博雄（Hiroo Kanamori）一起（Vidale and Kanamori, 1983）研究新赫布里底群岛的地震构造（但是，我已经不记得当初为什么选择这个研究项目）。然后，我与罗布·克莱顿（Rob Clayton）一起研究了地震波模拟的有限差分方法，特别是如何将二阶方法提升到四阶格式，并用汇编语言对内层循环进行编程，使其运行速度提高一倍（Vidale, 1990）。为了下一步的研究工作，我在实验室三楼的走廊里闲逛，寻找对我拿着的这堆随机的实际观测和合成地震图有独到见解的健谈导师。我越来越多地与唐（Don）进行交流，虽然偶尔也会去打扰罗布（Rob）和博雄（Hiroo）。到 1986 年底毕业时，我编写了一些数值方法（Vidale, 1986, 1988, 1990; Vidale et al., 1985）并探索了洛杉矶盆地的共振效应（Vidale and Helmberger, 1988; Helmberger and Vidale, 1988）、俯冲板片的结构（Vidale, 1987）、位于阿留申群岛的核爆驱动的近场瑞利波（Vidale and Helmberger, 1987），并放弃了许多不太成功的尝试。

　　值得注意的是，在我的记忆中，唐（Don）对我漫无目的的科研工作几乎没有任何要求或者阻挠。幸运的是，海迪·休斯敦（Heidi Houston）是比较严格的。也许是因为有奖学金，我可以自由地涉足地幔不连续面的微弱反射问题——至少在特里·华莱士（Terry Wallace）问了我一个显而易见的问题之前：这一反射信号与压倒性的噪音水平相比会有多微不足道。我一直在寻找俯冲板块导致的细微波形失真（Vidale, 1987），直到我们意识到早期一些麻省理工学院提出的板块异常模型中的强烈异常是错误的。板内的应力仍存在一些未解决的问题（我预先告知我的资格考试委员会不要对我的不成熟的第三个研究项目提问），所以我尝试用数字上的把戏来细化地幔不连续面对应的三重震相的认识，直到我想明白信息不可能凭空从无到有。我仍然想不通为什么我会尝试重新编写 Zoeppritz 方程或做一个基于网格的走时计算器（Vidale, 1988）和复杂的偏振滤波器（Vidale, 1986）。唐（Don）是一个和蔼的导师，罗布（Rob）和博雄（Hiroo）也是。

　　唐（Don）很大度。他原谅了我在他和戴夫·哈克赖德（Dave Harkrider）的课程中没做的作业，并决定让我在第二年担任这两门课程的助教，并重新调整成绩[（而在布拉德·黑格（Brad Hager）的地球动力学课程中我则是得了一个应得的 D，并且没有被调整]，还将助教工资添加到我的奖学金中。当我的论文答辩比我预期的要早时，他以双倍的薪水聘请我做了一两个月的博士后。

但大多数情况下，唐（Don）沉浸在数据中，直到波形可以用理论合成地震图合理地解释。我们首先排版好图，然后我补充论文的其余部分。地震图、解释它们是如何产生的示意图以及所需的模型是核心，而语言是次要的。如果故事没有说服力，我们会返回获取更多数据并计算更多更好的合成理论地震图。他认为我们应该接受尽可能多的想法，但不要太执着，地质学对我们来说远没有地震速度结构那么有趣。他很擅长他的工作，因为他知道许多不同程度和尺度的结构的影响，以及地震的特殊性、数据和合成波形的弱点，以及能找到更多数据的地方。我一直在努力追随他的脚步，无论好坏。

唐（Don）的许多故事都记录了他对探究地壳、地幔、地核、地震和爆炸的贡献。一篇他从未向我提到过的有先见之明的论文，让我觉得它具有潜在的开创性和被低估的价值。所以接下来，我想详细解释一下。1973 年与克拉伦斯·艾伦（Clarence Allen）合著的斯坦福卷中的论文（Allen and Helmberger, 1973）清楚地表明，尽管和"棕榈谷隆起"相关的速度时变的观点被广泛认可，但没有任何（观测到的）变化能够证实这一观点。据称，横跨莫哈韦沙漠的一个数英寸高的隆起是圣安德烈亚斯断层沿线膨胀扩散的征兆。这是当时流行的一种理论，认为地震很快就可以被预测，特别是洛杉矶有理由进入警戒状态（因此地震学家需要增加资金，这在 1976 年作为国家地震减灾计划出台）。几年后，大地测量学的迅猛发展证明这可能是光学水准测量的错误，而不是真正的隆起。唐（Don）清楚地证明了我们无法观测到可解析的速度变化，并继续去做其他工作了；而许多著名的地震学家花了几年时间，沿着这条路一直走下去。唐（Don）是真正能理解数据的人。

我与唐（Don）的一次比较间接的互动来自他的科研项目申请书。任何前沿的地震学家都认可唐（Don）的广泛贡献，尽管使用唐（Don）的近似理论的人与通常在圣迭戈或东海岸的纯粹主义者之间存在无法解释的竞争，那些纯粹主义者追求有正式的误差棒的精确解析解。但唐（Don）的申请书以古怪著称。不止一次，我发现自己在一个项目会评会议上，对唐（Don）的措辞感到困惑。唐（Don）从过去的资助中取得了很多成就，但除了他以前的学生以外，任何人都会觉得他提出的计划是不可思议的，幸运的是他的学生人数不少。在翻译成常人所能理解的和直截了当的语言表达后，这些申请书是令人印象深刻的，但翻译是必需的。

最后一则轶事：1984 年，唐（Don）在德纳利国家公园与灰熊相遇时表现突出。研究生史蒂夫·格兰德（Steve Grand）、海迪·休斯敦（Heidi Houston）和我，以及唐（Don）和刚毕业的索恩·莱（Thorne Lay），不明智地选择徒步穿越苔原，在行进的过程中，我们注意到越来越多的新鲜的熊迹。过了一会儿，我们在大约 100 m 外的山坡上发现了一只灰熊妈妈和它的两只幼崽。唐（Don）一定是觉得有些无聊——他大声地用一块石头撞击下水渠，提出"如果熊冲向我们，我不必是最快的，只要不是最慢一个爬进下水道的就好。"熊猛地转过身来，瞪大了眼睛，幸好它们并不饿。然后我们强行登上了沿路行驶的下一辆公共汽车，尽管他们说已经人满了。

和唐（Don）在一起，人们通常会找到通往下一次冒险的道路。

参 考 文 献

Allen CR and Helmberger DV (1973). Search for temporal changes in seismic velocities using large explosions in southern California. In: Proceedings of Conference on Tectonic Problems of the San Andreas Fault System. Stanford University, Palo Alto, pp 436–445.

Helmberger DV and Vidale JE (1988). Modeling strong motions produced by earthquakes with two-dimensional numerical codes. Bull Seismol Soc Am **78**(1): 109–121.

Vidale JE and Kanamori H (1983). The October 1980 earthquake sequence near the new hebrides. Geophys Res Lett **10**(12): 1137–1140.

Vidale JE, Helmberger DV and Clayton RW (1985). Finite-difference seismograms for SH waves. Bull Seismol Soc Am **75**(6): 1765–1782.

Vidale JE (1988). Finite-difference calculation of travel times. Bull Seismol Soc Am **78**(6): 2062–2076.

Vidale JE (1986). Complex polarization analysis of particle motion. Bull Seismol Soc Am **76**(5): 1393–1405.

Vidale JE (1987). Waveform effects of a high-velocity, subducted slab. Geophys Res Lett **14**(5): 542–545.

Vidale JE and Helmberger DV (1987). Path effects in strong motion seismology. In: Bolt BA ed. Seismic Strong Motion Synthetics. Elsevier, Amsterdam, pp 267–319.

Vidale JE and Helmberger DV (1988). Elastic finite-difference modeling of the 1971 San Fernando, California earthquake. Bull Seismol Soc Am **78**(1): 122–141.

Vidale JE (1990). Comment on "a comparison of finite-difference and fourier method calculations of synthetic seismograms". Bull Seismol Soc Am **80**(2): 493–495.

　　约翰·维达莱（John Vidale）目前是南加州大学的院长讲席教授。在耶鲁大学主修物理和地质学后，于 1986 年在加州理工大学亨伯格（Helmberger）和克莱顿（Clayton）教授的指导下完成了博士学位。此后，他成为加州大学圣克鲁斯分校和美国地质调查局的科研人员。随后，他分别在加州大学洛杉矶分校和华盛顿大学工作了十年，负责地球物理和行星物理研究所以及太平洋西北地震台网。在南加州大学，他曾短时间担任南加州地震中心主任一职。他是美国地球物理联合会麦凯尔温奖章的获得者，并且是美国国家科学院院士。个人主页是 https://dornsife.usc.edu/profile/john-vidale/。

Chapter 6. Memories of Donald V. Helmberger: Mentor and seismologist extraordinaire

Allison Bent[*]

Natural Resources Canada 7 Observatory Cres., Ottawa, Ontario K1A 0Y3, Canada

[*]**Correspondence:** allison.bent@nrcan-rncan.gc.ca

Citation: Bent A (2022). Memories of Donald V. Helmberger: Mentor and seismologist extraordinaire. Earthq Sci **35**(1): 19–21 doi: 10.1016/j.eqs.2022.01.018

I grew up in one of the most aseismic regions of the planet but decided as a child that I wanted to be a seismologist. Ignoring all the naysayers who claimed that no one really did that for a living and who told me I should choose something sensible like neurosurgery or engineering, I showed up at the Caltech Seismo Lab in the summer of 1985. I arrived equipped with the right skills but, as I quickly learned, no real knowledge of the breadth of seismological research. On day one I made the usual rounds of the faculty and soon thereafter began working on a project relocating earthquakes of a swarm in the Coso region.

A couple of months later, Don Helmberger stopped me in the hall and asked if I needed a project. I told him I was working on something but was also looking for a second project. He was wondering whether there could be a relation between stress drop and depth and was looking for a student to work on it. I thought it sounded interesting, agreed to take a stab at it and was thus introduced to the wonderful world of synthetic seismograms. It was one of the best decisions I ever made. Using a bunch of wiggles to unlock the secrets of earthquake sources and the Earth itself had an appeal that the seismicity based work, although interesting, didn't. I was hooked. By the way, the answer to the stress drop question is a definite maybe.

A decade prior to my arrival at Caltech, Don and his previous students and collaborators had developed methods to study earthquake sources through waveform modeling and the use of synthetic seismograms (e.g., Helmberger and Engen, 1980; Langston and Helmberger, 1975). Don explained the theory to me and sent me to one of his more senior graduate students, Vicky Lefevre, for a crash course on how to use the codes. He then handed me a paper (I've forgotten which one) and told me to come back when I could reproduce all of the synthetic seismograms in it exactly as they appeared. One of Don's strengths was that he didn't spoon feed his students but encouraged them to work out problems for themselves. At the same time, he provided guidance and acted as a sounding board. He wasn't constantly looking over our shoulders but if we went too long without talking to him, he would seek us out and ask about progress. His style of supervision was a perfect fit for my style of working. His enthusiasm was infectious.

I dislike asking for help but have learned that sometimes it's necessary. Any time I went to Don because I was stuck, I had already tried numerous solutions and come up empty. I'd go into his office, explain the problem and say I tried x, y, and z but none of them helped and this was why. More often than not, in the middle of the explanation I'd say "Never mind, I just figured it out". It happened enough that it wasn't lost on Don and he once made a comment "What am I, your confessor?" I think that by articulating the problem, it became better organized in my own mind and that led to the solution.

I got through the infamous "orals" and chose Don as my thesis advisor. I never regretted it. Initially, I worked on earthquakes in the "Big Bend" region of California, which, unlike much of California, is dominated by thrust faulting. The research involved modeling both regional (Pnl) and teleseismic body waves from the World-Wide Standardized Seismograph Network (WWSSN) and similar analog stations. Hand digitizing the data is a step I don't miss. Broadband stations were rarer than they are now, but we modeled both the long- and short-period data to assure that the source parameters fit multiple frequency bands. Don commented that it was easy to find a perfect fit for a single seismogram but that a solution which provided a very good fit to multiple seismograms and wave types recorded at different distance ranges, azimuths and frequencies was more likely to be correct than one that provided an excellent fit to only one seismogram. If the teleseismic and regional waveforms suggest different values for any parameter, there is something wrong and you need to dig deeper. He also taught me some tricks for using the PL part of the Pnl wavetrain to quickly identify whether the source mechanism was likely to be thrust or strike-slip. I saw him apply that knowledge in real time when the Loma Prieta earthquake occurred in 1989. As was typical whenever a large earthquake occurred, students, faculty and United States Geological Survey (USGS) staff rushed to gather around the seismograms on the second floor of the Seismo Lab. Don took one look at them and stated that the earthquake wasn't on the San Andreas Fault. That later became the subject of some debate but Don was correct in that this was not a typical San Andreas earthquake.

When the Whittier Narrows earthquake occurred on 1 October 1987 I was ready to tackle it. It soon became apparent that the source was complex and a simple triangular or trapezoidal source time function was inadequate to model it. Don, who had an amazing memory for seismograms, remarked that the waves reminded him of the 1971 Friuli earthquake and suggested I consult a paper by one of his former students (Cipar, 1981) and start with that. Sure enough, the same complex source did a great job fitting the Whittier Narrows data and needed only minor tweaking for a better fit. The Whittier Narrows earthquake led to my first experience as first author (Bent and Helmberger, 1989). It came back from review needing major revisions. The comments from one reviewer were quite negative identifying about thirty "major blunders". I was naturally somewhat concerned and showed the reviews to Don who merely shrugged them off and said the reviewer must have been in a snit that day. He pointed out two or three comments and told me to address those and ignore the rest. I did as he suggested, and the same reviewer subsequently commented on how much the paper had improved. There were no comments about the twenty—something supposedly major errors that had not been addressed.

As I continued to work with Don, we began to explore the idea of applying the same modeling techniques used to study contemporary earthquakes to historical ones. Given the relative paucity of high quality historical seismograms, we expanded on what could be gleaned from basic modeling by comparing the waveforms of the historical earthquakes to those of recent, well-recorded, well-studied events in the same region (Bent and Helmberger, 1991). This work could be considered a crude forbearer to the cut and paste method developed by Don and his students who succeeded me (Zhao LS and Helmberger, 1994; Zhu LP and Helmberger, 1996).

Conversations with Don were never boring. He asked lots of tough questions and I always tried and generally succeeded in coming up with an answer. However, there was one occasion when I was thoroughly stumped and responded with an emphatic "I don't know". Don said, "I don't either but I thought it was a good question". Ah-ha, it's OK if I don't always know the answer. Don had a habit of breaking off in mid sentence and staring off into space. A minute or so later he would pick up the conversation exactly where it left off. I got used to that. Another common occurrence was that he would say he was going for a coffee and would be back in a minute. Ten minutes later he often would not have returned leaving me to wonder whether I should continue to sit and wait or whether it was better to leave. When Don disappeared for days, I knew it was NBA play-off season and not to expect to see much of him until the play-offs were over.

Despite his countless contributions to seismology and his amazing insight into what seismograms were telling us, Don really didn't have an ego. I always felt that he was proudest of me (Figure 1) when I shot down one of his suggestions. He once told me that "We (meaning the Seismo Lab faculty) are all stupid. We know a lot about one or two things and nothing about anything else". Then he grinned and added "Except Hiroo. If he doesn't know, no one does".

Fig. 1   Don, coffee cup in hand, looked on as I opened a gift at my final Seismo Lab coffee break.

He also had a wicked sense of humor. I remember literally cutting and pasting data and synthetics to make a figure for my orals. This was the 1980s. Mercifully, some decent plotting codes were soon to be developed; I'm much better at science than arts and crafts. I recall saying in a sarcastic tone to a student who had stopped by to chat that this was stupendous and I was sure to impress the committee with its beauty. What I didn't know was that Don was in the hall eavesdropping. A few minutes later, he popped in and remarked that it was the ugliest thing he had ever seen.

I was saddened when Doug Dreger gave me the news of Don's passing. Seismology lost one of the great ones and I lost a mentor. However, his legacy will live on through his students and the subsequent generations of seismology they influence. More than a year later, conversations with other former students of Don always turn to how much we miss him. Don will not be forgotten.

Acknowledgments

I thank Laurel Sinclair for her review of the first draft. This paper is Natural Resources Canada Contribution Number 20210459. I would also like to thank Xiaodong Song and Thorne Lay for putting together this special issue in Don's memory.

References

Bent AL and Helmberger DV (1989). Source complexity of the October 1, 1987, Whittier Narrows earthquake. J Geophys Res: Solid Earth **94**(B7): 9548–9556.

Bent AL and Helmberger DV (1991). A re-examination of historic earthquakes in the San Jacinto fault zone, California. Bull Seismol Soc Am **81**(6): 2289–2309.

Cipar J (1981). Broadband time domain modeling of earthquakes from Friuli, Italy. Bull Seismol Soc Am **71**(4): 1215–1231.

Helmberger DV and Engen GR (1980). Modeling the long-period body waves from shallow earthquakes at regional ranges. Bull Seismol Soc Am **70**(5): 1699–1714.

Langston CA and Helmberger DV (1975). A procedure for modelling shallow dislocation sources. Geophys J Roy Astron Soc **42**(1): 117–130.

Zhao LS and Helmberger DV (1994). Source estimation from broadband regional seismograms. Bull Seismol Soc Am **84**(1): 91– 104.

Zhu LP and Helmberger DV (1996). Advancement in source estimation techniques using broadband regional seismograms. Bull Seismol Soc Am **86**(5): 1634–1641.

Allison Bent is a Research Seismologist at Natural Resources Canada where she has spent her professional career. She completed her Ph. D. at Caltech in 1990 with Prof. Helmberger as her thesis advisor. Throughout her career she has been an active member of the Seismological Society of America, formerly serving on the Board of Directors and currently as Editor-in-chief of *Seismological Research Letters*. She is the current Chair of the IASPEI Working Group on Magnitude Measurements.

第 6 章　追忆唐·亨伯格：杰出的导师和地震学家

艾莉森·本特

加拿大自然资源部

7 号观景台，安大略省渥太华，加拿大　K1A 0Y3

引用：Bent A (2022). Memories of Donald V. Helmberger: Mentor and seismologist extraordinaire. Earthq Sci **35**(1): 19–21 doi: 10.1016/j.eqs.2022.01.018

　　我在世界上地震最严重的地区之一长大，但我从小就决定要成为一名地震学家。1985年夏天，我无视所有反对的声音——他们声称没有人真正以此为生，并告诉我应该选择像神经外科或工程学这样明智的职业——来到了加州理工学院地震实验室。我来的时候已经拥有足够的技能，但是，正如我很快了解到的那样，我对地震研究的广度没有真正的了解。在第一天，我按照惯例在学院四处参观，此后不久就开始着手在科索地区的群震重定位的项目。

　　几个月后，唐·亨伯格（Don Helmberger）在大厅里拦住了我，问我是否需要一个项目。我告诉他我正在做一些事情，但也在寻找第二个项目。他想知道应力降和深度之间是否存在关系，并正在寻找一名学生来研究它。我觉得这听起来很有趣，同意试一试，我因此也被引入到合成地震图的奇妙世界。这是我做过的最好的决定之一。使用一堆摆动来解开震源和地球本身的秘密对我很有吸引力，而基于地震活动的工作虽然有趣，但不如前者有吸引力，我被迷住了。顺便说一句，应力降问题的答案是肯定的。

　　在我来加州理工学院的十年前，唐（Don）和他以前的学生和合作者已经开发出通过波形建模和使用合成地震图来研究地震源的方法（例如，Helmberger and Engen，1980；Langston and Helmberger，1975）。唐（Don）向我解释了这个理论，并把我送到他的一位更高级的研究生维基·勒费夫尔（Vicky Lefevre）那里参加使用代码的速成课程。然后唐（Don）递给我一张纸（我忘记了是哪一张），告诉我说，等我能完全重现其中的所有合成地震图时再回来。唐（Don）的优势之一是他不会向学生填鸭式灌输，而是鼓励他们自己解决问题。同时，他提供指导并检查我们的想法是否正确。他不会经常监督我们，但如果我们太久没有和他谈话，他会找我们问进展情况。他的监督风格非常适合我的工作风格。他的热情很有感染力。

　　我不喜欢寻求帮助，但我知道有时这是必要的。每当我为问题所困去找唐（Don）时，我已经试过了许多解决方案，但都一无所获。我会走进他的办公室，解释问题并说我尝试了 x、y 和 z，但它们都没有帮助，因此我才来找他。很多时候，在解释的中间我会说"没关系了，我刚刚想通了"。这种情况发生很多次，唐（Don）并不理解，他曾经说，"我是什么，你的忏悔者？"我想，通过阐明问题，它在我自己的脑海中变得更好地串联起来，从而导向了解决方案。

我通过了令人头疼的"口头报告"，并选择了唐（Don）作为我的论文导师。我从来没有后悔过。最初，我在加利福尼亚的"大湾"地区研究地震，与加利福尼亚的大部分地区不同，该地区以逆冲断层为主。该研究涉及对来自全球标准化地震仪网络（WWSSN）和类似模拟台站的区域（Pnl）和远震体波进行建模。手动数字化数据是我不会错过的一步。宽频带台站远比现在少，但我们对长周期和短周期数据进行了建模，以确保源参数符合多个频段。唐（Don）评论说，很容易为单个地震图找到一个完美的拟合，但相比于仅精确符合某一个地震图的震源机制，一个能提供非常符合多个地震图和在不同距离范围、方位角和频率记录的波类型的震源机制更可能是正确的。如果远震和区域震波形表明每个参数的值都不同，则说明有问题需要深入考虑。他还教了我一些使用 Pnl 波列的 PL 部分来快速识别震源机制是否可能是逆断层或走滑断层的技巧。我看到他在 1989 年洛马普列塔地震发生的时候实时地应用了这些知识。就像每次发生大地震时一样，在地震实验室二楼，学生、教职员工和美国地质调查局（USGS）的工作人员都争先恐后地围到地震图周围。唐（Don）看了一眼，说地震不在圣安地列斯断层上。这后来成为一些争论的主题，但唐（Don）是正确的，因为这不是典型的圣安地列斯地震。

1987 年 10 月 1 日惠蒂尔海峡发生地震时，我已做好应对的准备。很快就发现震源很复杂，简单的三角形或梯形震源时间函数不足以准确描述它。唐（Don）对地震图有着惊人的记忆力，他说这次的波形让他想起了 1971 年的弗留利地震，并建议我查阅他以前的一位学生（Cipar，1981）的一篇论文，并且以那篇论文开始着手研究。果然，同样的复杂震源对惠蒂尔海峡（Whittier Narrows）的数据拟合得很好，只需要稍作调整即可更好地拟合。惠蒂尔海峡地震的文章是我第一次作为第一作者（Bent and Helmberger，1989）。投稿得到的回复是需要重大修改。一位审稿人的评论相当负面，指出大约有 30 个"重大错误"。我自然有些担心，把评论展示给唐（Don），唐只是耸了耸肩，说审稿人那天一定很生气。他指出了两三个评论并告诉我解决这些并忽略其余的。我按照他的建议做了，同一位审稿人随后评论了这篇论文的改进程度，没有提及剩下尚未解决的 20 多个他曾称之为重大错误的地方。

随着我继续与唐（Don）合作，我们开始探索能否把用于研究当代地震的相同建模技术应用于历史地震。鉴于高质量的历史地震图相对缺乏，我们由可收集到的基础建模信息展开工作，将历史地震的波形与同一地区近期、记录良好、研究充分的事件的波形进行比较（Bent and Helmberger，1991）。这项工作可以被认为是唐（Don）和他的在我之后的学生开发的剪切粘贴方法的原始先驱（Zhao and Helmberger，1994；Zhu and Helmberger，1996）。

与唐（Don）的对话从不乏味。他问了很多棘手的问题，我总是尝试并且通常成功地想出答案。然而，有一次我完全被难住了，并斩钉截铁地回答"我不知道"。唐（Don）说："我也不知道，但我认为这是一个好问题。"啊哈，如果我不总是知道答案也没关系。唐（Don）有一个习惯，就是在谈话到一半时停下来，凝视着上方。大约一分钟后，他会准确地从中断的地方继续谈话。我已经习惯了。另一个常见的情况是，他会说他要去喝杯咖啡，一会儿就回来。十分钟后，他通常不会回来，让我思考是否应该继续坐等，还是离开比较好。当唐（Don）消失了好几天时，我知道这是 NBA 季后赛时间，在季后赛结束之前不要指望见到他。

　　尽管他对地震学做出了无数贡献，并且对地震图中蕴含的内容有着惊人的洞察力，但唐（Don）完全不自负。当我否决他的一个建议时，我一直觉得他以我为荣（图 1）。他曾经告诉我："我们（指地震实验室的教员）都是愚蠢的。我们对一两件事了解很多，而对其他任何事情一无所知。"然后他咧嘴笑着补充道，"除了博雄（Hiroo）。如果他不知道，没人知道。"

图 1　在我最后一次参加地震实验室（Seismo Lab）茶歇时，唐（Don）手里拿着咖啡杯，看着我打开礼物。

　　他也有良好的幽默感。我清楚地记得曾剪切粘贴并合成数据来制作我的口头报告中的图片时，那是 20 世纪 80 年代。幸运的是，一些不错的绘图代码很快被开发出来，比起艺术和手工艺，我更擅长科学。我记得我曾用讽刺的语气对一位过来聊天的学生说，这太棒了，我一定会用它的美丽给委员会留下深刻印象。我不知道的是，唐（Don）正在大厅里偷听。几分钟后，他突然出现并说这是他见过的最丑陋的东西。

　　当道格·德雷格（Doug Dreger）告诉我唐（Don）去世的消息时，我很难过。地震学失去了一位伟大的人，而我失去了一位导师。但是，他的精神将永存，他的贡献将由他的学生们和他们影响的未来几代地震学者传承下去。一年多之后，我与唐（Don）过去的其他学生聊天时，总是谈到我们多么想念他。唐（Don）不会被遗忘。

致谢

我感谢劳雷尔·辛克莱（Laurel Sinclair）对初稿的审阅。本文是加拿大自然资源部投稿，编号 20210459。我还要感谢宋晓东和索恩·莱（Thorne Lay）为纪念唐（Don）整理了这期特刊。

参 考 文 献

Bent AL and Helmberger DV (1989). Source complexity of the October 1, 1987, Whittier Narrows earthquake. J Geophys Res: Solid Earth **94**(B7): 9548–9556.

Bent AL and Helmberger DV (1991). A re-examination of historic earthquakes in the San Jacinto fault zone, California. Bull Seismol Soc Am **81**(6): 2289–2309.

Cipar J (1981). Broadband time domain modeling of earthquakes from Friuli, Italy. Bull Seismol Soc Am **71**(4): 1215–1231.

Helmberger DV and Engen GR (1980). Modeling the long-period body waves from shallow earthquakes at regional ranges. Bull Seismol Soc Am **70**(5): 1699–1714.

Langston CA and Helmberger DV (1975). A procedure for modelling shallow dislocation sources. Geophys J Roy Astron Soc **42**(1): 117–130.

Zhao LS and Helmberger DV (1994). Source estimation from broadband regional seismograms. Bull Seismol Soc Am **84**(1): 91– 104.

Zhu LP and Helmberger DV (1996). Advancement in source estimation techniques using broadband regional seismograms. Bull Seismol Soc Am **86**(5): 1634–1641.

艾莉森·本特(Allison Bent) 是加拿大自然资源部的地震学研究员，她在那里度过了自己的职业生涯。1990 年，她在加州理工学院完成了博士学位，亨伯格（Helmberger）教授是她的论文导师。在她的整个职业生涯中，她一直是美国地震学会的活跃成员，曾担任董事会成员，目前担任 *Seismological Research Letters* 的主编。她是国际地震学和地球内部物理学协会(IASPEI)震级测量工作组的现任主席。

Chapter 7. How Donald V. Helmberger inspired me

Robert Graves[*]

U.S. Geological Survey, Pasadena, California 91106, USA

[*]**Correspondence:** rwgraves@usgs.gov

Citation: Graves RW (2022). How Donald V. Helmberger inspired me. Earthq Sci **35**(1): 22−23 doi: 10.1016/j.eqs.2022.01.005

I first met Don Helmberger when I visited Caltech in the spring of 1984 as a prospective graduate student. During that visit, I was immediately impressed by Don's unbridled passion for science, in general, and seismology, in particular. Don made me feel quite at ease as we discussed mantle triplications, core phases and ray theory. Never mind that most of it was well above my head, he patiently continued the discussion while answering my many questions. Then he showed me a paper that literally changed my life: *Theory and Application of Synthetic Seismograms* (Helmberger, 1983). I was hooked. The notion of creating an earthquake and predicting the resulting ground shaking using a computer was simply amazing to me.

In the fall of 1984, I began my graduate studies at Caltech and was happy to find that I would be working with Don as my research advisor. Eager to start modeling earthquakes, I discovered another of Don's tenets: modeling is simply a tool to help us better understand and explain **observations**. Hence, I began my graduate research by hand digitizing numerous seismograms that were stored on microfiche. The goal was to look at multibounce SH waves recorded at sites across North America. While the hand digitizing was tedious, it was also very enlightening. As Don would say, all the bumps and wiggles on those records were telling us something about the Earth. Guided by Don and with help from fellow graduate student Steve Grand, I developed a keen appreciation for identifying phases on the records and seeing how they changed from station to station. Eventually, I guess Don figured I had done enough digitizing, and we finally started on modeling the data. This work culminated in my very first published paper, which focused on the study of laterally varying structure in the upper mantle beneath the Pacific Ocean (Graves and Helmberger, 1988).

Over the next couple of years, I worked on developing new methods for modeling wave propagation in complex 3D media. My interest was the Los Angeles Basin region, spurred on by the pioneering work on the 1971 San Fernando, California earthquake by Vidale and

Helmberger (1988). However, I wanted to analyze smaller magnitude events so I could concentrate on the effects of basin structure on the waveforms. But how to get these data? Once again, Don came to the rescue as he excitedly described a new seismic recording system that was being installed in southern California as part of the TerraScope network. These new instruments had high dynamic range, were broadband and fully digital (no more hand digitizing!). Don was like the proverbial kid in a candy shop!

As I neared completion of my Ph.D. thesis, I faced another dilemma: I needed to find a real job. I was discussing this with Don, and I asked him about Woodward Clyde Consultants (WCC), which I knew little about other than they had an office in Pasadena (that Don helped to establish) focused on seismic hazards. The next day I found myself joining Don at a lunch meeting with Larry Burdick and Paul Somerville, who jointly ran the Pasadena WCC office at the time. Shortly after this meeting a job offer from WCC arrived and that is where I spent the next 20 years of my professional life. None of it would have happened without Don.

In 2010, I moved to the USGS Pasadena office and, with closer proximity to the Seismo Lab, rekindled my interactions with Don. As always, one could not come away from a meeting with Don without an increased level of optimism, enthusiasm, and hope. During this time, I was also fortunate to participate in numerous collaborative studies with Don and his students and post-docs, in particular, Shengji Wei, Zhongwen Zhan, and Voon Hui Lai. Voon was Don's last graduate student, and I am grateful to have had the opportunity to work with her and Don on analyzing and modeling ground motions from small earthquakes in the Los Angeles basin region (Lai et al., 2020). I feel like I have come full circle.

Don, you are truly an inspiration, and I thank you from the bottom of my heart. You will be deeply missed.

References

Graves RW and Helmberger DV (1988). Upper mantle cross section from Tonga to Newfoundland. J Geophys Res **93**(B5): 4701–4711.

Helmberger DV (1983). Theory and application of synthetic seismograms. In: Kanamori H, and Boschi E eds. Earthquakes: Observation, Theory and Interpretation. North-Holland Publ. , Amsterdam, pp 173–222

Lai VH, Graves RW, Yu CQ, Zhan ZW and Helmberger DV (2020). Shallow basin structure and attenuation are key to predicting long shaking duration in Los Angeles Basin. J Geophys Res **125**(10): e2020JB019663.

Vidale JE and Helmberger DV (1988). Elastic finite-difference modeling of the 1971 San Fernando, California Earthquake. Bull Seismol Soc Am **78**(1): 122–141.

Robert Graves is currently a research geophysicist in the Pasadena, CA office of the U.S. Geological Survey (USGS). He completed his Ph.D. at Caltech in 1990 with Prof. Helmberger as one of his thesis advisors. He then joined Woodward-Clyde Consultants (later URS Corporation) and worked as a consulting seismologist for 20 years before moving to the USGS in 2010. In 2019, he was named the William B. Joyner Lecturer by the Earthquake Engineering Research Institute and the Seismological Society of America.

第 7 章　我的人生引路者：唐·亨伯格

罗伯特·格雷夫斯
美国地质调查局
美国加利福尼亚州帕萨迪纳

引用：Graves RW (2022). How Donald V. Helmberger inspired me. Earthq Sci **35**(1): 22–23 doi: 10.1016/j.eqs.2022.01.005

　　1984 年春天，当我作为一名准研究生访问加州理工学院时，我第一次见到了唐·亨伯格（Don Helmberger）。在那次访问中，唐（Don）对科学，尤其是对地震学的澎湃热情立即给我留下了深刻的印象。当我们讨论地幔三重震相、地核震相和射线理论时，唐（Don）让我感到很自在。尽管大部分内容远超我的理解，他仍然耐心地继续讨论，同时回答了我的许多问题。接着，他给我看了一篇真正改变了我人生的文章：合成地震图的理论和应用（Helmberger，1983）。我被迷住了，使用计算机模拟地震并预测由此产生的地面震动的想法对我来说简直不可思议。

　　1984 年秋天，我在加州理工学院开始了我的研究生学习，我很高兴地发现唐（Don）将作为我的研究导师和我一起工作。渴望开始模拟地震的同时，我发现了唐（Don）的另一个宗旨：建模只是用来帮助我们更好地理解和解释观测结果的工具。因此，我通过把存储在缩微胶片上的大量地震图手动数字化来开始我的研究生研究。我的目的是查看在北美各地记录的多次反射 SH 波。虽然手动数字化很乏味，但也很有启发性。正如唐（Don）所说，这些记录中的每个大起伏和小摆动都在告诉我们一些关于地球的事情。在唐（Don）的指导和当时同为研究生的史蒂夫·格兰德（Steve Grand）的帮助下，我形成了能敏锐地识别记录中的各个震相，并且观察它们如何随着台站变化而变化的能力。最终，我猜唐（Don）觉得我已经做了足够的数字化工作，于是我们终于开始对数据进行建模。这项工作以我发表第一篇论文而告终，该论文侧重于研究太平洋上地幔的横向变化结构（Graves and Helmberger，1988）。

　　在接下来的几年里，我致力于开发用于模拟复杂三维介质中的波传播的新方法。维达莱（Vidale）和亨伯格（Helmberger） 在 1988 年发表的一篇关于 1971 年加利福尼亚州圣费尔南多（San Fernando）地震的开创性工作引起了我对洛杉矶盆地地区的兴趣。不过，我想研究震级较小的地震事件，这样一来我可以专注于盆地结构对波形的影响。但是如何获取这些数据呢？唐（Don）再次出手相救，他兴奋地向我描述了一个新的地震记录系统，该系统作为 TerraScope 网络的一部分设在南加州。这些新仪器具有大动态范围、宽频带并且全数字化（不再需要手动数字化！）的特点。唐（Don）开心得就像我们常说的糖果店里的孩子一样！

当快要完成博士毕业论文时，我遇到了另一个难题：我需要找到一份真正意义上的工作。和唐（Don）讨论这个问题时，我向他询问了伍德沃德咨询公司（Woodward Clyde Consultants，WCC）的情况，除了知道他们在帕萨迪纳有一个研究地震灾害的办公室［唐（Don）帮助创立的那个］外，我就不了解别的了。第二天，我和唐（Don）一起参加了与拉里·伯迪克（Larry Burdick）和保尔·萨默维尔（Paul Somerville）的午餐会，他们当时共同管理帕萨迪纳的 WCC 办公室。这次会面后不久，我就得到了来自 WCC 的工作机会，并且在那里度过了接下来 20 年的职业生涯。如果没有唐（Don），所有的一切都不会发生。

2010 年，我搬到了美国地质调查局（United States Geological Survey，USGS）帕萨迪纳办公室，因为离地震实验室更近了，这使我又重新开始与唐（Don）的合作。像从前一样，与唐（Don）会面总是让我更加乐观、热情和充满希望。在此期间，我也有幸参与了唐（Don）及其学生和博士后的许多合作研究，特别是与韦生吉（Shengji Wei）、詹中文（Zhongwen Zhan）和赖文慧（Voon Hui Lai）的合作。文慧是唐（Don）的最后一个研究生，我很高兴有机会与她和唐（Don）一起分析和模拟洛杉矶盆地的区域小地震的地面运动(Lai et al., 2020)。我觉得自己仿佛又回到了最开始与唐（Don）共事的时候。

唐（Don），你是我的精神向导，我从心底里感谢你。我们将深深地怀念你。

参 考 文 献

Graves RW and Helmberger DV (1988). Upper mantle cross section from Tonga to Newfoundland. J Geophys Res **93**(B5): 4701–4711.

Helmberger DV (1983). Theory and application of synthetic seismograms. In: Kanamori H, and Boschi E eds. Earthquakes: Observation, Theory and Interpretation. North-Holland Publ. , Amsterdam, pp 173–222

Lai VH, Graves RW, Yu CQ, Zhan ZW and Helmberger DV (2020). Shallow basin structure and attenuation are key to predicting long shaking duration in Los Angeles Basin. J Geophys Res **125**(10): e2020JB019663.

Vidale JE and Helmberger DV (1988). Elastic finite-difference modeling of the 1971 San Fernando, California Earthquake. Bull Seismol Soc Am **78**(1): 122–141.

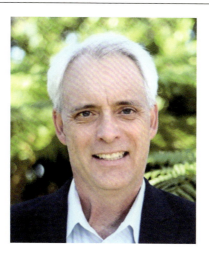

　　罗伯特·格雷夫斯（Robert Graves）目前是美国地质调查局（USGS）加利福尼亚州帕萨迪纳办事处的地球物理学研究员。他 1990 年在加州理工学院完成了博士学位，亨伯格（Helmberger）教授是他的论文导师之一。随后，他加入伍德沃德咨询公司（后来的 URS 公司）并担任咨询地震学家 20 年，之后于 2010 年转到美国地质调查局。2019 年，他被地震工程研究所和美国地震学会选为威廉湾乔伊纳（William B. Joyner）讲师。

Chapter 8. Working and playing with Don: Memories of Donald V. Helmberger

David Wald [*]

U.S. Geological Survey, Golden, Colorado 80401, USA

[*]**Correspondence:** wald@usgs.gov

Citation: Wald DJ (2022). Working and playing with Don: Memories of Donald V. Helmberger. Earthq Sci **35**(1): 24−25 doi: 10.1016/j.eqs.2022.01.016

You might find it hard to believe, but I went to Caltech's Seismological Lab for my Ph.D. on a football scholarship. Well, perhaps I should explain.

I received my M.S. in Geophysics (Earthquake Seismology) at University of Arizona in 1986, under the tutelage of Terry Wallace (Caltech Ph.D., 1983). Terry worked with Don prior to joining the faculty at the University of Arizona. And there the Helmberger stories began.

With Terry's connections in California, I leveraged my Master's degree in seismology into my first real job, at Woodward Clyde Consultants (WCC) in Pasadena, working with Paul Somerville and Larry Burdick (Caltech Ph.D., 1977). Larry's repeated mantra to me was, "Respect the data," a phrase that presumably came from his studies with Don a few years earlier, and one that has always stuck with me. Don happened to be a founding consultant at that WCC Pasadena office, and I worked with him regularly. Oh, and played.

Don led a league of one called "Helmberger Football." I played intramural football previously as an undergrad; my size and speed made me suitable only as a receiver, and in my own mind, one of Don's favorites. Don was a talented and athletic quarterback, and we loved to play together. When I applied only to Caltech for my Ph.D., and only to work with Don as my advisor, I somehow got in. The term "Helmberger Football," by the way, reflected the fact that Don stacked the teams by his knowledge of the changing roster over the years and occasionally changed the rules in his favor—during a game. His competitiveness came out on the field, sometimes resulting in a literal moving of the goalposts. But we did have fun.

Note I referred earlier to working "with" Don rather than "under" Don. He never pulled rank. Don was never intimidating or unkind, nor did he ever add pressure to what was otherwise a pressure-cooker of an experience at Caltech. His ability to play with his mentees, either with seismograms, over a beer, or on the football field, made for such a memorable experience that these words easily flow for me, and I smile just recollecting all this.

I don't recall hearing the term "Doctor" or "Professor" Helmberger. Informality was the name of the game, and Don was Don, which was part of his approachability. His famous quirkiness was indeed a barrier to entry, and while that may have been a speedbump to some, it too was a lesson at the Lab—communicating with gifted people whose thoughts and ideas are way out ahead of their words.

What Don provided students was a haven to learn about the makeup of a seismogram, as if they held the keys to the universe. Whether from phases impinging on D", reflecting off the 650 km discontinuity, the lithosphere, Pnl path through the crust, bouncing along the bottom of a basin, or those within the top 30 m; these were all ingredients that helped us understand at least the Earth … and Don. What Don didn't provide was tutoring in writing papers or proposals, nor in preparing slides and talks; those lessons came collectively from others in the Llab, primarily our peers, whom I thank immensely as I think back (I would not have survived Physics 106 without help from my friend, Kuo-Fong Ma).

One's success with Don depended on learning the critical ability to recognize the gems among the barrage of otherwise crazy ideas Don threw at you. Blessed with a flurry of earthquakes in my years at Caltech (1988–1992), every year I had another earthquake to study, and thus another thesis chapter (Wald, 1993). My work with Don was to resolve the spatial and temporal evolution of fault slip for each earthquake that came our way (Wald et al., 1990, 1991, 1992, 1993), with a full recognition of where the diagnostic waveforms came from and what circuitous paths they took. This might have gone on for years since we kept finding new ways to attack the problem. That is, until the 1992 Landers ($M7.3$) earthquake, and after chapter six, I'd had enough. After nearly four years, I was able to snatch the pebble from Don's hand, and it was time to leave. Luckily, moving across the street to the U.S. Geological Survey (USGS) in Pasadena allowed me another dozen years on the Caltech campus with hundreds of coffee hours with Don and the wonderful cast of characters at the Lab who came and went. And more seismograms.

After moving to the USGS National Earthquake Information Center in Golden, Colorado, I routinely revisited our Pasadena office and would drop in on Don every time. As if nothing had changed, he would start talking about what was sitting on his desk in front of him. He showed no sign of slowing down, nor boredom—just the unending inquisitiveness of a man blessed with tremendous curiosity.

I would be remiss to not mention all the great lessons I learned from Don's circle of influence and other students at the time, among them: Kuo-Fong Ma, Hong-Kie Thio, Monica Kohler, and colleagues Paul Somerville, Terry Wallace, Hiroo Kanamori, Tom Heaton, Steve Hartzell, Don Anderson, Rob Clayton, and Clarence Allen.

Whether my foray into the fantastic world of seismology with Don was due to my ability to catch a football or my passable knowledge of seismology learned during my Master's program will remain a mystery with Don's passing. But one way or the other, I got to work with Don Helmberger, and there, with Don, I thrived. I owe so much of my love and appreciation of seismology and scholarship to Don—both academic and football. Godspeed Don.

References

Wald DJ, Helmberger DV and Hartzell SH (1990). Rupture process of the 1987 Superstition Hills earthquake from the inversion of strong-motion data. Bull Seismol Soc Am **80**(5): 1079–1098.

Wald DJ, Helmberger DV and Heaton TH (1991). Rupture model of the 1989 Loma Prieta earthquake from the inversion of strong-motion and broadband teleseismic data. Bull Seismol Soc Am **81**(5): 1540–1572.

Wald DJ, Hartzell SH and Helmberger DV (1992). Reply to Arthur Frankel's "Comment on 'Rupture process of the 1987 Superstition Hills earthquake from the inversion of strong-motion data'". Bull Seismol Soc Am **82**(3): 1519–1533.

Wald DJ (1993). Source characteristics of California earthquakes. Dissertation. California Institute of Technology, Pasadena, California, pp 278

Wald DJ, Kanamori H, Helmberger DV and Heaton TH (1993). Source study of the 1906 San Francisco earthquake. Bull Seismol Soc Am **83**(4): 981–1019.

David Wald a seismologist with USGS at the National Earthquake Information Center. He completed his Ph.D. at Caltech in 1993 with Prof. Helmberger as his primary thesis advisor. Wald leads development and operations of real-time information systems including ShakeMap, Did You Feel it?, PAGER, ShakeCast, and Ground Failure. David is currently the Editor-in-Chief of the EERI's journal *Earthquake Spectra* and is an Adjunct Professor in the Geophysics at the Colorado School of Mines. He was an IRIS/SSA Distinguished Lecturer and EERI's Distinguished Lecture.

He also served on the Board of Directors for both SSA and EERI and was the 2009 recipient of SSA's Frank Press Public Service Award. In 2021, Wald was awarded the EERI-SSA Joyner Lectureship, an AGU Fellow, and received the USGS Shoemaker Lifetime Achievement Award in Communications, an award granted annually to a scientist who creates excitement and enthusiasm for science among non-scientists by using effective communication skills.

第 8 章 寓教于乐：追忆唐·亨伯格

戴维·沃尔德
美国地质调查局，高级地球物理研究员

引用：Wald DJ (2022). Working and playing with Don: Memories of Donald V. Helmberger. Earthq Sci **35**(1): 24-25 doi: 10.1016/j.eqs.2022.01.016

你或许会觉得难以置信，我是拿着橄榄球奖学金在加州理工学院地震实验室攻读博士学位。那么，我或许应该解释一下。

1986 年，我在亚利桑那大学获得了地球物理学（震源地震学）硕士学位，师从特里·华莱士（Terry Wallace，加州理工学院博士，1983 级）。特里（Terry）在来到亚利桑那大学之前，曾与唐（Don）一起合作过。我与唐·亨伯格（Don Helmberger）的故事从这里开始。

凭借特里（Terry）在加州的关系，我以地震学硕士的身份找到了第一份正式工作，在帕萨迪纳的伍德沃德咨询公司（WCC）与保尔·萨默维尔（Paul Somerville）和拉里·伯迪克（Larry Burdick，加州理工学院博士，1977 级）一起工作。拉里（Larry）常对我说的口头禅是"尊重数据"，这句话大概是他几年前从唐（Don）那里学到的，这句话也一直伴随着我。唐（Don）恰巧是 WCC 帕萨迪纳办事处的创始顾问，所以我常和他一起工作，哦对了，我们也经常一起玩乐。

唐（Don）组织了一个名为"亨伯格（Helmberger）橄榄球"的球队。我以前在本科时参加过校内橄榄球比赛，我的体型和速度让我只适合作为一名接球手，而在我看来，这是唐（Don）最爱的位置之一。唐（Don）是一位才华横溢、运动能力强的四分卫，我们喜欢一起打球。当时我只申请了加州理工学院的博士，而且只申请了唐（Don）作为我的导师，不管怎么说我还是成功地被录取了。顺便提一下，从"亨伯格（Helmberger）橄榄球"这个球队名称也可以看出，唐（Don）通过多年来对不断变化的球队阵容的了解，偶尔会在一场比赛中随自己的喜好修改一些规则。他的好胜心在球场上表现得淋漓尽致，有时甚至会移动球门柱。但我们确实一起玩得很开心。

要强调的是，我上文提到过"与唐（Don）一起工作"，而不是"在唐（Don）手下工作"。他平易近人，从不恶言厉色，也从不给加州理工学院的高压氛围再增添压力。无论是研究地震图、喝啤酒还是在球场上，他都能和学生们打成一片，而这些都给我留下了如此难忘的回忆，以至于现在想起来还仿佛就在昨日。每当回忆起那些日子，我都不自觉地扬起了嘴角。

我不记得听过"亨伯格（Helmberger）博士"或者"亨伯格（Helmberger）教授"这

样的称呼。唐（Don）就是唐（Don），我们无须拘泥于这些礼节，这是他平易近人的一部分。他著名的小毛病是他说的话需要我们仔细琢磨，虽然这对一些人来说可能是一个考验，但这也是我们从实验室中学到的一点：如何与那些思想和想法远超言语的天才交流。

唐（Don）为学生们提供了一个学习地震图构成的港湾，在这里，他们仿佛掌握着宇宙的钥匙。无论是经过 D″ 的震相、650 km 不连续界面的反射波、岩石圈、穿过地壳的 Pnl 路径、沿着盆地底部的多次波，还是 30m 以浅的研究，这些东西帮助我们理解地球，也理解唐（Don）。唐（Don）不辅导我们如何撰写论文或项目申请书，也不辅导如何准备幻灯片和演讲，这些宝贵经验往往来自实验室的其他人，主要是我的同学们，回想起来我非常感谢他们［如果没有我朋友马国凤（Kuo-Fong Ma）的帮助，我不可能通过我的物理 106 课程］。

一个人能否在唐（Don）那里的成功取决于他是否学会了一种关键能力，即能否在唐（Don）向你抛出的一连串天马行空的想法中提取到其中的精华部分。我在加州理工学院的那些年（1988～1992）里，有幸经历了一连串的地震，因此每年我都可以研究一场地震，我的论文的内容也就更丰富一些(Wald, 1993)。我和唐（Don）的工作是解决每次地震时断层滑动的时空演化（Wald et al.，1990，1991，1992，1993），并充分研究这些特定的波形来自何处、经过了什么路径。这项工作持续了好几年，因为我们一直在寻找解决这个问题的新方法。直到 1992 年 Landers（M7.3）大地震，在完成了论文的第六章后，我已经取得了足够的成果。在学习了将近四年后，我终于在唐（Don）这里学有所成，也发表了几篇像样的论文，是时候离开了。幸运的是，搬到街对面的帕萨迪纳市的美国地质调查局，让我在加州理工学院又待了十几年，有数百个小时的时间和唐（Don）以及实验室里来来往往的杰出人物一起喝咖啡、聊地震图。

搬到科罗拉多州戈尔登（Golden）市的国家地震信息中心后，我经常会回到帕萨迪纳市的办公室，每次都会去看看唐（Don）。就像什么都没变一样，他依旧会谈论起摆在他面前桌子上的东西。他步履不停、饶有兴致——只是表现出一个拥有巨大求知欲的人无止境的好奇。

我不能忽视当时从唐（Don）的圈子和其他学生那里学习到的所有重要经验教训，其中包括马国凤（Kuo-Fong Ma）、洪基·蒂欧（Hong-Kie Thio）、莫妮卡·科勒（Monica Kohler）以及保尔·萨默维尔（Paul Somerville）、特里·华莱士（Terry Wallace）、金森博雄（Hiroo Kanamori）、汤姆·希顿（Tom Heaton）、史蒂夫·哈策尔（Steve Hartzell）、唐·安德森（Don Anderson）、罗布·克莱顿（Rob Clayton）和克拉伦斯·艾伦（Clarence Allen）等诸多同仁。

我能与唐（Don）共同进入奇妙的地震学世界，究竟是因为我有打橄榄球的能力，还是因为我在硕士课程中学到的地震学知识尚可，这都将随着唐（Don）的离去而成为一个谜。但无论如何，我曾经与唐·亨伯格（Don Helmberger）共同工作过，在那里，和唐（Don）一起，我茁壮成长。我对地震学和科研的热爱和欣赏都要归功于唐（Don）——无论是学术上还是橄榄球上。一路走好，唐（Don）。

参 考 文 献

Wald DJ, Helmberger DV and Hartzell SH (1990). Rupture process of the 1987 Superstition Hills earthquake from the inversion of strong-motion data. Bull Seismol Soc Am **80**(5): 1079–1098.

Wald DJ, Helmberger DV and Heaton TH (1991). Rupture model of the 1989 Loma Prieta earthquake from the inversion of strong-motion and broadband teleseismic data. Bull Seismol Soc Am **81**(5): 1540–1572.

Wald DJ, Hartzell SH and Helmberger DV (1992). Reply to Arthur Frankel's "Comment on 'Rupture process of the 1987 Superstition Hills earthquake from the inversion of strong-motion data'". Bull Seismol Soc Am **82**(3): 1519–1533.

Wald DJ (1993). Source characteristics of California earthquakes. Dissertation. California Institute of Technology, Pasadena, California, pp 278

Wald DJ, Kanamori H, Helmberger DV and Heaton TH (1993). Source study of the 1906 San Francisco earthquake. Bull Seismol Soc Am **83**(4): 981–1019.

　　戴维·沃尔德是美国地质调查局国家地震信息中心的地震学家。在主要论文导师亨伯格教授的指导下，他 1993 年在加州理工学院获得了博士学位。沃尔德主管实时信息系统的开发和运营，包括"ShakeMap""Did　You Feel it？""PAGER""ShakeCast"和"Ground Failure"。他目前是 EERI *Earthquake Spectra* 杂志的主编，也是科罗拉多矿业学院地球物理学兼职教授。他是 IRIS/SSA 和 EERI 杰出讲师。他还曾在 SSA 和 EERI 的董事会任职，并于 2009 年获得 SSA 的弗兰克·普雷斯公共服务奖。2021，沃尔德被授予了 EERI-SSA 乔伊纳杰出学术报告奖、美国地球物理联合会会士，并获得美国地质调查局"Shoemaker Lifetime Achievement Award in Communications"奖项，该奖项每年授予通过有效的沟通技巧点燃科学家以外的人们对科学的兴趣和热情的科学家。

Chapter 9. Donald V. Helmberger memoir — exceptional seismologist, teacher, mentor, friend

Douglas Dreger[*]
University of California, Berkeley, CA 94720, USA

[*]**Correspondence:** ddreger@berkeley.edu

Citation: Dreger D (2022). Donald V. Helmberger memoir — exceptional seismologist, teacher, mentor, friend. Earthq Sci **35**(1): 26−28 doi: 10.1016/j.eqs.2022.01.002

Donald V. Helmberger was an unparalleled observational seismologist, and theoretician. His pioneering work in seismic waveform modeling, and the numerical methods he developed to simulate seismograms to study the structure of the Earth and the nature of earthquake sources have become techniques that are now commonplace. But, that wasn't always the case. He once confided in me that when he was first proposing the modeling of whole waveforms there were not many who believed him that it was possible, and was 'laughed at.' I don't know if that later part is true or not, but perhaps it was his way of teaching a young scientist about humility, and to give him confidence that the current scientific struggle will succeed with tenacity and hard work.

I first met Don while visiting Caltech's Seismo Lab at coffee break. The topic was the core-mantle boundary — to me it was mysterious, fascinating and inspiring, though for a prospective student the coffee break dynamic was daunting. At one point in the conversation I was asked what I had been working on. As I described the shallow applied geophysics work I was doing at the time I was feeling it wasn't very significant given what was just being discussed. However, Don took great interest in what I shared, particularly my description of how I was able to see the structures I imaged, the reflectors/refractors (various weathering horizons) and scatterers (hard rock knockers) after the bulldozers stripped away the soft material, allowing me to make the connection between seismic observation and the actual materials. His unassuming nature was welcoming and we had a very nice discussion. It was during this conversation that he said 'arrival times are not the only information that one can measure from seismic experiments' and he introduced me to the idea that entire waveforms can be used to learn much more about the nature of seismic wave propagation, the structures imaged by the traveling waves, and the earthquake source that generated them. That began a wonderful 5-year journey with Don exploring the mysteries of the seismograms stored at Kresge and the new digital data from Terrascope, a brand new network of broadband seismic stations in southern California.

At the time, Terrascope was just getting underway, and there were numerous small-to-moderate earthquakes occurring throughout southern California. Don and I spent countless hours examining the waveforms, learning how to best filter them, numerically modeling the complete records, and untangling the complex local and regional distance seismograms, revealing both the source and propagation. It seemed that each earthquake had a new secret to discover. I was in awe of his ability to read seismograms and identify the often-times very subtle features that would lead to the greatest insight into the problem being tackled. It was as if he could invert a seismogram in his head, taking a bulldozer, stripping away the upper layers, and revealing the complexity of the Moho discontinuity or other such structure. With his initial assessment in hand, I would then go off and attempt to model the waveforms using a variety of tools we developed. Many times I would find a result often supporting his intuitive hypothesis, but sometimes not, leading to wonderful brainstorming sessions punctuated with reflective, wondering gazes outside his office window towards Mt. Wilson. Of course, Don's intuition was rooted by vast observational experience reading seismic waveforms as well as synthetic seismograms, allowing him to make the connection between the complex waveforms and Earth structure. Together we found PL type waves traveling in the upper weathered layer of the crust (Dreger and Helmberger, 1991a, 1993) and that S-wave multiple arrivals enabled reliable determination of earthquake source depth as well as providing information to constrain upper crustal structure (Dreger and Helmberger, 1990). Figure 1 illustrates the broadband S-wave modeling for the 1988 Upland earthquake from Dreger and Helmberger (1990). We also demonstrated the feasibility of inverting three-component records from a single station for the earthquake source mechanism, beneficial under the very sparse recording situations that was the norm at the time (Dreger and Helmberber, 1991b, 1993). This work ultimately led to the development of automated source determination methods that became part of the operational system shared between UC Berkeley, Caltech and the U.S. Geological Survey (e.g., Pasyanos et al., 1996; Dreger et al., 1998), and led to the use of regional moment tensor methods in source-type discrimination of nuclear explosions (Ford et al., 2009). The mentoring and inspiration Don provided to me was ultimately the driving force in many of the works by his 'grand-students.'

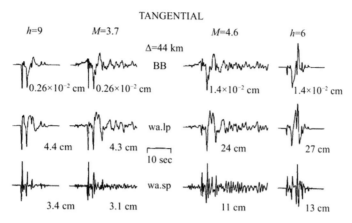

Fig. 1   Originally from Dreger and Helmberger (1990), tangential component synthetics (left- and right-most columns), and data (interior columns) for the 1988 M4.6 Upland mainshock and M3.7 aftershock are compared. Broadband displacement waveforms are shown in the first row, and long-period (wa.lp) and short-period (wa.sp) Wood-Anderson waveforms are shown in rows 2 and 3, respectively. The synthetics were computed using Generalized Ray Theory (Helmberger, 1974). The first two negative S-wave pulses are direct S and the first near-surface multiple, which is strongly source depth dependent. The long-period response that follows is the result of evanescent reverberations generating the Love wave.

In addition to being a great scientist, and exceptional mentor, he could also be your friend. Don was always interested in hearing about your life, and sharing his. For us the connection was football. Don, originally coming from Minnesota, was a Vikings fan, and me a 49ers fan. In his office reading seismograms, discussing our various projects, gazing at Mt. Wilson and contemplating the data, we would also discuss football. On occasion we would watch games together. But Saturday was the blowing-off-steam day. His students and postdocs (and those of other professors) would meet up Saturday morning for football scrimmage. It was great fun, building a strong camaraderie among the students, postdocs, and visitors – his team. Afterward we would go to Continental Burger on Lake Street for lunch, a pitcher of Shandy and great conversation. When I think back to the time I spent with Don Helmberger, I realize that it was perhaps the best time of my life, and I am forever grateful for his friendship, generosity, mentorship, and the hand he had shaping my career.

References

Dreger DS and Helmberger DV (1990). Broadband modeling of local earthquakes. Bull Seismol Soc Am **80**(5): 1162–1179.

Dreger DS and Helmberger D (1991a). Source parameters of the Sierra Madre Earthquake from regional and local body waves. Geophys Res Lett **18**(11): 2015–2018.

Dreger DS and Helmberger DV (1991b). Complex faulting deduced from broadband modeling of the 28 February 1990 upland earthquake (ML=5.2). Bull Seismol Soc Am **81**(4): 1129–1144.

Dreger DS and Helmberger DV (1993). Determination of source parameters at regional distances with three-component sparse network data. J Geophys Res: Solid Earth **98**(B5): 8107–8125.

Dreger DS, Uhrhammer R, Pasyanos M, Franck J and Romanowicz B (1998). Regional and far-regional earthquake locations and source parameters using sparse broadband networks: a test on the Ridgecrest sequence. Bull Seismol Soc Am **88**(6): 1353–1362.

Ford SR, Dreger DS and Walter WR (2009). Identifying isotropic events using a regional moment tensor inversion. J Geophys Res: Solid Earth **114**(B1): B01306.

Helmberger DV (1974). Generalized ray theory for shear dislocations. Bull Seismol Soc Am **64**(1): 45–64.

Pasyanos ME, Dreger DS and Romanowicz B (1996). Toward real-time estimation of regional moment tensors. Bull Seismol Soc Am **86**(5): 1255–1269.

Douglas Dreger is currently a Professor in the Earth and Planetary Science Department at the University of California, Berkeley (UCB). He completed his Ph.D. at Caltech in 1992 with Professor Helmberger as his primary thesis advisor. He then accepted postdoctoral scholar and assistant research positions at UCB. In 1996 he was appointed as Assistant Professor in the Department of Earth and Planetary Science at UC Berkeley, where he has remained to the present. His research site is https://vcresearch.berkeley.edu/faculty/douglas-dreger.

第 9 章　唐·亨伯格回忆录：杰出的地震学家、教师、导师和朋友

道格拉斯·德雷格

美国加州大学伯克利分校，加利福尼亚州，美国

引用：Dreger D (2022). Donald V. Helmberger memoir — exceptional seismologist, teacher, mentor, friend. Earthq Sci **35**(1): 26–28 doi: 10.1016/j.eqs.2022.01.002

　　唐·亨伯格（Don Helmberger）是一位无与伦比的观测和理论地震学家。在地震波波形模拟上，他进行了开创性工作，为研究地球结构和震源性质所开发的数值方法已成为常规的工具。但事实上波形模拟的工作并非一路坦途。他曾向我吐露，当他第一次提出对整个波形进行模拟时，没有多少人相信这是可能的，他也因此受到了"嘲笑"。我不确定这个故事后半部分是否真实，或许这只是他教导一位年轻科学家如何谦逊的方式，并让其相信当前科研中所经历的挣扎终将通过坚韧和努力来变为成功。

　　我第一次见到唐（Don）是在参观加州理工学院地震实验室时参加的"咖啡休息讨论时间"。当时讨论的主题是核幔边界。对我而言，这是一个神秘、迷人又令人振奋的话题。然而对于一个还未入学的学生来说，咖啡休息讨论的气氛令人望而生畏。在谈话中，有人问我在做什么工作。当我描述我当时正在做的浅层应用地球物理学工作时，我觉得和刚才讨论的内容相比这并不是很重要。然而，唐（Don）对我分享的内容非常感兴趣，尤其是我描述的在推土机剥离软的地表物质后，我如何能够亲眼看到自己成像出来的反射体/折射体（各种风化层）和散射体（硬的岩石露头）结构，可以让我把地震观测和实际物质联系起来。他谦和的天性令人舒服，我们进行了非常愉快的讨论。正是在这次谈话中，他提到"走时不是我们可以从地震实验中测量的唯一信息"，并向我介绍了利用整个波形来更多了解关于地震波传播的性质、地震波穿过的区域的结构以及产生它们的震源信息。从这，我开启了和唐（Don）一起的五年美妙旅程，在这期间，我们探索了存储在 Kresge 中的地震图和来自南加州一个全新的宽频带地震台网 Terrascope 的数字地震图的奥秘。

　　当时，Terrascope 刚刚起步，而且整个南加州发生了许多中小地震。唐（Don）和我花了无数时间检查波形，学习如何最好地滤波，对完整记录进行数值模拟，以及分离复杂的近场和区域的地震记录来同时揭示震源和传播路径的结构信息。似乎每次地震都潜藏着新的秘密。我对他的读取地震图的能力感到佩服，他往往能识别出地震图上非常微妙的特征，从而为解决正在困扰我们的问题提供很大的帮助。这就好像他可以在自己的脑袋里对地震图进行反演，正如用推土机剥离上层，揭示莫霍面或其他复杂的结构。有

了他的初步评估，我就开始尝试使用我们开发的各种工具对波形进行模拟。很多时候，我的结果支持他的直觉假设，但有时不支持，这导致了精彩的头脑风暴，其间不时有反思、好奇的目光从他的办公室望向窗外的威尔逊山。当然，唐（Don）的直觉源于他阅读大量观测和理论地震波形的经验，这些经验使他能够将复杂的波形与地球结构联系起来。我们共同发现了在地壳上部风化层中传播的 PL 型波（Dreger and Helmberger, 1991a, 1993），以及 S 波多次波能够可靠地确定震源深度，并提供对上地壳结构的约束信息（Dreger and Helmberger, 1990）。图 1 展示了 Dreger and Helmberger（1990）对 1988 年 Upland 地震的宽频带 S 波的模拟。我们还证明了从一个台站的三分量记录反演地震震源机制的可行性，这在当时台站非常稀疏的情况下是非常有用的（Dreger and Helmberber, 1991b, 1993）。这项工作最终引出了自动确定震源方法的开发。该方法已成为加州大学伯克利分校、加州理工学院和美国地质调查局共享的操作系统的一部分（例如, Pasyanos et al., 1996; Dreger et al., 1998），并推动了区域矩张量方法在核爆炸源类型识别中的应用（Ford et al., 2009）。唐（Don）给我的指导和灵感也成为了他的"徒孙"所做的很多工作的推动力。

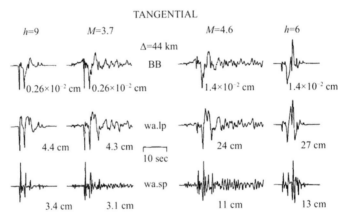

图 1　我们比较了 1988 年 Upland 的 4.6 级主震和 3.7 级余震的理论（最左侧和最右侧的列）和观测（中间两列）地震图的切向分量。第一行中展示的是宽频带位移记录，第二行和第三行则分别展示了伍德-安德森（Wood-Anderson）地震仪记录的长周期和短周期波形。理论波形是用广义射线理论计算的 (Helmberger, 1974)。前两个负的 S 波脉冲信号是直达 S 波和第一个近地表多次反射波，它们很大程度上取决于震源深度。接下来的长周期信号是瞬间混响造成的勒夫波。来自 Dreger and Helmberger(1990)。

　　作为一名伟大的科学家和杰出的导师，唐（Don）还可以成为你的朋友。他总是有兴趣了解你的生活并分享他的经历。对我们来说，这种联系就是美式橄榄球。唐（Don）的家乡在明尼苏达州，他是明尼苏达维京人队的球迷，而我是旧金山 49 人队的球迷。我们会在他的办公室里阅读地震图，讨论我们的各种项目，凝视威尔逊山，思考数据，同时我们还会讨论美式橄榄球。有时我们会一起看比赛。而星期六是一个舒缓压力的日子，他的学生和博士后（以及其他教授的学生和博士后）将在周六上午举行橄榄球"大混战"。这非常有趣，在他的团队（学生、博士后和访问学者）里建立了强烈的友谊。在"大混战"之后我们会去雷克街（Lake Street）的 Continental Burger 店吃午饭，喝一大杯 Shandy

酒，很开心地聊天。当我回想起与唐·亨伯格（Don Helmberger）共度的时光时，我意识到这可能是我一生中最美好的时光，我永远感激他的友谊、慷慨和给我的指导，当然还有他对我的职业生涯的亲手塑造。

参 考 文 献

Dreger DS and Helmberger DV (1990). Broadband modeling of local earthquakes. Bull Seismol Soc Am **80**(5): 1162–1179.

Dreger DS and Helmberger D (1991a). Source parameters of the Sierra Madre Earthquake from regional and local body waves. Geophys Res Lett **18**(11): 2015–2018.

Dreger DS and Helmberger DV (1991b). Complex faulting deduced from broadband modeling of the 28 February 1990 upland earthquake (ML=5.2). Bull Seismol Soc Am **81**(4): 1129–1144.

Dreger DS and Helmberger DV (1993). Determination of source parameters at regional distances with three-component sparse network data. J Geophys Res: Solid Earth **98**(B5): 8107–8125.

Dreger DS, Uhrhammer R, Pasyanos M, Franck J and Romanowicz B (1998). Regional and far-regional earthquake locations and source parameters using sparse broadband networks: a test on the Ridgecrest sequence. Bull Seismol Soc Am **88**(6): 1353–1362.

Ford SR, Dreger DS and Walter WR (2009). Identifying isotropic events using a regional moment tensor inversion. J Geophys Res: Solid Earth **114**(B1): B01306.

Helmberger DV (1974). Generalized ray theory for shear dislocations. Bull Seismol Soc Am **64**(1): 45–64.

Pasyanos ME, Dreger DS and Romanowicz B (1996). Toward real-time estimation of regional moment tensors. Bull Seismol Soc Am **86**(5): 1255–1269.

　　道格拉斯·德雷格（Douglas Dreger）目前是加州大学伯克利分校（UCB）地球与行星科学系的教授。他 1992 年在加州理工学院获得博士学位，主要论文导师是唐·亨伯格（Don Helmberger）。之后在加州大学伯克利分校进行博士后的研究，并任助理研究员。1996 年他在加州大学伯克利分校地球与行星科学系获得助理教授职位，并一直工作至今。他的主页是 https://vcresearch.berkeley.edu/faculty/douglas-dreger。

Chapter 10. Data and curiosity: Working with mentor Donald V. Helmberger

Edward Garnero[*]

School of Earth and Space Exploration Arizona State University Tempe, AZ 85287, USA

[*]**Correspondence:** Garnero E, email: garnero@asu.edu

Citation: Garnero E (2022). Data and curiosity: Working with mentor Donald V. Helmberger. Earthq Sci 35(1): 29−33 doi: 10.1016/j.eqs.2022.01.004

I arrived at Caltech in June 1986, with interests in both mineral physics and seismology. I was excited to either study mineral physics with Professor Tom Ahrens, or investigate great earthquakes with Hiroo Kanamori. Upon arriving, I decided seismology would be my path. I was particularly interested in Hiroo's work on earthquake size, from some papers I read as an undergraduate (Kanamori, 1978, 1983). In my first week, I met with Hiroo, and he asked me what my plan would be for studying great earthquakes. Well, I had no plan, no clue! He wisely noted that we are in need of more and better seismic data – which of course came during the decade that followed with the digital data explosion. Hiroo suggested I introduce myself to seismologist Don Helmberger next door – maybe he would have some interesting research projects for me to consider.

I knocked on Don's open door, and he welcomed me in with an enthusiastic smile. His office was big with an open feeling. Tall windows lined one wall, the long side of his rectangular office. A considerably large ficus tree sat off to one side, and a very large table space occupied most of the center of his office (it probably measured 2 by 4 meters). I mentioned I was a new graduate student and hoping to do seismology for my PhD. Don immediately invited me to sit down at his huge table. There were stacks of papers and seismograms on it. With no small talk, he grabbed a pile of printed seismograms, plopped them down in front of us, and started going through them, one page at a time, page after page. Each page was filled with "wiggles". They were printouts of microfiche film copies of World-Wide Standardized Seismograph Network (WWSSN) seismograms (Murphy, 1961). The sub-basement of Caltech's Seismological Laboratory had a room filled with file cabinets of WWSSN data which could be scanned and printed with a very big enlargement printing machine at the end of the room. Don had piles upon piles of file folders filled with these printouts. On each page, he pointed to wiggles he called "SKS", and talked about its wave shape, page after page after page. With each new page there was an excited, "…and look at *this* one!"

I had no idea what Don was talking about, and he gave me no indication that he was aware of my cluelessness about the seismogram after seismogram he was showing me. But his excitement and enthusiasm were so incredibly palpable. In that very first meeting I thought to myself that something this exciting to a Caltech seismology professor would probably be an excellent path forward for me! Little did I know that SKS would become my religion over the next many years. I quickly descended to the sub-basement, spending hours upon hours scanning and printing WWSSN records that contained SKS waves, then digitizing them on a table digitizer (Figure 1). This was a nearly daily routine until digital data became available (which was many years later). So, on day one I learned about Don's unbridled excitement and enthusiasm for seismic data. Don had such a wonderful demeanor of sharing things with you, regardless of your knowledge of the topic. He was like a kid sharing a new favorite toy, *every time* he showed you seismic data. His curiosity and joy were infectious.

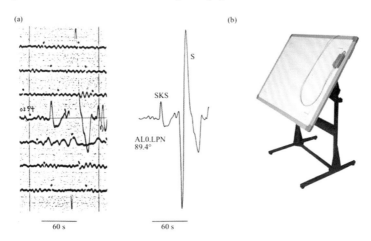

Fig. 1   (a) Scan of an original WWSSN long period recording of a Fiji earthquake recorded at station ALQ in Albuquerque New Mexico, with the digitized version to the right (image originally from Garnero (1994)). (b) An example of a digitizing table similar to the one used to digitize paper records (image from https://www.alibaba.com/product-detail/Jindx-Clothing-Plate-Making-Scanner-Gerber_62555983285.html)

After a whole summer of collecting data in the sub-basement, the Fall semester began and I found myself sitting in Don's "Advanced Seismology" course, with about four other students. I quickly learned of another side of my data loving advisor: theoretical and computational seismology. Don was not only an ultimate observer, he also actively pioneered ways to reproduce and explain seismic observations. It didn't take long to be buried in Cagniard de Hoop theory in class and generalized ray theory codes in research, which enabled us to explore the contribution to seismic data from individual layers in a velocity-depth model.

Several of Don's early papers covered these, such as Helmberger (1968) and Helmberger et al. (1985), as well as his nice summary paper, Helmberger (1983), all which became our daily scriptures. Many of us worked with Don's codes *aseries.f* or *bounce1or2.f*, and other flavors of the old Fortran codes in our research. It was common to arrive at my desk to see a yellow sticky note with the words, "See me, OK". When I went to Don's office, he usually had a printout of synthetic seismograms from these codes to explain some interesting aspect of SKS waves.

Our work quickly evolved to study an interesting phenomenon that happens to SKS when it encounters the core-mantle boundary (CMB). At the critical angle of incidence of an SV wave converting to a P wave at the CMB, diffracted P energy is created (i.e., an ScPdiff wave). This wave transmits P energy to the core to become SPdKS (and from reciprocity, on the upgoing K-leg of SKS, SKPdS is also made). Our first paper on the phenomena (Garnero et al., 1993) established how SPdKS, which first appears and then grows out of the shoulder of SKS, shows up earlier in distance for very strong P velocity reductions at the CMB (Figure 2). This would come to be called an ultra-low velocity zone, or ULVZ, and modeled as a thin layer (e.g., 5–40 km thick) at the CMB in later papers (Mori and Helmberger, 1995; Garnero and Helmberger, 1996). Restricting the low velocities to a thin layer at the CMB was Don's idea.

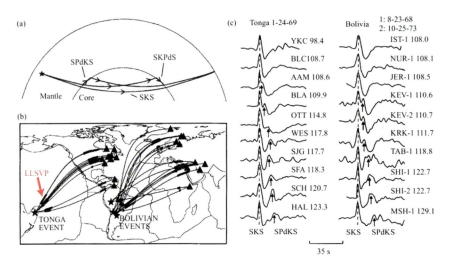

Fig. 2　(a) Seismic ray paths of the phases SKS, SPdKS, and SKPdS. (b) Paths from two source regions, the Fiji-Tonga area, which have the Pd parts of SPdKS (thicker line segments) traveling in the Pacific LLSVP, and South America (mostly Bolivia events). (c) Digitized long-period WWSSN SV data with arrows pointing to SKS and SPdKS arrivals (which is a combination of SPdKS and SKPdS). Seismographic station names and epicentral distances are to the right of each SV recording. The Tonga event has SPdKS developing at a sooner distance (e.g., see station AAM) than for the Bolivia data path geometry (e.g., see station JER at nearly the identical distance — there is no SPdKS yet). ULVZ structure causes SPdKS to arrive at earlier distances.

These figure panels are reproduced and slightly modified from Garnero and Helmberger (1996).

As another example of Don continuing to think about the problem happened after I moved to my first postdoc job at the University of California, Santa Cruz , to work with Don's former student Thorne Lay. In that first year I would receive faxes with pages upon pages of step function seismograms (output from Don's generalized ray theory codes that just needed a derivative and convolution with a seismic instrument to be compared to data). An example is presented in Figure 3, which shows that Don had identified a new and important feature in SKS data used to image ULVZ structure. Here, Don was showing that a multiple internal reflection in a low velocity boundary layer at the CMB also contributed significantly to the wavefield (Helmberger et al., 1996). This is just one example of Don's uncanny ability to dissect, model, and understand the seismic wavefield. This additional unique seismic arrival combines with SPdKS (and SKPdS) to make anomalous SKS waveforms.

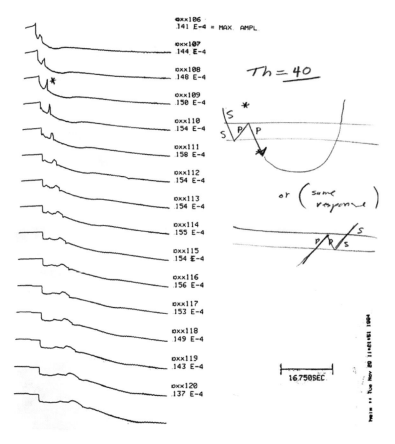

Fig. 3   A 1994 Fax message from Don Helmberger to me, several months into my first postdoc job, showing step (Green's) function responses for SKS and an additional arrival due to a multiple in a low velocity layer at the CMB (a 40 km thick ULVZ), SppKS (and SKppS). Epicentral distance is from 106 (top trace) to 120 (bottom trace). The asterisk depicts the arrival of interest for which Don sketched the ray paths in hand drawn cartoons on the right. This extra arrival contributes to creating anomalous SKS data that are used to map ULVZs.

Don's insight into data analyses and methods always seemed to be far ahead of his time. I recently looked at a binder I have called "DVH conversations" ('DVH' for Don's full name, Donald Vincent Helmberger). I learned to always write down anything Don said about data. I was very excited to find a page from nearly 30 years ago that is titled "DVH conversation summary" filled with bullets that summarized things Don told me to investigate over the previous year or two. The 15 or so bullets on that summary page have a number of things that, to this day, still have not been done and are incredible ideas!

I was incredibly fortunate to have Don Helmberger as an advisor. Of all the things he helped me with, the most profound for me was something he never explicitly verbalized. Don consistently showed me how the data, if you patiently study it without an agenda or a model you might want to prove, will *always* lead you to something. The data will always teach us and reveal Earth's secrets. Sure, we have our ideas, our intuition, our speculations and hypotheses. But turning these preconceptions off to openly look at all the data is where true discoveries lie. This was so compelling for me because Don's love of data always struck me as innocent, humble, and pure. No agenda. No ego. Rather, just pure curiosity. If you spent enough time with Don, you would see his wonderful innate curiosity towards a number of other things, for example, like human behavior, nature, politics, sports (basketball!), and more. Figure 4 shows two pictures from the SEDI 2016 meeting in France. Don, with great curiosity, looks at the beautiful tall trees. Standing there behind him, I marveled at him really pausing to take it all in.

Fig. 4　Photos of Don Helmberger during the "Gala Dinner" of the 2016 *Study of Earth's Deep Interior* Conference, at the Chateau de la Poterie, which is a Louis-XVI style castle built at the end of the 18th century. On the left, Don curiously takes in beautiful trees on the property. On the right, Don being Don, full of enthusiasm and joy.

Finally, to celebrate Don and his infectious curiosity, I purchased my own office ficus tree. It has grown quickly and almost reaches the ceiling. It is my own little daily reminder to *look at data*, as often as possible, with an open mind, without agenda or a model in mind, to innocently and curiously observe. Thank you Don!

Acknowledgements

I thank Xiaodong Song, Thorne Lay, and David Wald for providing edits and comments that helped to clarify this paper.

References

Garnero EJ, Grand SP and Helmberger DV (1993). Low P-wave velocity at the base of the mantle. Geophys Res Lett **20**(17): 1843–1846.

Garnero EJ (1994). Seismic structure above and below the core-mantle boundary. Dissertation. California Institute of Technology.

Garnero EJ and Helmberger DV (1996). Seismic detection of a thin laterally varying boundary layer at the base of the mantle beneath the central-Pacific. Geophys Res Lett **23**(9): 977–980.

Helmberger DV (1968). The crust-mantle transition in the Bering Sea. Bull Seismol Soc Am **58**(1): 179–214.

Helmberger DV (1983). Theory and application of synthetic seismograms. In: Kanamori H ed. Earthquakes: Observation, Theory and Interpretation. Società Italiana di Fisica, Bolgna, pp 173–222

Helmberger DV, Engen G and Grand S (1985). Notes on wave propagation in laterally varying structure. J Geophys **58**(1): 82–91.

Helmberger DV, Zhao LS, and Garnero EJ (1996). Construction of synthetics for 2D structures; core phases. In: Seismic Modelling of Earth Structure. Editrice Compositori, Bologna, Italy, pp 183–222

Kanamori H (1978). Quantification of earthquakes. Nature **271**(5644): 411–414.

Kanamori H (1983). Magnitude scale and quantification of earthquakes. Tectonophysics **93**(3-4): 185–199.

Mori J and Helmberger DV (1995). Localized boundary layer below the mid-Pacific velocity anomaly identified from a *PcP* precursor. J Geophys Res **100**(B10): 20359–20365.

Murphy LM (1961). World-wide network of standardized seismographs. Eos, Trans Am Geophys Union **42**(2): 184–186.

Edward Garnero is currently a Professor in the School of Earth and Space Exploration, at Arizona State University (ASU).　He completed his Ph.D. at Caltech in 1994 with Prof. Helmberger as his primary thesis advisor. Following his PhD, he was a US National Science Foundation Postdoctoral Fellow at University of California at Santa Cruz (UCSC, under the supervision of Prof. Thorne Lay). This was followed by an Assistant Researcher position at the University of California at Berkeley (UCB, under the supervision of Prof. Barbara Romanowicz), after which he began his faculty position at ASU. He is a fellow of the American Geophysical Union. His webpage can be found at: http://garnero.asu.edu.

第 10 章 数据和好奇心：与导师唐·亨伯格一起工作

埃德·加内罗

美国亚利桑那州立大学地球与空间探索学院，坦佩，亚利桑那州 85287

引用: Garnero E (2022). Data and curiosity: Working with mentor Donald V. Helmberger. Earthq Sci 35(1): 29–33 doi: 10.1016/j.eqs.2022.01.004

  1986 年 6 月，我来到加州理工学院，当时我对矿物物理学和地震学都感兴趣。无论是和汤姆·阿伦斯（Tom Ahrens）教授一起研究矿物物理，或是和金森博雄（Hiroo Kanamori）一起研究大地震都让我感到十分兴奋。在来到这里之后，我决定选择地震学。我对本科时读到的一些博雄（Hiroo）在地震大小方面的工作特别感兴趣（Kanamori, 1978, 1983）。在第一个星期，我见到了博雄（Hiroo），他问我对于研究大地震有何计划。事实上，我没有计划，毫无头绪！他独到地指出，我们需要更多更好的地震数据——这当然是在数字数据爆炸式增长后的十年里出现的。博雄（Hiroo）建议我向隔壁的地震学家唐·亨伯格（Don Helmberger）毛遂自荐，也许他会有一些有趣的研究项目供我参考。

  我敲了敲唐（Don）打开的门，他以热情的微笑欢迎我进来。他的办公室很大，给人一种开放的感觉。他长方形办公室的长边墙上排列着高高的窗户。一棵相当大的榕树位于一边，一张很大的桌子占据了他办公室中心的大部分空间（大概有 2×4 米）。我提到我是一名新的研究生，希望在博士期间研究地震学。唐（Don）立刻邀请我坐在他的大桌子旁。上面有成堆的文献和地震图。没有闲聊，他抓起一堆打印好的地震图，扑通一声放在我们面前，开始一页一页地浏览。每一页都画满了波形。它们是全球标准地震台网（WWSSN）地震图（Murphy, 1961）的缩微胶片拷贝的打印件。加州理工学院地震学实验室的地下室有一个房间，里面摆满了 WWSSN 数据的文件柜，可以在房间的尽头用一台非常大的放大打印机进行扫描和打印。唐（Don）有一堆堆的文件夹，里面都是打印出来的地震图。在每一页上，他都指着他称之为"SKS"的波形，一页又一页地谈论它的形状。每翻开新的一页，他都十分激动，"……看看这一页！"

  我对唐（Don）在说什么毫无头绪，他看起来也不知道我对他给我看的地震图一无所知。但他的兴奋和热情是如此的明显。在那初次见面后，我对自己说，能令加州理工学院地震学教授如此激动的事情可能对我来说会是极好的研究方向！我也没料到 SKS 会在接下来的许多年里成为我的信仰。我很快来到地下室，花了好几个小时扫描和打印包含 SKS 波的 WWSSN 记录，然后在桌上数字化仪上对它们进行数字化（图 1）。在数字记录可用（这是多年后的事）之前，这几乎是每天的例行公事。所以，在第一天我就了解到唐（Don）对地震数据的无限兴奋和热情，他有一种与你分享东西的绝妙风范，不管你对这个话题有多了解。每次他给你看地震数据时，他就像一个分享最喜欢的新玩具的孩子，他的好奇心和快乐很有感染力。

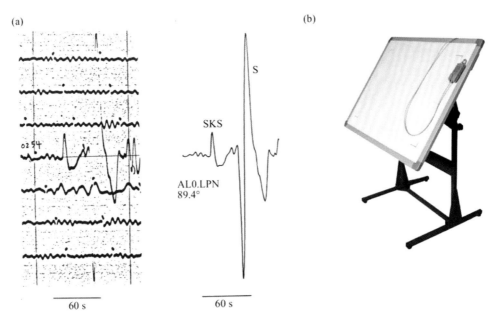

图1　（a）左边是来自于 WWSSN 的在新墨西哥州阿尔伯克基（Albuquerque）的 ALQ 台站记录到的斐济地震的长周期信号的扫描，右边是它的数字记录版本。（b）一个和当时用于将纸质信号转换成数字信号的装置相似的数字化台（图片来自于 https://www.alibaba.com/product-detail/Jindx-Clothing-Plate-Making-Scanner- Gerber_62555983285.html）

在地下室收集了整整一个夏天的数据后，秋季学期开始了，我和其他大约四名学生一起上了唐（Don）的"高等地震学"课程。我很快就了解到了我热爱数据的导师的另一面：理论和计算地震学。唐（Don）不仅是一个极优秀的观测者，他还积极开创了重现和解释地震数据的方法。没过多久，我们就在课堂上学习了卡尼亚尔-德胡普（Cagniard-de Hoop）理论，在研究中学习了广义射线理论的代码，这使我们能够探索速度-深度模型中各层对地震数据记录的贡献。唐（Don）的几篇早期论文都涉及了这些，比如 Helmberger（1968）和 Helmberger 等（1985），以及他出色的综述论文 Helmberger（1983），所有这些都成为了我们日常阅读的文献。我们中的许多人都使用唐（Don）的程序 *aseries.f* 或 *bounce1or2.f*，以及其他我们研究中要用到的老的 Fortran 代码。我时常在来到办公桌时看到一张黄色的便条，上面写着"来找我"。当我去唐（Don）的办公室时，他通常会打印出这些代码生成的合成地震图，用来解释 SKS 波的一些有趣的方面。

我们的工作很快发展到研究 SKS 遇到核幔边界（CMB）时发生的有趣现象。当 SV 波在核幔边界处以临界角入射并转化为 P 波时，会产生衍射 P 波能量（即 ScPdiff 波）。这个波将 P 波能量传送到地核，成为 SPdKS（从互易性出发，在 SKS 上行的 K 段上，也产生了 SKPdS）。我们关于这一现象的第一篇论文（Garnero et al., 1993）确立了由于 CMB 上存在非常强的 P 波速度降，在 SKS 波形"肩膀"上并逐渐远离的 SPdKS 波将在较近的震中距被观测到（图 2）。这在后来的研究中被称为超低速区（ULVZ），后续的论文（Mori and Helmberger, 1995; Garnero and Helmberger, 1996）中将其模拟为核幔边界的一个薄层（5～40 km 厚）。将低速体限制在 CMB 的一个薄层上也是唐（Don）的想法。

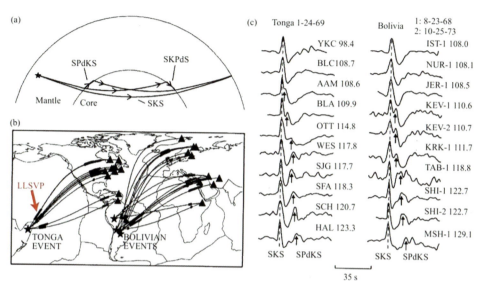

图 2　（a）SKS, SPdKS 和 SKPdS 震相的射线路径。（b）来自于斐济-汤加和南美（主要是玻利维亚）的两个震源产生的射线路径。射线路径包含了在太平洋超低速区中传播的 SPdKS 波的 Pd 部分（粗线）。（c）WWSSN 的数字化之后的长周期 SV 波数据,箭头标明了 SKS 波和 SPdKS(包含了 SPdKS 和 SPdKS)波的到时。每一条记录的右侧标注了台站名称和震中距。汤加地震比玻利维亚地震在更小的震中距产生了 SPdKS 波（例如 AAM 台记录到了 SPdKS 而相似震中距的 JER 台却没有）。超低速区的结构造成了 SPdKS 波出现在更小的震中距。这些图片来自于 Garnero and Helmberger（1996）并进行了少量的修改。

在我到加州大学圣克鲁兹分校和唐（Don）的学生索恩·莱（Thorne Lay）进行第一份博士后工作时，又一次感受到了唐（Don）一直在持续思考问题。在第一年里，我会收到一页又一页阶跃函数地震图的传真（这是广义射线理论程序的输出，只需要与地震仪器响应函数进行求导和卷积就可以与数据进行比较）。图 3 给出了一个例子，展示了唐（Don）在 SKS 数据中识别出的一个新的重要特征，这个特征可以用于超低速区结构成像。在这里，他展示了核幔边界低速边界层中的多次内反射也对波场产生了显著影响（Helmberger et al., 1996）。这只是唐（Don）解剖、建模和理解地震波场的神奇能力的一个例子。这种额外的独特地震波震相与 SPdKS（和 SKPdS）波一起形成异常的 SKS 波形。

唐（Don）对数据分析和方法的洞察力似乎总是远远领先于他的时代。我最近看了一本我称之为"DVH 对话"的活页夹（"DVH"代表他的全名，Donald Vincent Helmberger）。我学会了记下唐（Don）所说的关于数据的任何事情。我很兴奋地发现一个近 30 年前的页面，标题是"DVH 对话摘要"，里面用重点符号总结了唐（Don）在过去一两年里告诉我要探索的问题，这一页上 15 个左右的问题中很多到今天为止仍然没有被解决，这些都是无与伦比的想法！

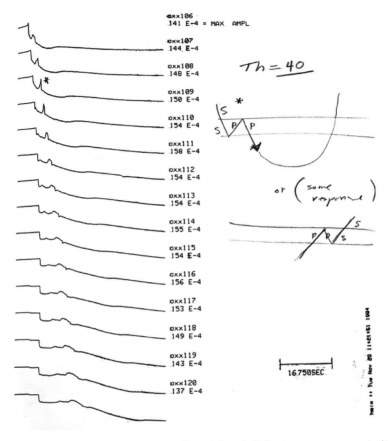

图3　1994年当我开始第一份博士后工作的几个月后唐·亨伯格（Don Helmberger）寄给我的一份传真，展示了阶跃函数产生的 SKS 波和一个额外的由于在核幔边界处的低速层（40km 厚的超低速区）内多次反射形成的 SppKS（以及 SKppS）波（相应的格林函数）震中距从最顶部的106°增加到最底部的120°。星号标注了我们感兴趣的震相到时，唐（Don）在右侧用手工示意图的形式画出了这一震相，这一额外的震相产生了异常的 SKS 波形，从而帮助我们探索超低速区的结构。

　　我非常幸运有唐·亨伯格（Don Helmberger）当导师。在他帮助过我的所有事情中，对我来说最受用的是他从未明确说过的事情。唐（Don）不断地向我展示，如果你不设议程或者在没有某个可能想要证明的模型的情况下耐心地研究数据，那么数据总是会引导你发现一些事情。这些数据总会教会我们一些知识，并帮助我们揭示地球的秘密。当然，我们有自己的想法、直觉、推测和假设，但真正的发现需要我们抛开这些先入之见来公正地查看所有数据。这对我来说很有吸引力，因为唐（Don）对数据的热爱总是让我觉得很触动，这种热爱天真、谦逊、纯洁，没有先入之见，不自负，而是纯粹的好奇心。如果你和唐（Don）相处的时间足够长，你会发现他对许多其他事物天生的好奇心，比如人类行为、自然、政治、体育（篮球！）等等。图4展示了2016年法国"地球深部研究"（study of earth's deep interior）学术会议期间拍摄的两张照片。唐（Don）怀着极大的好奇心看着那些美丽的大树，站在他身后的我惊讶于他真的停下来感受这一切。

图 4. 2016 年 "地球深部研究" 学术会期间拍摄的照片，这次会议在法国的 Chateau de la Poterie 举办，这是一个在 18 世纪末建成的路易十六式的城堡。左图中唐（Don）充满好奇心地观察着这些美丽的大树。右图中，唐（Don）像他平时一样，充满了好奇心和快乐。

最后，为了纪念唐（Don）和他有感染力的好奇心，我在自己的办公室买了一棵榕树，它长得很快，几乎到了屋顶。我每天都会提醒自己，要以开放的心态尽可能多地查看数据，不要先入为主，要天真而好奇地观察。谢谢你，唐（Don）！

致谢

感谢宋晓东、索恩·莱（Thorne Lay）和戴维·沃尔德（David Wald）对文章的评论以及编辑，这使得这篇文章更加清晰。

参 考 文 献

Garnero EJ, Grand SP and Helmberger DV (1993). Low P-wave velocity at the base of the mantle. Geophys Res Lett **20**(17): 1843–1846.

Garnero EJ (1994). Seismic structure above and below the core-mantle boundary. Dissertation. California Institute of Technology.

Garnero EJ and Helmberger DV (1996). Seismic detection of a thin laterally varying boundary layer at the base of the mantle beneath the central-Pacific. Geophys Res Lett **23**(9): 977–980.

Helmberger DV (1968). The crust-mantle transition in the Bering Sea. Bull Seismol Soc Am **58**(1): 179–214.

Helmberger DV (1983). Theory and application of synthetic seismograms. In: Kanamori H ed. Earthquakes: Observation, Theory and Interpretation. Società Italiana di Fisica, Bolgna, pp 173–222

Helmberger DV, Engen G and Grand S (1985). Notes on wave propagation in laterally varying structure. J Geophys **58**(1): 82–91.

Helmberger DV, Zhao LS, and Garnero EJ (1996). Construction of synthetics for 2D structures; core phases. In: Seismic Modelling of Earth Structure. Editrice Compositori, Bologna, Italy, pp 183–222

Kanamori H (1978). Quantification of earthquakes. Nature **271**(5644): 411–414.

Kanamori H (1983). Magnitude scale and quantification of earthquakes. Tectonophysics **93**(3-4): 185–199.

Mori J and Helmberger DV (1995). Localized boundary layer below the mid-Pacific velocity anomaly identified from a *PcP* precursor. J Geophys Res **100**(B10): 20359–20365.

Murphy LM (1961). World-wide network of standardized seismographs. Eos, Trans Am Geophys Union **42**(2): 184–186.

　　埃德·加内罗（Ed Garnero）目前是加利桑那州立大学（ASU）地球与空间探索学院的教授。他于 1994 年在加州理工学院完成博士学业，主要论文导师是唐·亨伯格（Don Helmberger）。博士毕业后，他作为美国自然科学基金博士后在加州大学圣克鲁兹分校（UCSC）进行研究，合作导师是索恩·莱（Thorne Lay）教授。之后，他在加州大学伯克利分校（UCB）担任助理研究员，合作导师是芭芭拉·罗曼诺维茨（Barbara Romanowicz）教授，并在亚利桑那州立大学获得教职。他是美国地球物理联合会（American Geophysical Union）的会士。他的主页是 http://garnero.asu.edu。

Chapter 11. My journey to the center of the Earth: A tribute to Professor Donald V. Helmberger

Xiaodong Song[*]

Institute of Theoretical and Applied Geophysics, School of Earth and Space Sciences, Peking University, Beijing 100871, China

[*]**Correspondence:** xiao.d.song@gmail.com

Citation: Song XD (2022). My journey to the center of the Earth: A tribute to Professor Donald V. Helmberger. Earthq Sci 35(1): 34−39 doi: 10.1016/j.eqs.2022.01.007

It has been more than a year since Don passed away suddenly. Thinking about it still makes my heart hurt. I did not know Don Helmberger or any other famous geophysicists before joining the Seismological Laboratory at Caltech in 1989. In fact, I had barely heard of the Seismo Lab before I landed there, to some extent, by chance or pure luck. At the time, graduate applications were filed by paper. A fellow student gave me a Caltech application form, as he thought he was not good enough, and encouraged me to apply instead. Despite the lack of information at the time and my own ignorance, I took the opportunity. Little did I know, my academic journey had begun at that moment.

Admission

The Seismo Lab received many Ph.D. students from Chinese mainland and Taiwan. An early graduate from the Seismo Lab was Professor Fu Chengyi (Ph.D. 1944; Adviser: Beno Gutenberg), who was probably the first Seismo Lab Ph.D. graduate from China and became one of the founding fathers of geophysics in China upon returning. Over the years, Don trained many students, including more than 20 Chinese students and postdocs, probably the most so far among all the Seismo Lab professors over its 100-year history. The Seismo Lab has also hosted some Chinese visiting scholars throughout this time, including Academician Yao Zhenxing and Professor Zhou Huilan in the earlier years.

Professors Yao and Zhou both wrote letters of recommendation for my application. Prof. Yao was Prof. Fu Chengyi's graduate student. In the early 1980s, he stayed at the Seismo Lab for 1.5 years working with Don, after staying at the University of Southern California for 1.5 years. Don remembered him well and said more than once that he was very smart (he would call him by the last name "Yao"). I did not know Prof. Yao, but he was kind enough to write a letter of recommendation for me after a brief conversation. He was very happy for the fact that the four students he recommended to Caltech were successful afterwards (Lianshe Zhao, Ph.D. 1991, Lianxing Wen, Ph.D 1998, Chen Ji, Ph.D. 2002, besides myself, who were all Don's students).

Prof. Zhou was my undergraduate teacher at the University of Science and Technology of China. She stayed at the Seismo Lab for two years working mainly with Hiroo Kanamori and Clarence Allen. Somehow, she had a very good impression of me, giving me opportunities and offering advice. Thus, when I was struggling at deciding which school to accept, she had a strong sway in my decision. In our recent phone conversation, she recalled her fond memories at the Seismo Lab and some of the thoughts on my choice at the time. She felt I knew what I wanted to do. I seemed to be the "academic type" and I was interested in seismic waves. "I didn't know whether it's the best place, but it would be a great place for studying seismology" she remarked on Caltech. It's also very easy to access seismic data. She recalled using the film chip records of the World-Wide Standardized Seismograph Network (WWSSN) in the Seismo Lab basement. The Seismo Lab also has a history of building and operating seismic networks. Thus, she thought Caltech would be a great match for me.

On July 7, 1989, I arrived at Caltech. It was a Friday afternoon after work, time for the Division beer gathering at the back yard of the South Mudd Building. Lianshe picked me up at LAX (Los Angles International Airport) and we went straight there, where I instantly found that my earlier practice of oral English was quite useful in helping adapt to the new life. As I arrived early, I was supported by Clarence Allen for the summer months before the Fall quarter started. Prof. Allen was an old friend to Chinese geologists and geophysicists. He served in the Army Air Corps in the Pacific during World War II and visited China many times later on. At the beginning of the Fall semester, I was told that the Run Run Shaw Foundation (of Hong Kong) would offer me a 3-year graduate fellowship (given to only two Caltech graduate students that year), for which I could not think of a good reason except perhaps I did well in my TOEFL exam.

The Seismo Lab

Soon after I joined the Seismo Lab, I realized that (creative) research was the thing that we needed to focus on. Unlike many institutions, students here were not tied to any particular professor or project at the start. To demonstrate the ability to do independent research, a new student in the Seismo Lab must take up two projects with two different faculty members and present the projects in an oral exam at the beginning of the second year.

One of the projects I did was with Don. It was to look at PKP waves (P waves passing through the core). The initial idea was to study the P wave structure at the D" region (lowermost ~200 km of the mantle). At the time, studies on D" had focused on S waves, including the initial work by Lay and Helmberger (1983), which first discovered the D" discontinuity (also known as the Lay-Helmberger discontinuity). Studies on P structure had been lacking.

PKP waves are sensitive to D" structure (Song and Helmberger, 1993a, 1997). But we quickly realized that we needed to understand the core first. Unlike SKS, which turns shallowly in the outer core, the PKP waves dive deeper and inevitably enter the inner core. That became my first Ph.D. project and my very first scientific paper (Song and Helmberger 1992; SH92). The key issue was that seismic models for the inner core boundary were quite variable (Figure 1). "The variety of models displayed indicates the richness of possible interpretations" (SH92). Figure 1 was later used in the classic textbook by Lay and Wallace (1995). It was a transformative start. I learned what research is about (which I did not really know before joining Caltech) and how it is carried out in the normal process (finding a problem, working out the method, searching for needed data, performing the analyses, drawing conclusions, summarizing the results, and going through the review process).

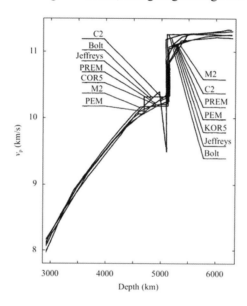

Fig. 1　P velocity models of the Earth's core compiled by Song and Helmberger (1992).

The approach we used is the so-called "waveform modeling". "It appears that the most detailed resolution of this discontinuity will come from the waveform modeling approach which will be followed in this study. This basic method relies on fitting observations with synthetics based on a model where the wave equations are satisfied" (SH92). Don wrote those quoted sentences in the paper (although he was not known for poetic English writing, I found his writing was always full of sparks of ideas). One tries to find high-quality (which usually means relatively few) record sections to study and to study well. Furthermore, because the deep structure of the Earth is not spherical, it must be sampled accordingly. Thus, a regionalization analysis is undertaken with a detailed investigation of a particular sample of the deep interior. This basic approach was a hallmark of Don's works, leading to many of his important discoveries (Lay, 2021). Synthetic waveforms need to be generated efficiently in order to adjust the model to fit the observed waveforms in the trial-and-error exercise. Don used synthetics for 1D Earth at the early stage (Helmberger, 1983), the famous Generalized Ray Theory (GRT) codes, and later expanded to 2D (Helmberger et al., 1996; Wen and Helmberger, 1998; Ni et al., 2000) and 3D (Helmberger and Ni, 2005; Ni et al., 2005) synthetics.

The data we used were analog in the beginning years when the new digital seismic stations were just starting to appear. Don enjoyed finding data himself in the basement film chip archive (Figure 2). After a while, I would spend time in the basement too. The digitization software (nXscan) developed in house was a great help and became instrumental for my later studies of inner core temporal changes that rely on historical earthquake data (below).

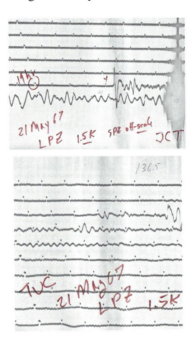

Fig. 2　Examples of seismic record copies from film chips obtained by Prof. Helmberger with his hand-written marks. The records were digitized and included in Song XD and Helmberger (1992).

Don had a natural talent for motivating students. He empowered them in their work and made them feel intelligent. Early on I needed to modify the GRT codes to double precision so that they could be used for the core phases. He would later call the modification "your codes". At times in our discussion, he would pause for a long time, staring out of the window. I would think I had probably said something dumb, but he would not point it out. His great scientific insights were penetrating and contagious and his genuine appreciation of good science ("terrific", "good stuff") boosted your confidence and interest.

Oral exam time came. I had been warned at the very start by senior fellow Chinese students to pay attention and not to "lose face". Fortunately, my exam went smoothly. David Stevenson asked an interesting question of why I paid attention to the waveform fit at the beginning part of the waveform but not the later part. When we talked later, Don clearly found the question hilarious. He joked that Dave had gotten better — he used to question how a seismologist can make a living solving only the wave equation. Peter Wyllie, the Committee Chair, wrote a short summary letter (which I have kept to this day), stressing the importance of broadening my research scope moving forward. I remember an interesting event around that time, which was a cultural education for me. At an annual Zilchbrau (a party of the Division to mingle and poke fun), graduate students shot a movie of an oral exam scene. The failed candidate got so agitated that he jumped across the table and choked the faculty. It struck me in particular because it was not only well done but also dramatized the stimulating environment of equality (and in a humorous way).

Another skill that all of us picked up was computing. Rob Clayton gave me a copy of Kernighan and Ritchie's C Programming in early days, alerting me the importance of coding. The Seismo Lab is very open and you learn a lot from your peers. But I took some additional computer science courses and ended up with a Computer Science minor in my Ph.D. Don asked one time: "Do you want to be a scientist or a scholar?". That was an interesting contrast that I had never thought about before. I certainly didn't want to be a bookworm. In retrospect, the experience was more useful in managing computational resources and needs in my own group, particularly at the beginning stage, than in my own research.

A Career

The training from Don and the Seismo Lab had a profound impact on my career. Habits from the training got ingrained into our minds and became part of our DNA. I continued to work on the Earth's core and to communicate with Don after moving to Lamont-Doherty Earth Observatory of Columbia University.

One of my Ph.D. studies with Don was the confirmation of the existence of the anisotropy of the inner core (Song and Helmberger, 1993b). The idea was proposed a while back (in 1986), but had remained controversial. The arrival time picks from the International Seismological Center (ISC) that were used are quite noisy and subject to biases (source errors and mantle heterogeneities); anomalous observations were in fact thrown out as noisy "outliers". We measured differential times between PKP phases based on actual waveforms, which is more precise and less biased by non-inner core factors, from a global search of paths with different ray directions. Obviously, the waveform-based approach is vastly outnumbered by the ISC data set, but the advantage of the approach is also equally obvious. The model can explain the first arrivals of the inner core phase (DF phase) well. However, the DF waveforms from the famous South Sandwich Islands (SSI) to Alaska and Canada appear unusually broad in the long-period records (Song and Helmberger, 1998; Figure 3). We thought the waveform complication in fact resulted from a "baby triplication", which appears as broad waveforms from the overlapping of multiple arrivals. The triplication is generated due to a velocity jump from the transition of the isotropic upper inner core to the anisotropic lower inner core along the pathway.

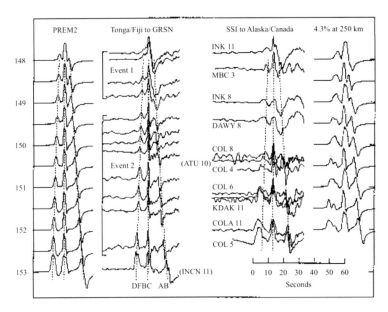

Fig. 3　Evidence leading to the proposal of an inner core transition zone by Song and Helmberger (1998). Note the DF pulses (the beginning ones) from SSI to Alaska are broadened, which can be explained by the synthetics at the right column.

In the work leading to the evidence for inner core super-rotation that Professor Paul Richards and I proposed (Song and Richards, 1996), attention to subtle differences was critical (Figure 4). The care to measure the relative times as precisely as possible helped reduce data scatter in the extraction of the delicate temporal change signal. Some measurements for the critical SSI to College, Alaska path had been made in my Ph.D. study, which made it easier to compare with the data in the early 1990s that were easily accessible at the International Research Institution of Seismology Data Management Center. The idea of overlaying and comparing observed seismograms (Figure 4) was a routine exercise, similar to how we tried to match a synthetic to the observed waveforms. In the follow-up hunt for historical data to confirm temporal changes from the inner core, the skills of working with analog data (finding, scanning, and digitizing the waveforms) in my graduate study became handy, which led me to archives around the world (Palisades, New York, USA; Golden and Denver, Colorado, USA; College, Alaska, USA; Beijing, China; and Tokyo, Japan) (Song, 2000; Song and Li, 2000; Xu and Song, 2003).

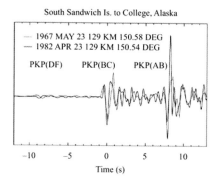

Fig. 4 Observation of temporal change of the inner core phase (PKP DF), leading to the proposal of inner core rotation, from Song and Richards (1996). The use of the outer core reference phase, PKP(BC), helps reduce other biases. The 1982 trace is digital data, while the 1967 trace was digitized from the WWSSN analog record.

My Caltech training has led me to a career that has focused on studies of the Earth's core for a great part: fruitful years as a postdoctoral fellow and young researcher at Lamont, tenured professor at University of Illinois at Urbana-Champaign, and visiting positions and recent full-time position in China. I've received virtually continuous support in this study area over the decades from the U.S. National Science Foundation, the National Natural Science Foundation of China, the U.S. National Aeronautics and Space Administration, and so on. At the heart of the issue is the limited sampling and resolution of the core, particularly the inner core. For half of the century after its discovery, the inner core had been a featureless sphere. However, over the last few decades, it has been shown to be quite complex and mysterious. I was fortunate to start working on this problem at the cusp of important breakthroughs under Don's mentorship.

Don Forever

Even though it had been decades since I graduated, Don was always present throughout my research career. I would run into him at the annual AGU Fall Meeting, which has played a big role in my career. It is a conference that I have participated continuously for more than 30 years ever since the first year of my arrival at Caltech, with Don's encouragement. I find it always exciting and stimulating and you want to be (or need to be) there (unfortunately the pandemic has taken a toll on the meeting in the last two years). It is an opportunity to showcase your latest works and thus students often work into late hours to get the latest results done. It is also a place to meet up with people and discuss the latest work and ideas. It was always a delight to see Don and catch up with him at the AGU meetings and other conferences. The last time I saw Don was at the 2019 Fall AGU Meeting (in December) in San Francisco. He was as sharp as ever. He was very happy that I decided to relocate to Beijing and told me that I should stop by the Seismo Lab before departure. Unfortunately, that didn't happen. Who would have thought that was the last chance to see Don?

Don will always live in my heart as one of the people who influenced my life the most. He introduced me to the wonderful world of science and seismology. As I tell my kids, the American branch of our family started at Caltech. As they grew up, I would pay attention to their interests and passions. My son is now pursuing a science Ph.D. with an interest in academia, a rarity among his peers of similar background. The academic father-like influence that Don had on me impacted the way I tried to guide my kids (Figure 5).

Fig. 5　Don with my son and daughter. The picture was taken in early January 2015 in Don's office during the holiday break.

In the current era of "big data", full-waveform inversion and machine learning are the fashion, where a large amount of data are thrown in a "black box". Details and subtle differences in the waveforms can get buried easily in the global averaging and optimization. However, Don and his students have shown amply that key details in the data need to be taken into account to sharpen up the resolution of tomographic images, particularly on discontinuities and sharp boundaries, where important physics often lies. These key features in the data will surely need to be optimized differently for future generations of high-resolution tomographic imaging.

A group of Don's students set up a social group "Don4Ever" after Don's passing. We believe Don's legacy and legend will live on for a long time. Don will be forever missed and remembered for his kindness, generosity, humor, encouragement, and great scientific insights.

Acknowledgments

I thank comments and edits from Thorne Lay, Ed Garnero, Lupei Zhu, Daoyuan Sun, Voon Hui Lai, and my son Tommy Song, which helped improve the manuscript.

References

Helmberger DV (1983). Theory and application of synthetic seismograms. In: Kanamori H ed. Earthquakes: Observation, Theory and Interpretation. Istituto Nazionale di Geofisica, Rome, pp 173–222

Helmberger DV, Garnero EJ and Ding XM (1996). Modeling two-dimensional structure at the core-mantle boundary. J Geophys Res Solid Earth **101**(B6): 13963–13972.

Helmberger DV and Ni SD (2005). Approximate 3D body-wave synthetics for tomographic models. Bull Seismol Soc Am **95**(1): 212–224.

Lay T and Helmberger DV (1983). A lower mantle S-wave triplication and the shear velocity structure of D″. Geophys J Int **75**(3): 799–837.

Lay T and Wallace TC (1995). Modern Global Seismology. Academic Press, San Diego, p305

Lay T (2021). Donald V. Helmberger (1938–2020). Seismol Res Lett **92**(2A): 624–622.

Ni SD, Ding XM and Helmberger DV (2000). Constructing synthetics from deep earth tomographic models. Geophys J Int **140**(1): 71–82.

Ni SD, Helmberger DV and Tromp J (2005). Three-dimensional structure of the African superplume from waveform modelling. Geophys J Int **161**(2): 283–294.

Song XD and Helmberger DV (1992). Velocity structure near the inner core boundary from waveform modeling. J Geophys Res Solid Earth **97**(B5): 6573–6586.

Song XD and Helmberger DV (1993a). Effect of velocity structure in D″ on PKP phases. Geophys Res Lett **20**(4): 285–288.

Song XD and Helmberger DV (1993b). Anisotropy of Earth's inner core. Geophys Res Lett **20**(23): 2591–2594.

Song XD and Richards PG (1996). Seismological evidence for differential rotation of the Earth's inner core. Nature **382**(6588): 221–224.

Song XD and Helmberger DV (1997). PKP differential travel times: Implications for 3-D lower mantle structure. Geophys Res Lett **24**(15): 1863–1866.

Song XD and Helmberger DV (1998). Seismic evidence for an inner core transition zone. Science **282**(5390): 924–927.

Song XD (2000). Joint inversion for inner core rotation, inner core anisotropy, and mantle heterogeneity. J Geophys Res Solid Earth **105**(B4): 7931–7943.

Song XD and Li AY (2000). Support for differential inner core superrotation from earthquakes in Alaska recorded at South Pole station. J Geophys Res Solid Earth **105**(B1): 623–630.

Wen LX and Helmberger DV (1998). A two-dimensional *P-SV* hybrid method and its application to modeling localized structures near the core-mantle boundary. J Geophys Res **103**(B8): 17901–17918.

Xu XX and Song XD (2003). Evidence for inner core super-rotation from time-dependent differential PKP traveltimes observed at Beijing seismic network. Geophys J Int **152**(3): 509–514.

Xiaodong Song is currently Chair Professor at School of Earth and Space Sciences, Peking University. He received his M.S. degree in 1991 and Ph.D. degree in 1994 at Caltech with Prof. Helmberger as thesis advisor. He then joined Lamont-Doherty Earth Observatory of Columbia University as a postdoc fellow and later as Associate Research Scientist and Storke-Doherty Lecturer. He subsequently served on the faculty of Department of Geology at University of Illinois at Urbana-Champaign from 1999 to 2020 before relocating to Beijing, China. His work on the inner core differential rotation was named as a breakthrough of the year by Science magazine (1996). He received Doornbos Prize by the Studies of Earth Deep Interior Committee of the International Union of Geophysics and Geodesy (1996), Outstanding Overseas Young Scientist Award by the Natural Science Foundation of China (1998), Solid Earth Distinguished Lectureship by the Asia Oceania Geosciences Society (AOGS) (2016). He currently serves as the Editor-in-Chief of Earthquake Science. His webpage can be found at: http://geophy.pku.edu.cn/people/songxiaodong/english/index.html.

第 11 章　我的地心之旅：致敬唐·亨伯格教授

宋晓东

北京大学理论与应用地球物理研究所，北京 100871，中国

引用: Song XD (2022). My journey to the center of the Earth: A tribute to Professor Donald V. Helmberger. Earthq Sci 35(1): 34−39 doi:　10.1016/j.eqs.2022.01.007

　　唐（Don）突然去世至今已经一年多了。想到这件事，我仍然感到心痛。在 1989 年进入加州理工学院地震实验室（Seismo Lab）之前，我并不认识唐·亨伯格（Don Helmberger）或那里其他任何著名的地球物理学家。事实上，在我凭借着某种程度的偶然或运气到那里之前，我几乎没有听说过地震实验室（Seismo Lab）。当时，研究生的申请是以纸质形式提交的。一位同学给了我一张加州理工学院的申请表，因为他觉得自己不够优秀，便鼓励我去申请。尽管当时缺乏信息而且我自己也很无知，我还是抓住了这个机会。我一点儿也没有意识到，我的学术之旅就在那一刻开始了。

录取

　　地震实验室（Seismo Lab）接收过许多来自中国大陆和中国台湾的博士生。傅承义教授［1944 年获得博士学位；导师：贝诺·古滕贝格（Beno Gutenberg）］是地震实验室（Seismo Lab）早期的毕业生。他可能是第一位毕业于地震实验室（Seismo Lab）的华人博士，并在回国后成为了中国地球物理学的奠基人之一。多年来，唐（Don）培养了许多学生，包括 20 多名中国学生和博士后，这可能是自地震实验室（Seismo Lab）成立的 100 多年以来所有教授中最多的。在此期间，地震实验室（Seismo Lab）还接待了一些来自中国的访问学者，包括早年的姚振兴院士和周蕙兰教授。

　　姚教授和周教授都为我的申请写了推荐信。姚教授是傅承义教授的研究生。20 世纪 80 年代初，他在南加州大学待了一年半之后，又去地震实验室（Seismo Lab）与唐（Don）一起工作了一年半。唐（Don）对他印象深刻，并不止一次地夸他很聪明（他以他的姓"姚"相称）。我当时不认识姚教授，但他很友善，在简短的交谈后为我写了一封推荐信。他在得知他推荐给加州理工学院的四名学生后来都获得了成功后非常高兴［赵连社（Lianshe Zhao），1991 年获得博士学位；温联星（Lianxing Wen），1998 年获得博士学位，纪晨（Chen Ji），2002 年获得博士学位；包括我，我们都是唐（Don）的学生］。

　　周教授是我在中国科学与技术大学的本科生老师和班主任。她在地震实验室（Seismo Lab）工作了两年，主要是与金森博雄（Hiroo Kanamori）和克拉伦斯·艾伦（Clarence Allen）合作。她对我印象很好，给了我机会，并给了我建议。因此，当我在纠结该接受

哪所学校时，她很大程度地影响了我的决定。在我们最近的通话中，她回忆起了她在地震实验室（Seismo Lab）的美好回忆，以及当时对我选择的一些想法。她觉得我知道自己想做什么。我似乎属于"学术型"，而且对地震波很感兴趣。"我不知道那里是不是最好的地方，但将是研究地震学的好地方。"这是她对加州理工学院的评价。在那里，获取地震数据也很容易。她回忆了在地震实验室（Seismo Lab）的地下室使用全球标准化地震台网（WWSSN）的胶片记录的经历。地震实验室（Seismo Lab）还负责布设并运作地震台网。因此，她认为加州理工学院会很适合我。

1989 年 7 月 7 日，我来到了加州理工学院。那是一个周五下午，正是下班后在南马德楼后院举行学部里啤酒聚会的时间。连社（Lianshe）来洛杉矶国际机场接我，然后我们直接去了那里。在那里，我很快意识到我先前的口语练习对适应新生活非常有用。由于我的提前到来，在秋季学期开始前的几个月里，我得到了克拉伦斯·艾伦（Clarence Allen）的帮助。艾伦（Allen）是中国地质和地球物理学者们的老朋友。第二次世界大战期间，他曾在太平洋地区的美国空军服役，后来多次访问中国。在秋季学期开始的时候，我收到通知，邵逸夫基金会（香港）将为我提供 3 年的研究生奖学金（这一年只颁发给了两个加州理工的研究生）。我猜这大概归功于我的托福考试成绩不错。

地震实验室（Seismo Lab）

在我加入地震实验室（Seismo Lab）后不久，我意识到（创新性的）研究是我们需要关注的事情。与许多院校不同，这里的学生一开始并没有固定的导师和研究课题。为了展示独立研究的能力，地震实验室（Seismo Lab）的新生必须与两名不同的教授各完成一项课题，并在第二年年初的口试中展示这些工作。

其中一个项目我是跟唐（Don）做的。这项工作是关于 PKP 波（穿过地核的 P 波）。我们最初是想要研究 D″区域（地幔底部约 200km 厚度的区域）的 P 波结构。当时，对 D″区域的研究主要集中在 S 波上，包括最早的 Lay 和 Helmberger（1983）的工作，他们第一个发现了 D″不连续面（也称为"Lay-Helmberger 不连续面"）。然而一直缺少对 D″区域 P 波结构的研究。

虽然 PKP 波对 D″结构很敏感（Song 和 Helmberger，1993a，1997），但我们很快意识到，我们需要先去了解地核。与在外核浅部折射的 SKS 不同，PKP 波穿透得更深，会不可避免地进入内核。这成为我博士的第一个课题和第一篇学术论文（Song and Helmberger 1992；SH92）。关键问题是，内核边界的地震波模型相当多样（图 1）。"展示的模型的多样性表明了丰富的可解释空间"（SH92）。图 1 后来被收录于 Lay 和 Wallace（1995）的经典教科书。这个开端是变革性的。我理解了什么才是科研（在进入加州理工之前我并未真正了解），以及科研的正常流程（发现问题，制定方法，搜索所需数据，进行分析，得出结论，总结结果，并经历一段评审过程）。

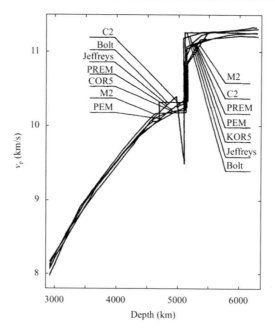

图 1　Song 和 Helmberger（1992）编制的地核 P 波速度模型。

我们使用的方法是所谓的"波形建模"。"对于研究这个不连续面而言，分辨率最高的方法似乎就是本研究所用的波形建模方法。这个基本方法在于用某个假设模型计算的满足波动方程的合成波形来拟合观测波形"（SH92），唐（Don）在论文中写道（虽然他的英语写作并不以富有诗意而出名，但我发现他的字里行间总是充满思想的火花）。为了进行细致的研究，研究者努力寻找质量高（通常意味着数量较少）的记录剖面。此外，由于地球的内部结构不是球对称的，因此必须对应采样。这样的一个区域性研究是对地球深部特定样本区域的详细调查。这一基本方法是唐（Don）的工作的特色，并为他带来了许多重要的发现（Lay，2021）。在反复的试错、调整模型的过程中，需要高效生成合成波形，来拟合观测记录。唐（Don）在早期阶段（Helmberger，1983）使用一维地球模型计算合成图，即著名的广义射线理论（GRT）程序，后来合成方法扩展到了二维（Helmberger et al.，1996；Wen and Helmberger，1998；Ni et al.，2000）和三维（Helmberger and Ni，2005；Ni et al.，2005）。

开始几年我们用的数据是模拟信号，那时新的数字化地震台站才刚刚兴起。唐（Don）喜欢在地下室的胶片记录档案中自己寻找数据（图 2）。不久后，我也开始在地下室倒腾了。实验室内部开发的数字化软件（nXscan）非常有用，对我后来基于历史地震数据的内核时变研究起到了很大的帮助（见下文）。

唐（Don）很有激励学生的天赋。他会充分赋权给学生从事工作，并让他们觉得自己很聪明。早些时候，我需要将 GRT 代码修改为双精度用于内核震相。他后来就将我的修改称为"你的代码"。在我们讨论的时候，他有时会停顿很长时间，盯着窗外。我会反思我可能哪里说得不对，但他不会说穿。他对科学的见解具有穿透力和感染力，而且他对好的科学的发自内心的欣赏（"很棒""好东西"）也会提高你的信心和兴趣。

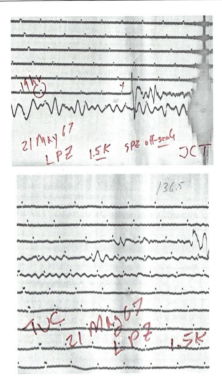

图2　唐·亨伯格（Don Helmberger）教授手写标注的从地震记录胶片打印的地震图样本。这些记录被数字化并收录在 Song 和 Helmberger（1992）中。

口试时间到了。刚来的时候，高年级中国同学就提醒我要注意，不要"丢面子"。幸运的是，我的考试进行得很顺利。戴维·斯蒂文森（David Stevenson）问了一个有趣的问题，为什么我关注拟合波形开始的部分，而不管后面的部分。当我们后来聊天时，唐（Don）被这个问题逗笑了。他开玩笑说，戴维（Dave）已经好多了——他过去常常质疑一个地震学家是怎样做到仅靠求解波动方程谋生的。考试委员会主席彼得·怀利（Peter Wyllie）写了一小段总结（我一直保留至今），强调了拓宽我的科研视野的重要性。我记得当时有一件有趣的事，给我上了一堂文化课。在一年一度的 Zilchbrau（学部里的一场调侃打趣的聚会）上，研究生们拍摄了一部关于口试的情景电影。考试没通过的博士生情绪激动，翻过桌子掐住教授的脖子。它给我留下了特别的印象，因为它不仅拍得很好，而且还戏剧化地表现了刺激的平等环境（以幽默的方式）。

另外，我们所有人都掌握了计算机。罗布·克莱顿（Rob Clayton）给了我一本克尼根（Kernighan）和里奇（Ritchie）早期的 C 语言编程的书，这提醒我写代码的重要性。地震实验室（Seismo Lab）非常开放，你可以从同龄人那里学到很多东西。但我选修了一些额外的计算机科学的课程，并最终拿到了计算机科学的副科学位。唐（Don）有一次问我："你想成为科学家还是学者？"我以前从未进行过这样一个有意思的对比。我当然不想变成书呆子。现在回想起来，这段经历对日后我管理自己研究团队的计算资源和需求有很大帮助，甚至比对我自己的研究的帮助更大。

事业

我在唐（Don）和地震实验室（Seismo Lab）那里接受的锻炼对我的学术生涯产生了深远的影响。在这些训练中养成的习惯根深蒂固，如同刻进了我们的 DNA 里。来到哥伦比亚大学拉蒙特-多尔蒂（Lamont-Doherty）地球观测站后，我继续研究地核，并与唐（Don）保持交流。

我在博士期间与唐（Don）的一项研究是确认内核各向异性的存在（Song and Helmberger，1993b）。这个概念是在那之前不久（1986 年）提出的，但一直存在争议。当时使用的国际地震中心（ISC）的地震波到时噪音很大，并且存在其他因素引起的偏差（震源误差和地幔的非均匀性）；事实上，重要的异常的观测数据被当作杂乱的"异常值"扔掉了。我们搜索了全球范围不同射线方向的路径，并测量了 PKP 震相之间的走时差。相对走时更加精确，且除内核以外的因素引起的偏差更小。显然，ISC 数据集的数据量远远超过基于波形的方法，但后者的优势也同样明显。得到的模型能很好地解释到内核的初至震相（DF 震相）。然而，在长周期记录中，从著名的南桑威奇群岛（SSI）到阿拉斯加和加拿大这一路径上的 DF 波形似乎异常得宽（Song and Helmberger，1998；图 3）。我们认为波形的复杂性实际上是由"小型的三叉现象"引起的，它表现为由多个震相重叠产生的宽波形。这个三叉现象是由于射线路径穿过了从各向同性的上内核到各向异性下内核的过渡带的速度跳变而产生的。

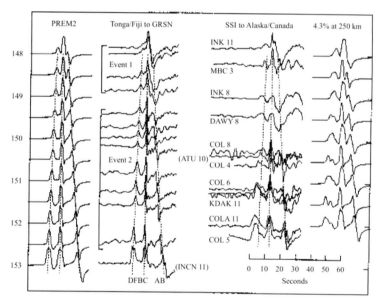

图 3　Song 和 Helmberger（1998）提出内核过渡带的证据。注意，从 SSI 到阿拉斯加的 DF 脉冲（第一个脉冲）变宽，这可以通过右侧的合成图来解释。

在保尔・理查兹（Paul Richards）教授和我提出的关于内核超速旋转的证据的研究中（Song and Richards，1996），对细微差异的关注是至关重要的（图 4）。在提取微小的时变信号时，尽可能精确地测量相对到时有助于减小数据的离散程度。我在博士期间的研究中，对从 SSI 到阿拉斯加的 College 台站这条关键路径进行过一些测量，不难用来与20世纪90年代早期从美国地震学联合研究会数据管理中心（IRISDMC）获取的数据相比较。叠置并比较观测到的地震图（图4）对我们是一个常规操作，类似于用合成波形来匹配观测波形。在随后寻找历史数据以确认内核时变的过程中，我在研究生阶段学习到的和模拟数据打交道的技能（查找、扫描和数字化波形）使我得心应手，并应用于世界各地的模拟记录（帕里萨德斯，美国纽约州；戈尔登和丹佛，美国科罗拉多州；大学城，美国阿拉斯加州；中国北京；日本东京）（Song, 2000; Song and Li, 2000; Xu and Song, 2003）。

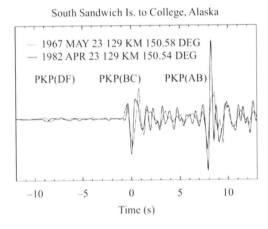

图4　内核震相（PKP DF）时变现象的观测，引出了内核旋转的概念，来自 Song 和 Richards（1996）。使用外核参考震相 PKP (BC)有助于减少偏差。这里1982年的数据是数字记录，而1967年的是经数字化的 WWSSN 模拟记录。

我在加州理工的经历使我的学术生涯大部分的时间专注于地核的研究：在拉蒙特作为博士后和青年研究者时硕果累累，在伊利诺伊大学厄巴纳-香槟分校被聘为终身教授，并在回国后先后担任了访问职位和全职工作。几十年来，我在这一研究领域获得了来自很多机构几乎不间断的支持，例如美国科学基金会、中国自然科学基金会、美国国家航空航天局等。这项研究的核心难点是对地核有限的采样率和分辨率，尤其是内核。在发现球形内核之后的半个世纪里，人们没有发现它的任何特征。然而，在过去几十年里，它的复杂性和神秘性被发现。能够在唐（Don）的指导下，在取得重大突破的关键时刻开始研究这个问题，我真是非常幸运。

永远的唐（Don）

虽然我毕业已经几十年了，但在我的整个学术生涯中，唐（Don）总是在场的。我会在 AGU 秋季会议上碰到他，这个年会在我的学术生涯中扮演了重要角色。自从我来到加州理工学院的第一年起，在唐（Don）的鼓励下，我已经连续参加了30多年的 AGU 会议。我发现它总是令人兴奋到让你想要（或需要）参加（不幸的是，在过去两年中，疫情对会议举办造成了很大的影响）。这是你展示最新成果的机会，因此学生们经常工作到深夜，以获得最新的成果。这也是一个与人们见面、讨论最新成果和想法的地方。

在 AGU 或者其他会议上见到唐（Don）总是一件令人高兴的事。我最后一次见到唐（Don）是在旧金山的 2019 AGU 秋季会议（十二月）上。他还是那样一如往常地敏锐。他得知我决定搬到北京后很开心，并叮嘱我出发前应该回一趟地震实验室（Seismo Lab）。只可惜事与愿违。谁又会想到那是见到唐（Don）的最后一面呢？

作为对我的一生影响最大的人之一，唐（Don）将永远活在我心中。他将我领进了科学和地震学的奇妙世界。我对我的孩子们讲，我们家的"美国分支"始于加州理工学院。随着他们的长大，我会关注他们的兴趣和爱好。我的儿子现在正带着对学术的兴趣攻读科学博士学位，这在跟他有类似背景的同龄人中是很少见的。唐（Don）对我的影响像一个"学术父亲"一样，并影响了我教导孩子的方式（图 5）。

图 5　唐（Don）和我的儿子女儿的合照。摄于 2015 年 1 月初的寒假，背景是唐（Don）的办公室。

在当前的"大数据"时代，全波形反演和机器学习成为了一种时尚，大量数据被扔进了"黑匣子"。波形中的细节和微小的差异容易被淹没在全局平均和优化中。然而，唐（Don）和他的学生已经充分证明，要提高层析成像的分辨率，特别是在间断面和尖锐的边界处，需要考虑数据中的关键细节，因为这些细节通常蕴藏着重要的物理成因。数据中的这些关键特征必然需要以不同的方式进行优化，以用于未来的高分辨率层析成像。

唐（Don）去世后，唐（Don）的一群学生成立了一个叫做 "Don4Ever" 的社交群。我们相信唐（Don）的遗产和传奇将持续很长时间。我们将永远怀念唐（Don），怀念他的善良、慷慨、幽默、鼓励和对科学的深刻见解。

致谢
我感谢索恩·莱（Thorne Lay）、埃德·加内罗（Ed Garnero）、朱露培（Lupei Zhu）、孙道远（Daoyuan Sun）、赖文慧（Voon Hui Lai）和我儿子宋嘉辚（Tommy Song）的评价和编辑，他们帮忙改进了手稿。

参 考 文 献

Helmberger DV (1983). Theory and application of synthetic seismograms. In: Kanamori H ed. Earthquakes: Observation, Theory and Interpretation. Istituto Nazionale di Geofisica, Rome, pp 173–222

Helmberger DV, Garnero EJ and Ding XM (1996). Modeling two-dimensional structure at the core-mantle boundary. J Geophys Res Solid Earth **101**(B6): 13963–13972.

Helmberger DV and Ni SD (2005). Approximate 3D body-wave synthetics for tomographic models. Bull Seismol Soc Am **95**(1): 212–224.

Lay T and Helmberger DV (1983). A lower mantle S-wave triplication and the shear velocity structure of D″. Geophys J Int **75**(3): 799–837.

Lay T and Wallace TC (1995). Modern Global Seismology. Academic Press, San Diego, p305

Lay T (2021). Donald V. Helmberger (1938–2020). Seismol Res Lett **92**(2A): 624–622.

Ni SD, Ding XM and Helmberger DV (2000). Constructing synthetics from deep earth tomographic models. Geophys J Int **140**(1): 71–82.

Ni SD, Helmberger DV and Tromp J (2005). Three-dimensional structure of the African superplume from waveform modelling. Geophys J Int **161**(2): 283–294.

Song XD and Helmberger DV (1992). Velocity structure near the inner core boundary from waveform modeling. J Geophys Res Solid Earth **97**(B5): 6573–6586.

Song XD and Helmberger DV (1993a). Effect of velocity structure in D″ on PKP phases. Geophys Res Lett **20**(4): 285–288.

Song XD and Helmberger DV (1993b). Anisotropy of Earth's inner core. Geophys Res Lett **20**(23): 2591–2594.

Song XD and Richards PG (1996). Seismological evidence for differential rotation of the Earth's inner core. Nature **382**(6588): 221–224.

Song XD and Helmberger DV (1997). PKP differential travel times: Implications for 3-D lower mantle structure. Geophys Res Lett **24**(15): 1863–1866.

Song XD and Helmberger DV (1998). Seismic evidence for an inner core transition zone. Science **282**(5390): 924–927.

Song XD (2000). Joint inversion for inner core rotation, inner core anisotropy, and mantle heterogeneity. J Geophys Res Solid Earth **105**(B4): 7931–7943.

Song XD and Li AY (2000). Support for differential inner core superrotation from earthquakes in Alaska recorded at South Pole station. J Geophys Res Solid Earth **105**(B1): 623–630.

Wen LX and Helmberger DV (1998). A two-dimensional *P-SV* hybrid method and its application to modeling localized structures near the core-mantle boundary. J Geophys Res **103**(B8): 17901–17918.

Xu XX and Song XD (2003). Evidence for inner core super-rotation from time-dependent differential PKP traveltimes observed at Beijing seismic network. Geophys J Int **152**(3): 509–514.

　　宋晓东现任北京大学地球与空间科学学院讲席教授，国家级人才计划专家。于 1994 年在加州理工学院获得博士学位，亨伯格教授是他的论文导师。随后，他加入哥伦比亚大学拉蒙特-多尔蒂地球观测站，做博士后，后来担任副研究员和讲师。他于 1999 年加入伊利诺伊大学厄巴纳-香槟分校地质系，从助理教授到终身正教授工作 20 多年，于 2020 年全职回国。他在内核差速旋转方面的工作被《科学》杂志（1996）评为年度十大突破之一。他曾获得国际地球物理和大地测量学联合会（IUGG）地球深部内部研究委员会多恩博斯奖(1996)，中国自然科学基金委海外杰出青年基金（B 类) (1998)，亚洲大洋洲地球科学学会(AOGS)固体地球杰出讲座奖(2016)。目前担任国际英文期刊《地震科学》主编。他的主页是：http://geophy.pku.edu.cn/people/songxiaodong/english/index.html。

Chapter 12. In memory of Donald V. Helmberger

Lupei Zhu [*]

Department of Earth and Atmospheric Sciences, Saint Louis University St. Louis, MO 63108, USA

[*]**Correspondence:** lupei.zhu@slu.edu

Citation: Zhu LP (2022). In memory of Donald V. Helmberger. Earthq Sci 35(1): 40−43 doi: 10.1016/j.eqs.2022.01.012

When I received the shocking news on August 13, 2020 that our beloved Don passed away, I was deeply saddened. The feeling was worsened by the COVID-19 pandemic that essentially locked down everything so most of us were not able to attend his memorial ceremony. On Nov. 11, 2021, more than a year later, I took an early flight from St Louis to LAX to attend the memorial observance and reception honoring him in the Athenaeum of Caltech. While sitting in the 4-hour-long flight fully packed with passengers wearing masks, I tried to recollect the times I spent with Don almost 30 years ago. For a moment, my faded memory woke up and those images flashed through my mind like a river through a floodgate. They went so quickly that I was only able to write down a few glimpses of them.

I knew Don by name through my undergraduate advisor, Prof. Huilan Zhou, who visited the Seismo Lab and worked with him in the early 1980s. I first met Don on a sunny day in the summer of 1993 when I arrived at Caltech as a new graduate student. Upon entering the Seismo Lab's South Mudd building, I followed the standard procedure to see my designated academic advisor Professor Rob Clayton. After a brief conversation, he gave me a tour of the lab's facilities. While chatting with him by the drinking water station on the third floor, I saw a tall and athletically fit man holding a cup walking towards us from the other end of the hallway. Rob introduced me to him and told me this was Professor Helmberger. I had seen his photo in the Seismo Lab's brochure when I applied to Caltech, but the person before me definitely did not fit in my stereotype of professors at that time. He was wearing a colorful Hawaiian short-sleeve shirt and a pair of two-strap sandals, like he was just back from the beach. He said to me something funny. Although I didn't get his joke, his casual outfit and humorous demeanor helped me relax and made me like him immediately.

The first year of Caltech for graduate students was hectic and stressful (Figure 1). In addition to taking required courses of math, physics, and intros to geology, geophysics, and planetary sciences, we needed to conduct two research projects with two faculty members and to take the oral exam at the beginning of the second year. Those who failed the exam were usually asked to leave, with a consolation master's degree. Some did get a second chance, but the psychological damage seemed irreversible. For my first project, I proposed to work with Don to model seismic regional waveforms of stations on the Tibetan Plateau for its crustal structure. I had participated in the first Sino-US broadband seismic recording experiment on the plateau between 1991 and 1992 (Owens et al., 1993) and had a copy of the data with me. Don seemed quite interested in this unique data set. My second project was with Prof. Hiroo Kanamori to estimate crustal thickness variation in Southern California using the receiver function technique. After a summer of intense work, I presented the two propositions and preliminary results to my exam committee. After the exam, I was asked to wait in the library next to the exam room while they had a closed-door discussion on the outcome. It seemed to me forever before they finally walked out the room to congratulate me for passing the exam. Don signed the form the next day to become my dissertation advisor.

Fig. 1   Photo of Seismo Lab faculty, staff, and graduate students in 1994. Don is sitting 2nd from the right in the 2nd row, with Rob Clayton (5th), and Hiroo Kanamori (6th). The author is sitting at the center of the 1st row.

Being Don's advisee was a pleasant as well as productive experience. As I acknowledged late in my dissertation: "He seemed always enthusiastic in whatever I did. He is truly a waveform master. Under his guidance, I learned how to appreciate the beauty of a seismogram. It is amazing that once you devote yourself to it, each wiggle of the waveform is willing to tell you a secret about our Earth" (Zhu, 1998). Years later, after becoming a professor and having my own graduate students, I tried to emulate Don's advising style and realized that it was not an easy task to motivate students to excel in their research endeavor. Don did it by being a role model for his students. He made himself available to students all the time and made us feel that he was truly interested in what we were doing.

In 1995 I started to work with Don on determining focal mechanisms and depths of earthquakes using their regional seismic waveforms. His student Lianshe Zhao had just developed a novel method called "cut and paste" (CAP) to cut the waveforms into the Pnl and surface wave segments and to compare them with synthetic waveforms separately by waveform cross-correlation (Zhao and Helmberger, 1994). I am sure that Lianshe got the idea by watching how Don compared observed and synthetic seismograms. At that time, there were no graphical computer terminals. Don simply printed the observed seismogram on a transparency and synthetics on a piece of paper. He then overlaid the transparency on top of the paper, shifted the data back and forth, and evaluated the similarity between the two. Lianshe implemented this manual process with computer code. While using Lianshe's code, I noticed that his use of waveform cross-correlation coefficient as the waveform fitness discarded the data's amplitude information which should help constrain the earthquake's focal mechanism and depth. I rewrote the code by replacing it with the L2 norm of the waveform differences. Though an incremental improvement in my opinion, Don was quite excited about it and encouraged me to turn it into a paper with his suggested title "Advancement in source estimation techniques using broadband regional seismograms". The manuscript was submitted to BSSA in April, 1996. Surprisingly, it was accepted, without revision, just two month later (Zhu and Helmberger, 1996a). So far, this first paper with Don still holds the record of shortest acceptance time of all my publications.

My second paper with Don was also published in 1996 (Zhu and Helmberger, 1996b). By applying my new CAP method to the 1991–1992 Tibet data, I found three earthquakes at depths ~70 km beneath the southern Tibetan Plateau. Because the Plateau has a very thick (~70 km) crust, there was a question of whether these events occurred in the lower crust or the uppermost mantle, given the uncertainties of the focal depths and crustal thicknesses. I used what I learned in Don's GE261 class of synthetic seismograms and Don's generalized ray theory code to show convincingly that these three earthquakes occurred 5 to 10 km below the Moho. In other words, the seismic waveform data provided much better relative positions of the earthquakes with respect to the Moho than their absolute depths.

The high-water mark of my PhD research with Don came in 1998. I was analyzing teleseismic waveforms of seismic stations on the Tibetan Plateau and was puzzled by some anomalous azimuthal variations of P-wave waveform shape and travel time at a few stations located in the northern margin of the plateau. The first P waves of events from the north arrived about 1s earlier than events from the south (Figure 2). This was not uncommon because of Earth's lateral velocity variation. What was intriguing was that the first P-wave pulse split into two pulses separated by about 1s for events from the east or west (Figure 2). One day, after a sleepless night, I came up with an idea that the anomalous variations were caused by a sudden decrease of crustal thickness of the plateau, i.e., a Moho step, at its northern boundary (Figure 2). I talked with Don about the idea and sought his advice of how to compute the waveform of a plane wave through an arbitrarily shaped Moho. He quickly pulled out a paper in which he and his former student, Patricia Scott, developed an efficient numerical method using the Kirchhoff-Helmholtz integration (Scott and Helmberger, 1983). With this method, I was able to constrain the location, width, and height of the Moho step by modeling the observed waveforms and to infer its tectonic implications. The work was published in journal Science (Zhu and Helmberger, 1998), two months after I got my PhD degree from Caltech.

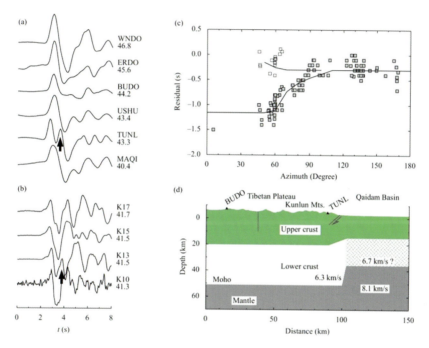

Fig. 2   The left panel shows vertical components of seismic records from two earthquakes that occurred beneath the Kuril Islands. Arrows point to the anomalous double-pulse P waveform shape at stations TUNL (a) and K13 (b). (c) shows travel-time residuals of the first P-wave arrivals (the shaded squares) at station TUNL from earthquakes in distance range of 30 to 50 degrees. (d) denotes a north-south cross section along the 95°E meridian showing the surface topography (exaggerated by a factor of two), major faults, and the possible crustal structure used in modeling P waveforms at TUNL, from Zhu and Helmberger (1998).

Looking back, I would say that the five years of graduate study at Caltech were the happiest and most productive time of my life. I attribute this mostly to Don because not only did he provide insightful guidance to my research, he also supported me financially. During that time, my wife and I were living in a Caltech-owned lease property with our daughter. Worrying that my graduate assistantship might not be enough to support a family of three, Don tried to hire my wife to scan and digitize old seismogram film records for him. He also got me a consulting job from Woodward Clyde Consultants firm in Pasadena. There was, however, a problem. My wife didn't have the work permit then and my student visa didn't allow me to work off campus. Don came up with a solution to offer us to live in his rental property in Altadena for free as compensation. My wife and I checked out the house. It was definitely bigger than our bungalow on Wilson avenue, but we declined Don's generous offer because of the extra commute to work and because Caltech provided those on-campus housing properties to students at very low cost. Nevertheless, I was grateful to Don who always took care of his students in every way.

All of us knew that Don was a great scientist, but not many know that he was also an entrepreneur. In 2001 while I was a post-doctoral associate at USC, Don, Chandan Saikia, and I started a company called Global SeisNet. We were equal share partners of the limited liability company. Each of us put in $313.59 cash to get the company set up and registered. I remember that our first board meeting was in a coffee shop on California Blvd. Don was quite optimistic about the prospect of the company to grow into a multi-billion-dollar enterprise in the seismic consulting business, like the Woodward Clyde Consultants. When that happened, he suggested to me, I could quit my up-coming faculty position at Saint Louis University which I just accepted. Global SeisNet did successfully get an SBA Phase-I grant in the first year from DoE to develop a waveform-based method of locating earthquakes and explosions. We completed the project in time. Unfortunately, we were not selected for Phase II. The company ran out of money and was dissolved in 2003, along with my hope of early retirement.

Don retired from Caltech in 2017. I last met Don in August, 2018 in a symposium in Singapore organized by his former students to celebrate his 80th birthday and more than half century of academic career. He looked as sharp as when I first met him 25 years ago. It is very unfortunate that he left us two years later. In his memorial observance and reception at Caltech, I told others that I owe Don a lot for what I have today. I can only repay my debt by educating my students the way he did and hope that they will do the same to their students, so that Don will live among us forever.

Acknowdgements

I would like to thank Xiaodong Song, Thorne Lay, Zhongwen Zhan, and Yan Zhu for their comments that helped to improve the manuscript.

References

Owens TJ, Randall GE, Wu FT and Zeng R (1993). PASSCAL instrument performance during the Tibetan plateau passive seismic experiment. Bull Seismol Soc Am **83**: 1959–1970.

Scott P and Helmberger D (1983). Applications of the Kirchhoff-Helmholtz integral to problems in seismology. Geophys J Int **72**(1): 237–254.

Zhao LS and Helmberger DV (1994). Source estimation from broadband regional seismograms. Bull Seismol Soc Am **84**(1): 91–104.

Zhu LP and Helmberger DV (1996a). Advancement in source estimation techniques using broadband regional seismograms. Bull Seismol Soc Am **86**(5): 1634–1641.

Zhu LP and Helmberger DV (1996b). Intermediate depth earthquakes beneath the India-Tibet Collision Zone. Geophys Res Lett **23**(5): 435–438.

Zhu LP (1998). Broadband waveform modeling and its application to the lithospheric structure of the Tibetan Plateau. Dissertation. California Institute of Technology.

Zhu LP and Helmberger DV (1998). Moho offset across the northern margin of the Tibetan Plateau. Science **281**(5380): 1170–1172.

Lupei Zhu is currently a Professor of Geophysics at the Department of Earth & Atmospheric Sciences of Saint Louis University (SLU) in Missouri, USA. He got his Ph.D. at Caltech in 1998 under the supervision of Prof. Helmberger. He then did his post-doctoral research in University of Southern California and Caltech before joining SLU as an assistant professor in 2001. He is a recipient of the F. Beach Leighton Fellowship in geophysics at Caltech in 1996, Citation of the SLU President and Dean of the Graduate School for excellence in research in 2005, and was appointed a fellow of Research Institute of SLU in 2022. His webpage can be found at https://www.eas.slu.edu/People/LZhu/home.html.

第 12 章　纪念唐·亨伯格

朱露培
美国圣路易斯大学地球与大气科学系

引用：Zhu LP (2022). In memory of Donald V. Helmberger. Earthq Sci 35(1): 40–43 doi: 10.1016/j.eqs.2022.01.012

2020 年 8 月 13 日得知我们深爱的唐（Don）去世的震惊消息时，我深感悲痛，而当时的 2019 年冠状病毒疫情又加重了我的悲伤，因为疫情居家令，我们大多数人都无法参加他的葬礼。一年多后的 2021 年 11 月 11 日，我乘坐早班飞机从圣路易斯飞往洛杉矶国际机场，参加当天在加州理工学院为唐（Don）举行的追思会，坐在满载戴着口罩的乘客的 4 小时飞行中，我试图回忆 30 年前我和唐（Don）一起度过的时光。刹那间，我褪去的记忆苏醒了，那时的画面如洪水穿越闸门一样在脑海中闪过。这些画面走得如此之快，以至于我只能记下它们中的一些片段。

我是通过我的科大本科导师周惠兰教授知道了唐（Don）的名字，她在 20 世纪 80 年代初访问了加州理工学院地震实验室并与他一起工作过。我第一次见到唐（Don）是在 1993 年夏天，一个阳光明媚的日子，当时我刚到加州理工学院读博。那天我迈入地震实验室的南马德楼后，我先按照程序见指定给我的学术导师罗布·克莱顿（Rob Clayton）教授。简短交谈后，他带我参观了实验室的设施。在三楼的饮水机旁和他聊天的时候，我看到一个运动员体型的高个男人端着杯子从走廊的另一头向我们走来。罗布（Rob）把我介绍给他，并告诉我这是亨伯格（Helmberger）教授。我申请加州理工学院时，在地震实验室的宣传册上看到过他的头像，但眼前的这个人绝对不符合我当时脑海中教授的形象。他穿着一件花花绿绿的夏威夷短袖衬衫和一双凉鞋，就好像他刚从海滩回来一样。他对我说了几句打趣的话，虽然我没听懂他的笑话，但他悠闲的着装和幽默的举止让我放松下来，让我立刻喜欢上了他。

加州理工学院研究生的第一年忙碌且压力大（图 1）。我们除了要选修数学、物理、地质、地球物理和行星科学导论等必修课外，还需要与两名教授做两个研究项目，并在第二学年初参加口试，考试不及格的人通常被要求离开，尽管会获得一个安慰性硕士学位。有些人会得到第二次考试机会，但心理上的伤害似乎是难以愈合。我的第一个研究计划是与唐（Don）合作，模拟青藏高原台站的区域地震波形，以了解其地壳结构。我参加了 1991～1992 年在高原上的第一次中美宽频带地震记录实验（Owens et al., 1993），并拥有一份完整的记录的波形数据。唐（Don）似乎对这个独特的数据集很感兴趣。我的第二个项目是与金森博雄（Hiroo Kanamori）教授一起使用接收函数技术估算南加州的地壳厚度变化。经过一个夏天的紧张工作，我向考试委员会报告了两个计划的内容和初步结果。考试结束后，我被告知在考场旁边的图书馆等候他们关门讨论的结果。熬过一段我觉得漫长的时间后，我终于等到委员会成员一个个走出房间祝贺我通过考试。唐（Don）第二天签署了表格，正式成为我的博士论文导师。

在唐（Don）的指导下做博士论文是一段愉快而充实的经历。正如我在后来的论文致谢中写的那样：“他似乎总是对我所做的一切充满热情。他是一位真正的波形大师。在他的指导下，我学会了如何欣赏地震图的美。令人惊奇的是，如果你真心投入，波形的每一个摆动都会告诉你一个关于地球的秘密”（Zhu，1998）。多年后，我也成为一名教授并有了自己的学生，我尝试效仿唐（Don）的指导风格，这才意识到激励学生在他们的研究工作中力争上游并非易事。唐（Don）通过以身作则做到了这一点。无论多忙，他的办公室门总是向学生敞开的，而且他让我们感到他对我们所做的事情真心感兴趣。

1995 年，我开始与唐（Don）一起利用区域地震波形确定地震的震源机制和深度。他的学生赵连社刚刚开发了一种称为“剪切和粘贴”（CAP）的新方法，将地震波形切割成 Pnl 和面波段，并通过波形互相关将它们分别与理论波形进行比较（Zhao and Helmberger，1994）。我猜连社是通过观察唐（Don）如何比较观测和理论地震图而得到这个想法的。那时还没有计算机图形终端。唐（Don）总是将观测到的地震图打印在透明胶片上，然后将理论波形打印在一张纸上。然后他将透明胶片覆盖在纸上，通过来回移动透明胶片来评估两个波形之间的相似性。连社用计算机程序实现了这个手工过程。我在使用连社的程序时，注意到他用波形互相关系数作为波形的拟合度，这就忽略了数据的振幅信息，而振幅信息应该有助于约束地震的震源机制和深度。我重写了代码，将其替换为波形差异的 L2 范数。当时在我看来这是一个小小的改进，但唐（Don）对此非常兴奋，鼓励我将其写成一篇论文，并将其标题定为“利用宽频区域地震波进行震源估计的进展”。稿件于 1996 年 4 月提交给《美国地震学会通报》（BSSA）。让我惊讶的是，仅仅两个月后，它就被接收了，而且没有要求修改（Zhu and Helmberger，1996a）。到目前为止，这篇与唐（Don）合作的第一篇论文仍然保持着我所有发表论文中接收时间最短的纪录。

我与唐（Don）的第二篇论文也在 1996 年发表（Zhu and Helmberger，1996b）。通过将我的新 CAP 方法应用于 1991~1992 年的西藏数据，我在青藏高原南部约 70 km 深处发现了 3 个地震。由于青藏高原有一个非常厚的地壳（约 70 km），考虑到震源深度和地壳厚度的不确定性，这些事件是发生在下地壳还是上地幔顶部很难回答。我使用了在唐（Don）教授的 GE261 这门课学习到的理论地震图知识和唐（Don）的广义射线理论，令人信服地说明了这 3 个地震发生在莫霍面以下 5~10km 处。换句话说，相对于震源的绝对深度，地震波形数据能更好地约束震源与莫霍面的相对位置。

我的博士论文研究的最高光时刻是在 1998 年，当时我正在分析在青藏高原的地震台站的远震波形，对位于高原北缘的几个台站的 P 波波形的形状和走时的一些与方位角相关的异常变化感到困惑。来自北方的地震事件的第一个 P 波初至比来自南方的提前约 1 秒（图 2）。由于地球的横向速度变化，这种情况并不少见，但有趣的是，来自东方或西方的事件的 P 波初至脉冲分裂成两个间隔约 1 秒的脉冲（图 2）。有一天，经过一个不眠之夜后，我突然想到了这些异常变化可能是由于台站下方地壳厚度突然减薄造成的，即高原在其北部边界存在一个莫霍面阶跃（图2）。我与唐（Don）讨论了这个想法，并征求了他如何计算一个平面波通过一个任意形状的莫霍面后的波形。他很快拿出了一篇论文，他和他以前的学生帕特里夏·斯科特（Patricia Scott）开发了一种用基尔霍夫-亥姆霍兹积分计算理论地震波形的有效数值方法（Scott and Helmberger，1983）。使用这种方法，我能够通过对观察到的波形进行模拟来约束莫霍台阶的位置、宽度和高度，并推断其构造意义。这项工作在我从加州理工学院获得博士学位两个月后发表在《科学》杂志上（Zhu and Helmberger，1998）。

回首往事，我想说在加州理工学院读博的五年是我一生中最快乐、最充实的时光，这主要归功于唐（Don），因为他不仅为我的研究提供了有见地的指导，而且还为我提供了经济上的支持。在那段时间里，我和妻子女儿住在加州理工学院提供的出租屋。唐（Don）担心我的奖学金可能不足以养活一个三口之家，提出聘我的妻子为他扫描和数字化旧的地震记录胶片记录。他还想帮我在帕萨迪纳的伍德沃德-克莱德咨询公司找到一份额外的咨询工作。但是这里有一个问题，那时我的妻子没有工作许可，我的学生签证也不允许我在校外工作。唐（Don）想出了一个变通方案，让我们免费住在他在阿尔塔迪纳的出租房中作为补偿。我和我的妻子去看了那房子。它肯定比我们在威尔逊街上住的小房子大，但我们最后婉拒了唐（Don）的好意，主要是因为从那上学校需要额外的通勤时间，而且我们住的学校的出租房租金很低。尽管如此，我还是很感谢唐（Don），他总是在各个方面照顾他的学生。

我想大家都知道唐（Don）是一位伟大的科学家，但很少有人知道他也是一位企业家。2001年我在南加州大学做博士后时，唐（Don）、钱丹·赛基亚（Chandan Saikia）和我一起创办了一家名为全球地震网的公司。我们仨是这个有限责任公司的平等股份合伙人，我们每个人都投入了313.59美元现金来成立公司并进行注册。我记得我们的第一次董事会会议是在加利福尼亚大道的一家咖啡店举行的。唐（Don）非常看好该公司在地震咨询业务中成长为一个价值数十亿美元的企业的前景，就像伍德沃德-克莱德咨询公司一样。他说到那时我就可以辞去我刚刚接受的圣路易斯大学的教职退休了。全球地震网公司在第一年就成功地从美国能源部获得了微小企业第一阶段的一个资助，以开发一种基于波形的地震和爆炸定位方法。我们按时完成了项目。不幸的是，我们没有被选中进入第二阶段。公司资金耗尽并于2003年解散了，与其一起消失的还有我早早就可以退休的梦想。

唐（Don）于2017年从加州理工学院退休。我最后一次见到唐（Don）是在2018年8月的新加坡，一个他以前的学生为庆祝他80岁生日和半个多世纪的学术生涯而举办的研讨会上。他看起来就像我25年前第一次见到他时一样精神。很遗憾两年后他离开了我们。我在加州理工学院举行的追思会上告诉其他人，我今天所拥有的都多亏有唐（Don）。我只能通过像他那样培养我的学生来回报他，并希望他们也对他们的学生也这样做，薪火相传，让唐（Don）永远和我们在一起。

致谢

我要感谢宋晓东、索恩·莱（Thorne Lay）、詹中文和朱颜提出的帮助改进手稿的建议。

图 1　1994 年地震实验室教职员工和研究生的合影。唐（Don）坐在第二排右起第二位，和罗布·克莱顿（Rob Clayton）（第 5 位）、金森博雄（Hiroo Kanamori）（第 6 位）一起。本章作者坐在第一排的中央。

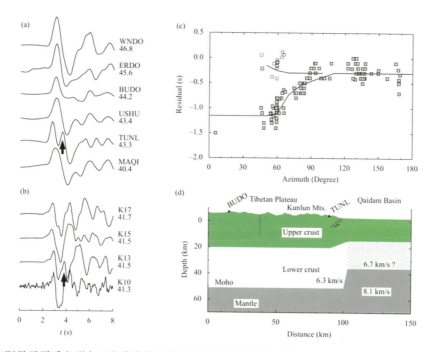

图 2　左图显示了千岛群岛下方发生的两次地震的地震记录的垂直分量。箭头指向 TUNL（a）和 K13（b）站的异常双脉冲 P 波形形状。（c）显示了 30 到 50 度距离范围内地震在 TUNL 站的第一个 P 波到达（阴影方块）的走时残差。（d）表示沿 95°E 子午线的南北横截面，显示地表地形（放大两倍）、主要断层和用于模拟 TUNL 的 P 波形的可能地壳结构，来自 Zhu 和 Helmberger（1998）。

参 考 文 献

Owens TJ, Randall GE, Wu FT and Zeng R (1993). PASSCAL instrument performance during the Tibetan plateau passive seismic experiment. Bull Seismol Soc Am **83**: 1959–1970.

Scott P and Helmberger D (1983). Applications of the Kirchhoff-Helmholtz integral to problems in seismology. Geophys J Int **72**(1): 237–254.

Zhao LS and Helmberger DV (1994). Source estimation from broadband regional seismograms. Bull Seismol Soc Am **84**(1): 91–104.

Zhu LP and Helmberger DV (1996a). Advancement in source estimation techniques using broadband regional seismograms. Bull Seismol Soc Am **86**(5): 1634–1641.

Zhu LP and Helmberger DV (1996b). Intermediate depth earthquakes beneath the India-Tibet Collision Zone. Geophys Res Lett **23**(5): 435–438.

Zhu LP (1998). Broadband waveform modeling and its application to the lithospheric structure of the Tibetan Plateau. Dissertation. California Institute of Technology.

Zhu LP and Helmberger DV (1998). Moho offset across the northern margin of the Tibetan Plateau. Science **281**(5380): 1170–1172.

朱露培，美国密苏里州圣路易斯大学地球与大气科学系地球物理学教授。1998 年在亨伯格（Helmberger）教授的指导下获得加州理工大学博士学位；紧接着在南加州大学和加州理工大学完成博士后研究；最终于 2001 年作为助理教授加入圣路易斯大学。1996 年在加州理工大学获得地球物理弗里曼·比奇·礼顿奖学金（F. Beach Leighton Fellowship），2005 年获得圣路易斯大学校长和研究生院院长卓越研究奖，并于 2022 年被任命为圣路易斯大学研究所研究员。个人主页：https://www.eas.slu.edu/People/LZhu/home.html。

Chapter 13. Donald V. Helmberger the Mentor

Timothy Melbourne [*]

Department of Geological Sciences, Central Washington University, WA 98926, USA

[*]**Correspondence:** tim@geology.cwu.edu

Citation: Melbourne TI (2022). Donald V. Helmberger the Mentor. Earthq Sci 35(1): 44–50 doi: 10.1016/j.eqs.2022.01.019

Don is certainly missed, by me, and by so many others. I particularly miss the constancy I derived by thinking of him down in Pasadena on the third floor of South Mudd, under the tree in his office, looking at waveforms. I have myriad memories with him, formed not just as a student at the Caltech Seismo Lab but over the two decades following. It is therefore a bit difficult to choose which I might use to paint a picture of the person I knew, the person who did more to shape me scientifically than anybody except my father, and the person for whom I felt such affection. Obviously, pure science, waveform modeling done purely for curiosity to tease out Earth's secrets, should take center stage, particularly for this venue, but Don was a rich tapestry of humanity and science, so I thought I might tell a few offbeat stories, interwoven with the work I did with him, to offer up my sense of him.

Don was, at his core, salt-of-the-earth, and he had a lot of sayings for a lot of situations. One I heard more than once, and which I think he was proud of, was "I grew up on a ranch and when something broke, you fixed it". The first I heard it was early on, just a few months into graduate school, when he wandered into my office. He'd been back-burner thinking, as was his wont, about some Mammoth Lakes waveforms I'd shown him and had started modeling. Rather than working diligently on my betterment through my science, he instead found me and my officemate pouring over a newly milled and acid-bathed aluminum head for my hideous late '70s Mazda hatchback car' that had previously died and which my roommate and I had decided, based on no evidence or prior experience, that we could fix. I recall kind of trying to hide the head from Don, since I was putatively modeling shallow caldera anisotropy in that office and it being very un-Caltech to have an engine head sitting on your office desk, but Don saw it nonetheless. To my surprise, rather than chew me out like I might have expected, he lit right into it. He poked at it, flopped it over, asked for a book to push down on and test the valve stems so he could see their seatings, peered into water jackets, etc. He asked a bunch of questions that clearly indicated he knew what he was talking about, and concluded we were right in our diagnosis. When I commented that he seemed to know a lot about engines, voila- "I grew up on a ranch and when something broke, you fixed it". It was wondrous to me, at my young age, squaring Don-the-Cagniard-de-Hoop-path-integral-through-complex-ray-parameter-space abstractician with Don-the-small-engine-repair-guy. But that was the thing with Don, the more you got to know him, the more layers you discovered there were to him.

Don was a gentle soul and to get him to yell at you, and I mean really let loose, took some doing. It happened precisely once, playing Don's version of American football, a game affectionately known as Helmberger Ball. The rules of this game, held on Saturday mornings, pretty much went as follows: Don always played quarterback, all Helmberger students were duly expected to show up to populate both teams, and Don's team always won. When I first arrived at the Seismo Lab, being a big American guy, Don assumed I could play football, when in fact I had never previously played, or even watched, a football game, so I was no good. But I was fast, as was he, and the incident of note happened when I failed to catch a pass inbound to me while Don was covering me. We both jumped into the air to catch the pass, I missed it in a way no receiver should ever miss, and it hit Don squarely on the middle finger and he went down howling. When he came up, cradling his hand, his middle finger was terribly broken, a step function right at the middle joint. I remember telling him we needed to take him to the ER, but he was looking at his hand, turning it over, this way and that, clearly in a lot of pain. Finally, he mumbled "It's not broken. Dislocated". And then, to my horror, he held his finger up right at me and said "Pull". Dismayed (to say the least), I said "Don you need to get to the ER and have that thing set." And then he let loose, and I mean he bellowed at the top of his lungs: "PULL!! GRAB IT AND PULL IT!!". So commanded, I took his finger in my hand, pulled hard, and there followed the grinding, rending-cartilage vibrations you get when you bend a chicken wing backwards to break it apart, followed by a pop, and suddenly the finger was straight. When something broke, you fixed it. At our regular meeting the following Monday, I could tell Don was deeply irritated with me. His finger was terribly swollen, black and blue, and duct-taped to an adjacent finger. Clearly, had not bothered with a doctor. When I asked how it was doing, he was obviously bitter, and muttered something along the lines of "It's fine. I don't see how you could possibly have missed that ball". Perhaps, but we were all back playing Helmberger Ball once the quarterback's finger healed up.

Don's waveform intuition, developed through modeling of countless datasets, was remarkable, arguably the singular best in the world, for the fifty or so years he was active. I learned early on the trick of bringing him new waveforms to hide the fact that I'd gotten little done since our last meeting. It was remarkable just to watch him muse over new waveforms and tease out physical structure within the Earth with his simple raypath drawings that could explain the coarse attributes of whatever it was we were looking at. The Seismo Lab at that time was in an interesting state because TriNet, as the original broadband network was then called, had only recently been funded and the first Streckheisen STS-1s had been around only a couple years and were showing all sorts of amazing things. But it was tedious to get the data out of the archives. It seemed wise to me at the time to figure out how to write some routines that would automatically parse incoming NEIC emails for hypocentral information, extract the relevant TriNet waveforms, sort by distance into record section and zoom into any particular phase, and then print it out on paper, paper being the only format Don could use. Once I got it working, every NEIC email automatically triggered the production of a record section of some phase waiting on the printer. The record sections piled up, Don was in heaven, and this endeavor yielded a very fun time spent looking at all sorts of lateral variation within the deep earth. There was no real focus to it, we just looked at phases that varied rapidly across the network from whichever earthquakes Mother Nature threw our way, from regional to nearly antipodal. For a few months, anyways, after which at some point even Don had had enough and started pushing me to actually finish modeling and write up some of the many small projects I had started.

All of the work I did end up publishing with Don came out of this tinkering. One record section yielded a remarkable range discrepancy between SCSN short-period recordings versus broad-band TriNet recordings of the back-branch of the 410 triplication from a perfect southern Baja California, Mexico low magnitude 6 event that lit up all of California and produced an extraordinarily clean full-bowtie triplication (Figure 1; Melbourne and Helmberger, 1998). The back-branch frequency dependence allowed us to constrain the thickness of the discontinuity fairly precisely; Cagniard synthetics done with a 5-km thick discontinuity produced quite different waveforms than did a 15-km thick discontinuity, for instance, and the best-fitting synthetics required a composite discontinuity that caused destructive interference and effectively quenched the short-period arrival beyond about 13 degrees of distance.

Another anomalous record section yielded a project of modeling diffracted precursors to SS along the Pacific-North American plate boundary that were very sensitive to lithospheric thickness. SS is a maximum travel-time phase and modeling the interference of these precursors with rays was tedious. But eventually I switched to a Frequency-Waveform code written by Lupei Zhu which was also a complete solution (with diffraction), fast and clean to use even if you didn't get the raypath information, so determining the structure was largely trial-and-error. But it allowed us to map out the E-W edge of Pacific plate lithosphere along the California and Baja borderlands, which we could then compare to the long-term velocity field that had recently come out of the new continuous GPS networks all over California (Figures 2 and 3; Melbourne and Helmberger, 2001). For all of the continental dynamics theories that are still argued over today, from our work, it sure looked like the steady-state strain rates along the California plate boundary, as measured with then-new continuous GPS networks, simply mirror the whole lithospheric thickness of the Pacific plate, what Don always called "the 800-lb gorilla of earth plate tectonics". The idea that the thickness of the whole lithosphere, rather than dynamics attributed California's overlying crust, which seems to be passively carried at a rate proportional to the thickness of the underlying mantle lithosphere, was controversial then and remains so today.

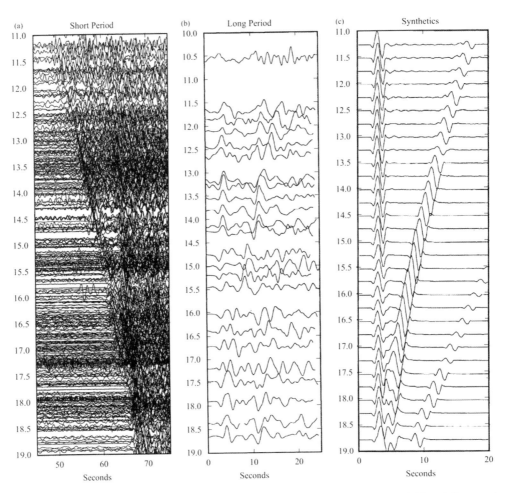

Fig. 1　Fine structure of the 410 km discontinuity, from Melbourne and Helmberger (1998). (a) Short-period vertical data plotted with reduction velocity of 10.5 km/s. The 394 traces shown in this array are 1-Hz lowpass filtered and normalized to the maximum amplitude in the window shown. The 410 reflection is clearly visible out to near 13 degrees, where it rapidly disappears. (b) Long-period recordings show 410 reflection to ~11 degrees. (c) Best-fitting Cagniard synthetics yield a composite 410 discontinuity in which a 3% velocity increase is overlain by an additional 3.5% increase spread over 14 km radial distance.

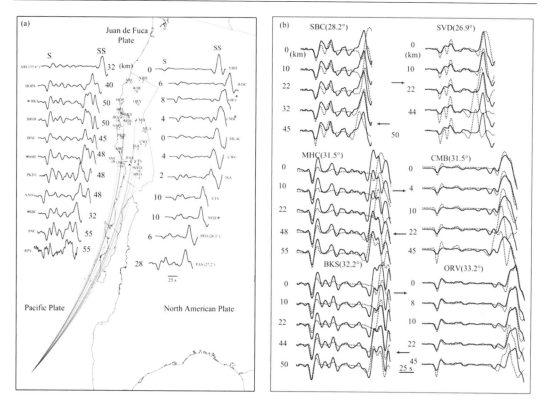

Fig. 2　Mapping the Edge of the Pacific Plate Lithosphere, from Melbourne and Helmberger (2001). (a) Observed (solid) and calculated (dashed) shear body waveforms recorded along Pacific-North American plate boundary, with corresponding lid thickness printed beside each trace. Westernmost raypaths uniformly require substantially thicker lithospheric lid structure, averaging 50 km, while eastern paths require thin or no lithospheric lid structure, consistent with known Basin and Range upper mantle shear structure. S2-S travel time anomalies relative to TNA (Grand and Helmberger, 1984) in seconds are shown below station name. FK synthetics are computed for 1D average lithospheric lid thicknesses indicated adjacent to waveform traces. (b) Infuence of Lithospheric lid thickness on S2-S travel times and S2 waveforms. Varying lid thickness between 0 and 50 km produces over 20 seconds change in S2-S travel time, and strongly alters S2 pulse shape. Each shear wave seismogram is repeated 5 times, and overlaid with synthetics with a single 1D model in which the thickness of the high velocity lid (v_S=4.55 km/s versus v_S=4.4 km/s, non-lid) varies according to thickness printed to left of data trace. Lid thickness providing minimal synthetic-data mist is identified with arrow.

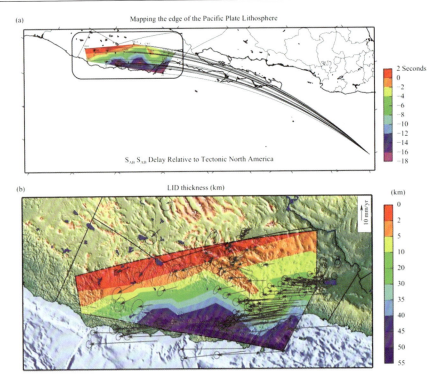

Fig. 3　Mapping the Edge of the Pacific Plate Lithosphere, from Melbourne and Helmberger (2001). (a) Contoured delay in accrued SS (AB branch) arrival times relative to the Tectonic North America model of Grand and Helmberger (1984) for waveforms propagating along the Pacific Plate edge from the source at the East Pacific Rise. Inset square corresponds to bottom panel. (b) Contoured seismic lithosphere thicknesses beneath North American continental margin derived from broadband S2 waveforms and S2-S travel times.

Lithospheric lid thicknesses range systematically from 55 km along margin coastal paths (Peninsular Baja-Western California), typical of Miocene-aged oceanic lithosphere and similar to that observed beneath eastern Pacific, to effectively 0 km along Eastern California-Eastern peninsular Baja paths, typical of Basin and Range upper mantle. Intraplate dextral strain, indicated by geodetic GPS measurements conducted across thick lithospheric lid regions, is substantially lower than interplate dextral strain, indicated by measurements taken across regions.

A third related project showed conclusively that the transition zone under the East Pacific Rise has no idea there's a spreading center above it (Figure 4; Melbourne and Helmberger, 2002). With the full development of California broad-band networks and the high earthquake productivity of the southern East Pacific Rise, we could map out transition zone structure and depth under and away from the spreading center itself, and I remember how fascinated Don was that I could find no systematic variation with distance away from the rise. Given the sensitivity of how the multiple branches of the triplication interfered to produce the observed waveforms, interference we could readily replicate in synthetics, Don felt it would be hard to ever come up with a more robust constraint on transition zone variability under the East Pacific Rise than these well-modeled record sections presented.

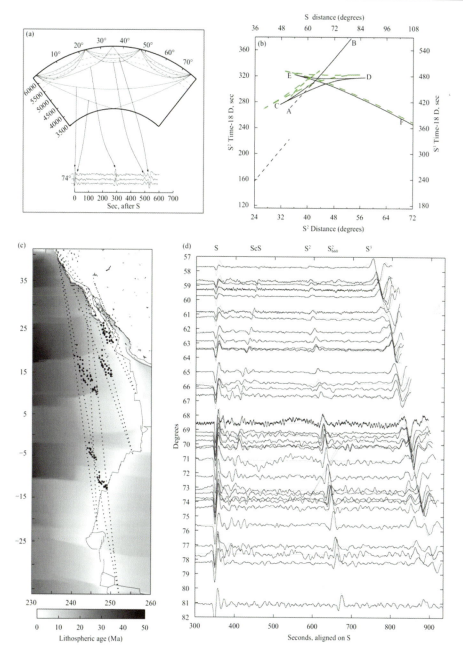

Fig. 4   Transition Zone Variability Beneath East Pacific Rise, from Melbourne and Helmberger (2002). (a) Generalized ray paths showing discrete phases of the upper mantle triplication of multiple (in this case, triple) S. Doubled and tripled time separation of triplicated S2 and S3 subphases, respectively, facilitate their slowness identication and synthetic replication relative to S. (b) Triplication plots for the TNA model with (solid) and without (thick dashed) a lid. (c) Crustal age map indicating the position of four events used to constrain lateral variation in mantle structure. Shading density indicates plate age. (d) Modeled waveforms containing S, ScS, S2, and triplicated S3, aligned on S. No systematic misfit in subphases of the S3 triplication is observed.

These were just three of the projects that I saw through to publication with Don, but I was always struck by the fact that the three were just three among dozens that I could have chosen from those automated record sections spat out like clockwork with every NEIC email. At some point, perhaps in my 5th year at Caltech, something clicked and I decided that I had done enough and that it was time to move on. I more or less announced this to Don one day, he didn't disagree, and that was that.

One of the gut instincts I took away from my work with him is that, at a 10 second period at least, the deep earth is a real mess and clean figures and simple velocity profiles really belie the complexity therein. There are many crazy structures, and, presumably processes, at work, whose signatures all blend together and become invisible in waveforms at longer periods or are smeared out or missed entirely by tomographic inversion. Don really gave me the freedom and liberty to pretty much pursue what I was interested in, and only if I pushed his patience too far, for instance by disappearing to climb mountains in Alaska, did he gently reign me in, in his way. But he was remarkably gracious and generous to a fault. For instance, my work with him was interrupted in the middle because I was serendipitously given an $M8$ earthquake that ruptured just offshore a GPS network that Joann Stock (also at Caltech) had built in Jalisco that I had partaken in as a first-year orals project. We were able to easily measure the coseismic deformation, but we were also able to image all sorts of transient creep events propagating around the plate interface following the mainshock. The creep events both triggered and were triggered by aftershocks, and the fact that we could image these was all very new in 1995. Don never hesitated when I told him I'd like to work on this gift-from-god-and-Joann-Stock; he knew I was totally motivated by the science and that was enough for him so he was very supportive. Two years and three papers later when I came back into his office to resume my work with him, it was like I had never left and we picked up where we had left off. That's unusual in science these days and testament to Don's love of science and his recognition that paths forward on the cutting edge are often tangled and take strange turns.

I'm going to stop now only because, while there are many more stories I could relate, I feel I've only scratched the surface of my time with Don. I was shocked to learn he had passed since I did not see it coming. I sat at my desk processing the news for a minute or two, and then walked down the hall to tell Craig Scrivner, another former Helmberger student with whom I work (PhD, 1998), who was equally stunned. We knew Don was 80ish, but he personified human time-invariance and I had just seen him at the SCEC meeting a few months earlier, where he seemed the same Don as ever. I suppose at great age a sudden departure can be preferable in some ways to a drawn-out decline, but I would have liked some warning so I could have made an effort to track him down and say, more than anything, thanks. Thanks for the tutelage, for the role model of kindness and generosity and extraordinary but quiet productivity, and thanks for giving so much to so many of us. So I'll say it here, instead:

Thanks, Don.

References

Grand SP and Helmberger DV (1984). Upper mantle shear structure of North America. Geophys J Int **76**(2): 399–438.

Melbourne T and Helmberger D (1998). Fine structure of the 410-km discontinuity. J Geophys Res: Solid Earth **103**(B5): 10091–10102.

Melbourne T and Helmberger D (2001). Mantle control of plate boundary deformation. Geophys Res Lett **28**(20): 4003–4006.

Melbourne T and Helmberger DV (2002). Whole mantle shear structure beneath the East Pacific Rise. J Geophys Res: Solid Earth **107**(B9): 2204.

Tim Melbourne is currently Professor of Geophysics at Central Washington University (CWU). He completed his Ph.D. at Caltech in 1999 with Prof. Helmberger as his primary thesis advisor and moved to CWU from Caltech. He has been Director of the Pacific Northwest Geodetic Array since 2002. His webpage can be found at: http://www.panga.org/about/tim/.

第 13 章　恩师唐·亨伯格

蒂莫西·墨尔本

美国中央华盛顿大学地质科学系，埃伦斯堡，华盛顿州 98926

引用：Melbourne TI (2022). Donald V. Helmberger the Mentor. Earthq Sci 35(1): 44–50 doi: 10.1016/j.eqs. 2022.01.019

　　我和其他很多人一样，都很想念唐（Don）。我特别怀念那种永恒感，回想起他在帕萨迪纳（Pasadena），南马德楼（South Mudd）三楼，大树下的办公室里观察波形的时光。我和他有着无数的回忆，这些回忆不止形成于我在加州理工学院地震实验室（Caltech Seismo Lab）做学生时期，还有接下来的 20 多年。这让我不好选择用哪些回忆来描述我所认识的他，那个在科学上比父亲以外的任何人都更多地塑造我的他，以及那个我深爱着的他。显然，纯粹的科学，纯为好奇而做的地震波形建模，并以此去揭开地球的秘密，应该占据中心舞台，尤其是在这个场合。但是，唐（Don）更像一幅人文和科学交融的丰富的画卷，所以我想我会讲一些不一样的故事，与我跟他合作的工作经历交织在一起，来表达我对他的感情。

　　唐（Don）是一个高尚而又朴实谦逊的人，他说过很多名言。其中有一句我不止听过一次，而且我觉得他很引以为豪，他说："我在一个牧场长大，有东西坏了，你就把它修好。"我第一次听到这句名言，是在我研究生刚入学几个月的时候，他走进我的办公室。就像他习惯的那样，他一直在思考我给他看的一些猛犸湖区（Mammoth Lakes）的波形，并开始建模。他没有看到我通过努力在科学上获得的进步，而是发现我和我的同事一头栽在一个新磨好的、酸洗过的铝制汽缸盖上，这是我那辆坏掉的 70 年代马自达掀背式轿车的汽缸盖。我和我的室友没有证据也没有经验，但我们觉得我们能修好它。还记得我试图不让唐（Don）发现，因为我当时在办公室模拟浅火山口的各向异性，在桌上放一个汽缸盖，这很不"加州理工"。但唐（Don）还是看见了。让我惊讶的是，他并没有像我原本担心的那样痛骂我一顿，而是直接对汽缸盖产生了兴趣。他戳了戳，把它翻过来，要了一本书试着往下压阀杆，方便他观察阀座，以及看一眼水套之类的。他问了一系列问题，很明显他懂自己在说什么。最终他得出结论，我们的判断是对的。当我说他似乎很懂发动机的时候，"喏——我在一个牧场长大，有东西坏了，你就把它修好。"对年轻的我而言，将抽象学者唐· 复射线参数域上卡尼亚尔·德胡普（Cagniard-de-Hoop）路径积分（Don-the-Cagniard-de-Hoop-path-integral-through-complex-ray-parameter-space）和唐·机修师傅（Don-the-small-engine-repair-guy）联系在一起的感觉很奇妙。但这就是唐（Don），你对他了解得越多，你就发现他身上有越多的层次。

　　唐（Don）是一个温柔的人，如果想让他对你大喊大叫，真的发飙的那种，得费点功夫。这种情况只发生过一次，是在玩"唐式橄榄球"的时候。那是一种被亲切地称为"亨伯格球"（Helmberger Ball）的游戏。比赛在周六上午举行，规则大致如下：唐（Don）要当四分卫，所有亨伯格的学生都要来，凑够两队人，唐（Don）在的队要赢。我刚来到地震实验室（Seismo Lab）的时候，作为一个美国大汉，唐（Don）原以为我会玩橄榄球，但事实上我从来没有参加过，甚至没有看过橄榄球比赛，所以我完全不会。但我跑得很快，他也跑得很快。当我漏掉了一个弹地球，唐（Don）来补位的时候，意外发生了。我俩都跳起来接球，这是一个没有人会漏掉的球，而我却把它漏过去了，这球正中唐（Don）的中指，他嚎着倒在地上。他抱着手起来，中指严重受伤，中间关节成了一个阶跃函数。我记得我说得带他去急诊室，但他看着手，转来转去，显然非常疼。最后，他喃喃地说："没断，只是脱臼了。"紧接着，他握着手指对着我，说："拉！"，这吓坏我了。我多少有些惊慌失措了，我说："唐（Don），你得去急诊室处理一下。"然后他发飙了，我的意思是他用最大的声音吼："拉！！抓紧它，拉！！"在这样命令式的语气下，我拽着他的手指，铆足劲拉，接着听到劈开软骨似的咯咯声，那是你反着掰断一根鸡翅时发出的声音，接着清脆的一声，他的手指一下子变直了。的确，有东西坏了，你就把它修好。在下个周一的例会上，我看得出唐（Don）在生我的气。他的中指肿得厉害，又青又紫，用管道胶带固定在另一根手指上。很显然，他没去看医生。当我问他情况怎么样时，他明显不开心，喃喃地说了几句大概是"没事。我搞不懂那样个小破球你怎么可能漏掉。"也许吧，但四分卫的手指痊愈后，我们又玩起了亨伯格球。

　　唐（Don）对波形的直觉是在对数不清多少数据集进行建模的过程中形成的，在他活跃的五十多年中，这种直觉是出了名的，可以说是世界上独一无二。我很早就学会了用给他带点新波形这一招，来掩盖自己在前一次见面之后几乎没什么进展。他沉浸在新的波形里，用他简单的射线路径图分析地球内部的物理结构，基本可以解释我们所看到的大致特征，我仅仅是看着都觉得非常的厉害。当时的地震实验室（Seismo Lab）受到关注，这归功于才刚获得资助的"TriNet"，也就是早期的宽频台网，距第一台斯特里克海森 STS-1s 地震仪问世才几年，展示了各种令人惊叹的东西。但从档案中取出数据是很乏味的。我觉得当时我写了一些自动化程序是明智的，这些程序能自动解析收到的国家地震信息中心（NEIC）邮件中的震源信息，提取对应的 TriNet 波形，得到按震中距排列的记录剖面，放大到任意震相，然后打印在纸上，纸是唐（Don）唯一可以使用的格式。如果我让它开始运行，每一封来自 NEIC 的电子邮件都会自动触发生成某个震相的记录剖面，在打印机上等待。记录的片段堆积如山，唐（Don）乐开了花，这样的努力产生了一段非常有趣的时光，用来观察地球深处的各种横向变化。我们没有真正的关注点，"自然母亲"丢给我们从区域性的到来自地球另一端的许多地震，而我们就在这个台网里观察快速变化的震相。不管怎样，在那之后的几个月里，就连唐（Don）都受够了，开始督促我完成实实在在的建模，并将我正在进行的一些小工作整理成文。

　　我所有的最终和唐（Don）一起发表的工作，都是在这样"试试看"的过程中完成的。有一场发生在墨西哥下加利福尼亚州（Baja California）南部的 6 级地震完美地照亮了整个加利福尼亚，产生了相当干净的蝴蝶结式三叉震相。在一个记录剖面上，南加州地震台网（SCSN）的短周期记录和 TriNet 的宽频带记录的 410 三叉震相尾支的可见范围明显不一致（图 1；Melbourne and Helmberger, 1998）。尾支的这种频率依赖性让我们能相对精确地约束不连续界面的厚度；例如，与 15 km 厚的不连续面相比，5 km 厚的不连续面在用卡尼亚尔（Cagniard）方法合成的波形中截然不同，而和观测拟合最好的合成波形需一个混合的不连续面，引起相消干涉，并将短周期地震波有效地抑制在大约 13° 的距离之外。

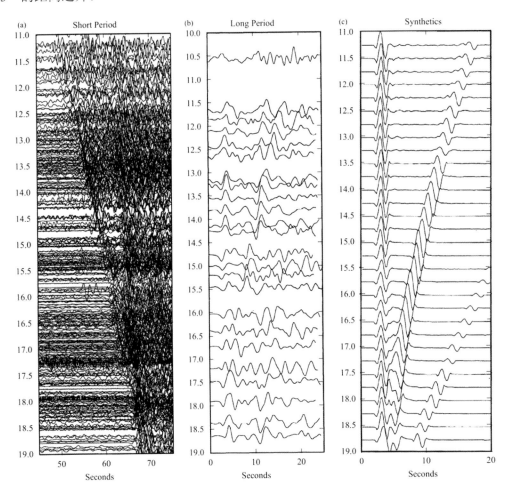

图 1　410 km 不连续面的精细结构，来自 Melbourne and Helmberger（1998）。（a）短周期垂向分量记录，按照 10.5 km/s 的视速度绘制。图中显示的 394 道波形经过了 1 Hz 低通滤波，并按在所示时窗内的最大振幅做了归一化。一直到 13° 震中距，410 反射都清晰可见，并在更近距离上很快消失。（b）长周期记录中的 410 反射的可见范围近达约 11° 震中距。（c）最优模型给出的卡尼亚尔（Cagniard）合成记录，采用一个复合的 410 不连续面来解释，其中在一个 3% 的正的速度界面之上 14km 处还有一个 3.5% 的正界面。

　　另一个异常记录剖面催生了一个模拟太平洋-北美板块边界上衍射的 SS 前驱波的项目，这些前驱波对岩石圈厚度很敏感。SS 是一个最大走时震相，[用卡尼亚尔（Cagniard）

方法）]模拟前驱波和直达波的干涉非常烦琐。最终我还是改用了朱露培（Lupei Zhu）写的频率波形代码，这也是一个完整解（考虑衍射），即使没有射线路径信息也可以快速、干净地运行，然后，确定结构需要大量反复试错过程。但它让我们能绘制出沿加利福尼亚（California）和巴哈（Baja）边界的太平洋板块岩石圈的东西向边缘，然后我们将它跟从加利福尼亚各地连续 GPS 台网中最近新得出的长期速度场进行比较（图 2 和图 3；Melbourne and Helmberger, 2001）。根据我们研究，对于今天仍然存在争议的所有大陆动力学理论来说，与当时新的连续 GPS 台网观测到的一样，沿着加利福尼亚处的板块边界的稳态的应变率，看起来确实反映了太平洋板块的整个岩石圈厚度。这个板块一直被唐（Don）称为"地球板块构造学里的 800 磅大猩猩"。加利福尼亚上覆地壳似乎以与下伏地幔岩石圈厚度成比例的速度被带着运动，是整个岩石圈的厚度，而不是动力学影响了加利福尼亚上覆地壳。

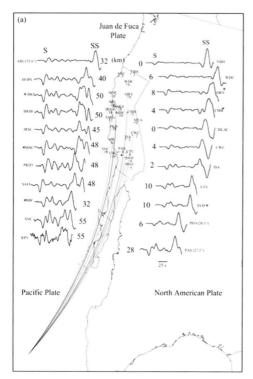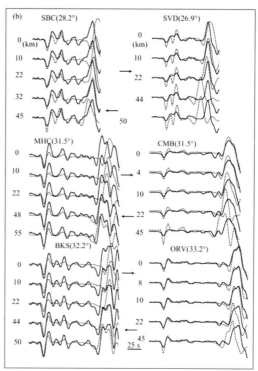

图 2　太平洋板块岩石圈边缘图，来自 Melbourne and Helmberger（2001）。（a）沿着太平洋板块和北美板块的交界传播的剪切体波的观测（实线）和合成（虚线）波形，每道数据旁标有相应台站位置处的盖层厚度。最靠西侧的射线路径一致反映出相对较厚的岩石圈盖层结构，平均 50 km 厚；与之相反，东侧的射线路径反映出的盖层结构相对较薄甚至几乎不存在，这与关于盆地和山脉下方的上地幔剪切波结构的常识相一致。在图中台站名下方标注了相对于 TNA 模型（Grand and Helmberger, 1984）的 S2-S 走时异常值，以秒为单位。和观测波形同时画出的 FK 合成波形是用一维模型计算得到，模型的岩石圈盖层厚度是各台站反映的厚度的平均值。（b）岩石圈盖层厚度对 S2-S 走时和 S2 波形的影响。在 0 km 和 50 km 之间改变岩石圈盖层厚度可产生超过 20 秒的 S2-S 走时变化，同时产生 S2 脉冲形状的畸变。每个横波地震记录重复 5 次，同时画有一维盖层模型的合成波形，模型中高速盖层（v_s=4.55 km/s 与非盖层范围 v_s=4.4 km/s）的厚度印在数据道左侧。图中箭头指示残差最小的盖层厚度对应的合成数据。

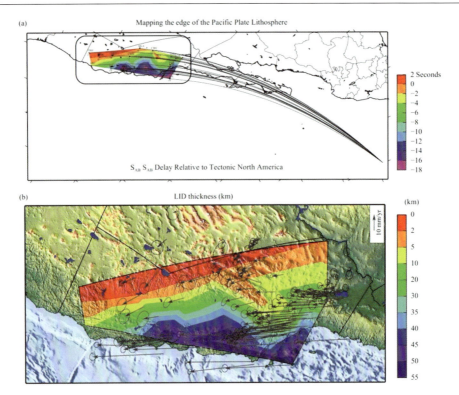

图 3　太平洋板块岩石圈边缘（Edge of the Pacific Plate Lithosphere）图，来自 Melbourne and Helmberger
（2001）。（a）相对于 Grand and Helmberger（1984）中的北美构造（Tectonic North America，简称 TNA）
模型的 SS（AB 分支）震相累积的走时延迟等值线图，涉及的震源位于东太平洋隆起处，且射线路径
沿着太平洋板块边缘延伸。嵌入的方框对应于底部图。（b）北美大陆边缘下方的地震学岩石圈厚度等
值线图，岩石圈厚度是根据宽频带记录中的 S2 波形和 S2-S 走时差得出的。岩石圈盖厚度存在从沿海
岸线路径（巴哈半岛−西加利福尼亚，Peninsular Baja-Western California）的 55 km 到沿东加利福尼亚−
东巴哈半岛（Eastern California-Eastern peninsular Baja）路径的约 0 km 的系统性差异。前者是典型的中
新世年龄海洋岩石圈，与在东太平洋下方观察到的岩石圈相似；后者是典型的盆地和山脉上地幔。板
块内部的右旋应变（来自岩石圈盖层较厚区域内部的大地 GPS 测量）远低于相邻板块之间右旋应变（来
自岩石圈该层厚度横向变化梯度较大的区域的 GPS 测量）。

　　第三个相关的项目最终表明，东太平洋隆起（East Pacific Rise）之下的地幔过渡带
不受它上方的扩张中心的影响（图 4；Melbourne and Helmberger, 2002）。借着加利福尼
亚宽频带台网的全面发展和东太平洋隆起南部的高地震发生率，我们可以绘制出在扩张
中心正下方和远离扩张中心的位置上的过渡带各深度的结构。我记得当我发现找不到随
着到隆起距离的系统性变化时唐（Don）有多入迷。虽然三叉震相的各支互相干涉会影
响观测波形的敏感性，我们仍不难在合成记录中复现这种干涉。唐（Don）认为，对东
太平洋隆起之下的过渡带结构横向变化，很难找到比这些漂亮的模拟记录剖面更有力的
约束。

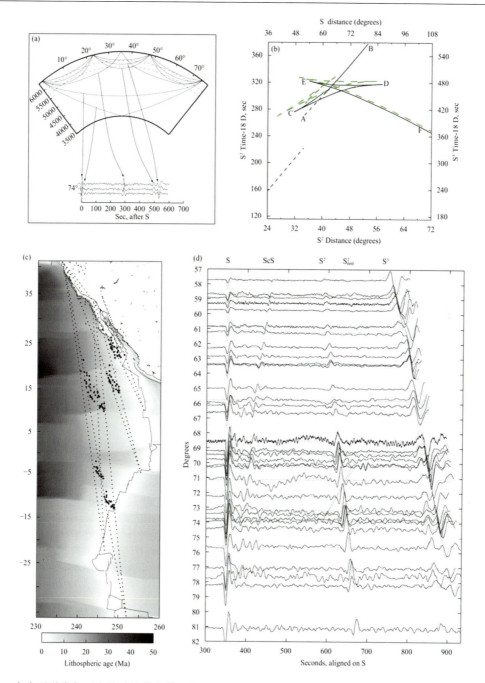

图 4　东太平洋隆起下方的过渡带变化，来自 Melbourne and Helmberger（2002）。（a）广义射线路径图，图中展示了上地幔中多次（本例中为三次）S 波三叉离散震相。S2 和 S3 震相的三叉子震相间的时间间隔分别是 S 震相的两倍和三倍，这便于识别它们的慢度并在合成中复现这些波形。（b）用有（实线）和没有（粗虚线）盖层的 TNA 模型合成的三叉震相图。（c）地壳年龄图，显示了用于约束地幔结构横向变化的四个地震事件的位置。阴影密度表示板块年龄。（d）包含 S、ScS、S2 和 S3 三叉震相的合成波形，按照 S 对齐。在 S3 的三叉分裂后的子震相中未观察到系统性残差。

这仅仅是我跟唐（Don）一起进行直到发表的项目中的三个，但我总是被这样一个事实所打动：NEIC 邮件像装了发条一样发出了几十个自动记录剖面供我选择，而这些只不过是这几十条记录中的三个。在某个时刻，也许是我在加州理工学院的第五年，我突然觉得自己已经做得够多了，是时候往前走走了。于是有一天，我直接或者间接地向唐（Don）宣布了这一点，他没有异议，就这样结束了。

我从与他合作的工作中获得的直觉之一是，至少在 10 秒周期，地球深处是一片混乱，干净的图像和简单的速度剖面确实掩盖了其中的复杂性。有许多疯狂的结构，可能还有一些过程在起作用，它们的特征都融合在一起，在较长周期的波形中变得不可分辨，或者被层析成像反演完全模糊掉或忽略掉。唐（Don）真的给了我很大的自由和自主去追求我感兴趣的东西，只有当我把他的耐心逼得太过分时，比如玩失踪跑去阿拉斯加（Alaska）爬山，他才会以他的方式温柔地鞭策我。但他对一些小错误非常慷慨大方。例如，我和他的工作在中间被打断了，因为我偶然发现了一个八级地震，在哈利斯科州（Jalisco）外海，就在乔安·斯托克（Joann Stock，也在加州理工）布设的一个 GPS 台网附近；作为第一年资格考试的一个项目，我也参与了这个工作。我们能够很容易地测量同震形变，但我们也能够成像主震后在板块界面周围传播的各种瞬态蠕滑事件。蠕滑事件既是触发余震，也是受到余震触发的，我们能够对这些进行成像，这在 1995 年是非常新颖的工作。当我告诉他我想从上帝和乔安·斯托克（Joann Stock）那里得到这份礼物时，唐（Don）毫不犹豫；他知道我完全被科学所激励，这对他来说已经足够了，所以他非常支持我。两年后，当我回到他的办公室继续和他一起工作时，我感觉自己好像从未离开过，我们又回到了我们分开的地方。这在当今的科学界里并不常见，这证明了唐（Don）对科学的热爱，以及他认识到，在前沿的道路往往是错综复杂的，并且会存在奇怪的转折。

我先写到这里，虽然我还有很多故事可以讲述，但我觉得这些只是我和唐（Don）相处的时光的皮毛。得知他过世的消息，我很震惊，因为我没想到这一刻会到来。我坐在办公桌前浏览了一两分钟的新闻，然后走进大厅告诉克雷格·斯克里夫纳（Craig Scrivner），他是另一位与我一起工作过的亨伯格以前的学生（1998 年获得博士学位），他同样感到震惊。我们知道唐（Don）是个 80 多岁的人，但他是人类时间不变性的化身，几个月前我才刚在南加州地震中心（SCEC）会议上见过他，在那里他似乎和以前一样。我想，当人年龄大了，突然的离世也许在某种程度上比缓慢的衰老更好一些，但我仍希望我曾得到一些提示，让我能够有机会去找他，并对他说出最重要的话：谢谢。感谢您的指导，感谢您树立的善良、慷慨、非凡而又静心工作的榜样，感谢您给予我们这么多。所以我要在这里说：谢谢，唐（Don）。

参 考 文 献

Grand SP and Helmberger DV (1984). Upper mantle shear structure of North America. Geophys J Int **76**(2): 399–438.

Melbourne T and Helmberger D (1998). Fine structure of the 410-km discontinuity. J Geophys Res: Solid Earth **103**(B5): 10091–10102.

Melbourne T and Helmberger D (2001). Mantle control of plate boundary deformation. Geophys Res Lett **28**(20): 4003– 4006.

Melbourne T and Helmberger DV (2002). Whole mantle shear structure beneath the East Pacific Rise. J Geophys Res: Solid Earth **107**(B9): 2204.

蒂莫西·墨尔本现任中央华盛顿大学（Central Washington University，CWU）地球物理学教授。他于 1999 年在加州理工学院取得博士学位，师从亨伯格教授，并在同一年从加州理工到了中央华盛顿大学。自 2002 年起，他一直担任太平洋西北大地测量阵列网（Pacific Northwest Geodetic Array）的负责人。更多关于他的信息，见网页：http://www.panga.org/about/tim/。

Chapter 14. The Lost and the Found: Memories of Donald V. Helmberger

Brian Savage [*]

University of Rhode Island, Kingston, RI 02879, USA

[*]**Correspondence:** savage@uri.edu

Citation: Savage B (2022). The lost and the found: Memories of Donald V. Helmberger. Earthq Sci 35(1): 51−53 doi: 10.1016/j.eqs.2022.01.006

My first exposure to Don Helmberger's work was during a seismology class in my 2nd year in college where several students, including myself, were to present on Grand and Helmberger (1984). It was over my head, but seeing the beauty of the seismograms, tracking the upper mantle triplication, and what it revealed about the Earth was just transformative. During my time as an undergraduate at Berkeley, I also digitized (Dreger and Savage, 1999) and forward modeled seismic data under the advisement of Dr. Doug Dreger (a Helmberger student) for about two years, had an academic advisor who went to Caltech (Dr. Mark Richards) and took a couple of courses from Dr. Lane Johnson (Don's friend from Minnesota). Little did I know the path I needed to take was already laid out – I just had to follow it.

During the graduate school "decision" period, I had the opportunity to visit the Seismo Lab in Pasadena. Don picked me up in his blue Peugeot from the Burbank airport. I think he purchased the car in Europe many years before; it was well-loved. On that particular day, there was a torrential rainstorm in southern California that flooded the highway (I-5). As a result, we had to take surface streets and the drive to Pasadena took what seemed like forever. At some point, I asked Don, "Why is that pen stuck there?" while pointing to where the windshield met the roof of his car, to which he responded: "To stop it from leaking". The pen didn't work, it continually fell out, and the windshield slowly leaked onto my pants. No worries, I was already soaked from the short scamper on the tarmac from the airplane to the terminal. We eventually arrived at South Mudd, where Don kindly pulled up under the walkway, told me to run inside, go to the 2nd floor and tell them I was here while he went and parked the car.

After nonetheless deciding to go to Caltech, I started as a graduate student working with Don in 1998. Whatever the project, Don was always there to assist in the seismogram perusal, hard thinking, derivations, or cutting and tapping of figures (Don liked to do it that way, I normally just remade them digitally). He was always there to guide me and fellow grad students through the complexities of getting research done from the basic work, the writing process, to the inevitable and unwelcome return of the paper from review "like an ex-girlfriend". The first paper I wrote with Don (Savage and Helmberger, 2001) was about an explosion on a Russian submarine. We were asked to get a quantitative measure of the size of the explosion; Don used his Air Force connections to get the data. He also worked diligently with me on the theory for an underwater, explosive source and how to model the data; the manuscript was sent out 4 months later, I was thrilled.

Typically, I was left to my own devices for a several weeks to work up a set of seismic data, from the newly installed regional network in southern California. Local and regional earthquake data were utilized to examine the crust and mantle structure. I would look for oddities in the data. The seismic data were always treated with special care as the amplitude and phasing were what we tried to reproduce. I was given the freedom to look at interesting responses and try to model them in the absence of Don's advisement. It was a great learning experience, but the modeling aspect always left me lost, and from what I was told, something called "the Fog"; grasping around for something, really anything to improve the fit between the data and synthetics. This was where Don stepped in to provide needed guidance.

Eventually, I would get Don's attention on the seismograms I was struggling with. The conversation often started with, "Hey this looks great! Who are you again?" I would normally play along and tell him my name. One day I told him my name was Pete. Don proceeded to call me Pete for the next six months; my Seismo Lab coffee mug with Pete on it broke a decade after I graduated. After capturing Don's attention, we would work on the data and think about the possible structures (I had chosen structure over source) and the models that would best match the data in question.

In the early years, I would ask many questions while we talked, but I would never get much of a response. I would ask a question and Don would either stare out the window to his beautiful view of the mountains just north of Pasadena or he would look up and stare at the ceiling. I would think and ask another question before he had a chance to respond to the first. At some point, I decided to just let Don think. This worked much better. I have a sneaky suspicion that every time I asked a question, he had to reboot his brain to address the most recent inquiry. I now find myself doing similar things with students in my office, thinking intently about the problem at hand to provide the best guidance.

Eventually, a possible solution, or multiple solutions, would be created by Don and myself and we would talk about why the solution would or would not work, Don always drawing on his engineering notepad and throwing broken pens behind his map case. I always thought my ideas were good and workable. After our long meetings, I would run the simulations (usually 1D or 2D at this point), mine first, of course. Eventually realizing my ideas were not feasible, I ran Don's structures. To my surprise then (but not now) Don's structures were good, always. Don learned so much by looking at and modeling lots of data, helping him generate the appropriate response. Sometimes that response took a while, in more way than one

Quite early in my graduate work, Don took me to an Air Force meeting in New Orleans, LA. He was doing his best to introduce me to important people, guiding me, and kept buying me beers during the initial night's social event; he also did this during a meeting in Jackson Hole. When the event was winding down, he indicated we should go get dinner, "somewhere with good food". We wandered around a bit, me mostly following Don, and ended up at a place that served deep-fried seafood where we each ordered a large platter and more beer. Sometime in the middle of the meal, Don off-handedly said, "You are going to get me in trouble with my wife for eating all this". Early the next morning, I barely caught the image of Don zipping past my hotel window on a morning run.

At a later stage as a graduate student, I took a lengthy research cruise across the Pacific. Around the same time, Don told me a story about a research cruise he took during his time at Scripps. This would have been sometime in the 1960s, pre-GPS, and the cruise was in and around the Aleutian Islands. During the cruise they got caught in what Don described as a bad storm which carried the research vessel to the opposite side of the island chain, without the crew's knowledge. At that point, Don said he was never going on another cruise again. He probably gave me this guidance before I left, thanks, Don. He was still kind enough to let me be gone for as long as I was, it was a good experience and I was able to focus and get work done and some papers written.

Following graduation from Caltech, I had an impromptu discussion with Don at AGU about an incredibly odd piece of data in the late afternoon poster session. Of course, Don was wearing his leather jacket. I described the problem to him and drew out the seismograms on the back of some paper scraps. I knew what they looked like as I had been staring at them for a long time, probably months. Don took a quick look at them and said "Why do we look at seismograms? Because they are pretty", he then thought for a few moments, and gave me some options of possible models to try, including models he and previous students had tried some decades before. Again, Don was darn close, but as always guiding and supportive. But this time Don's models were also similar to those I had come up with (Savage, 2012).

There was one more interaction between Don and myself that I remember fondly that happened at an Air Force meeting in New Mexico. I had just wrapped up my talk about a tomography project and following a couple of questions from other attendees, Don started asking question after question about the methodology, what I was seeing, and if I believed the results. This seemed like the usual "Don is interested, this is fun, let's go." The questioning continued for 20 minutes or so and it was as if we were back in Don's office working through a dataset with him. Following the talk, many attendees asked me if I had enjoyed my 2nd oral examination or not. Don always asked the hardest questions but, in a way, to get at the source of an issue or data set.

Thank you Don for always being there to lend a guiding hand as I stumbled around in the fog "putting yellow ribbons on every single one of those trees in the forest".

References

Dreger D and Savage B (1999). Aftershocks of the 1952 Kern County, California, earthquake sequence. Bull Seismol Soc Am **89**(4): 1094–1108.

Grand SP and Helmberger DV (1984). Upper mantle shear structure of North America. Geophys J Int **76**(2): 399–438.

Savage B and Helmberger DV (2001). Kursk explosion. Bull Seismol Soc Am **91**(4): 753–759.

Savage B (2012). Seismic constraints on the water flux delivered to the deep Earth by subduction. Geology **40**(3): 235–238.

Brian Savage is currently a Professor of Geoscience at the University of Rhode Island (URI) in the Department of Geosciences, of which he is the Chair. He completed his Ph.D. at Caltech in 2004 with Prof. Helmberger as his primary thesis advisor. His work focuses on using seismic waveform data to image plate-scale continental-like structures to better understand the formation, deformation and stability of tectonic plates. He has also been the sole developer of the Seismic Analysis Code for over 18 years. His webpage can be found at https://web.uri.edu/geo/brian-savage/.

第 14 章 朝花夕拾：回忆唐·亨伯格

布赖恩·萨维奇
美国罗得岛大学，罗得岛州金斯顿校友大道 9 E，罗得岛 02879

引用： Savage B (2022). The lost and the found: Memories of Donald V. Helmberger. Earthq Sci 35(1): 51−53 doi: 10.1016/j.eqs.2022.01.006

　　我第一次接触唐·亨伯格（Don Helmberger）的工作是在大学二年级的一节地震学课上，当时包括我在内的几个学生要介绍格兰德（Grand）和亨伯格（Helmberger）发表在 1984 年的一项工作。这项工作超出了我的理解范围，但在我见识到了地震图的美感、追踪上地幔三重结构，以及它所揭示的地球的情况后，我大受震撼。在我在伯克利大学读本科期间，在道格·德雷格（Doug Dreger）博士［亨伯格（Helmberger）的学生］的指导下，我将地震数据进行数字化处理（Dreger and Savage, 1999），并正演模拟地震数据，这项工作大约用了两年时间，有一个学业导师［马克·理查兹（Mark Richards）博士］的帮助，他后来去了加州理工学院工作，还在莱恩·约翰逊（Lane Johnson）博士［唐（Don）在明尼苏达州的朋友］那里学习了几门课程。我将要走的路，尽管我还对它不太明晰，但已经在我面前展开，于是我只需要沿着它走下去就好。

　　在研究生院决定期间，我有机会参观了帕萨迪纳市的地震实验室。唐（Don）开着他的蓝色标致到伯班克机场接我。我猜他是多年前在欧洲买了这辆车，他也很喜欢这辆车。那天南加州下起了特大暴雨，淹没了高速公路(I-5)。因此，我们不得不走地面街道，开车去帕萨迪纳的路似乎永远也走不完。在某个时刻，我指着挡风玻璃和车顶的接缝处问唐（Don），"为什么那支笔卡在那里?"他回答道:"为了防止它漏水。"那支钢笔并没有起到作用，它不断地掉出来，挡风玻璃的水慢慢地漏到我的裤子上。但这并没有什么好担心的，因为从飞机到候机楼的短暂奔跑中，我已经浑身湿透了。我们最终到达了南马德楼，唐（Don）好心地把车停在了人行道下，让我跑进去，到二楼告诉他们我在这里，他去把车停好。

　　尽管如此，我还是决定去加州理工学院，1998 年，我作为研究生开始了与唐（Don）的合作。无论项目是什么，唐（Don）总是为我们在阅读地震图以及努力思考、扩展派生或者剪切拼接和推敲数据图［唐（Don）喜欢打印出来研究地震波形，而我通常把波形重新数字化后再进行研究］等方面提供帮助。他总是在那里指导我和我的研究生同学们如何完成复杂的研究：从基础工作到写作过程，再到论文不可避免地被审核"像前女友一样"退回。我和唐（Don）（Savage and Helmberger, 2001）写的第一篇论文是关于一艘俄罗斯潜艇的爆炸。我们得到的要求是对爆炸的规模进行定量测量，唐（Don）利用他在空军的关系得到了数据。他还勤奋地和我一起研究水下爆炸源的理论以及如何为数据建模。手稿在 4 个月后发出，我当时激动极了。

通常情况下，我要花上几个星期的时间用自己的设备从南加州新安装的区域网络中收集一组地震数据。利用局部和区域地震资料研究地壳和地幔结构。我会在数据中寻找奇怪之处。地震数据总是要特别小心地处理，因为它们的振幅和相位是我们试图再现的。我可以自由地查看有趣的响应，并尝试在没有唐（Don）的建议的情况下对它们进行建模。这是一个很好的学习经历，但建模方面总是让我迷茫，据我所知，有一种东西叫作"迷雾"：我试图抓住一些东西，真的是任何东西来改善实际数据和合成数据之间的契合度。这正是唐（Don）介入的地方，他提供了我需要的指导。

最终，我在苦苦挣扎的地震图上引起了唐（Don）的注意。谈话的开头通常是："嘿，这个看起来太棒了！你是谁来着？"我通常会配合他，告诉他我的名字。有一天我告诉他我叫皮特（Pete）。接下来的 6 个月里，唐（Don）一直叫我皮特（Pete）；我在地震实验室的咖啡杯上面就印着皮特（Pete），这个杯子在我毕业 10 年后坏了。在引起唐（Don）的注意之后，我们会研究数据，并思考可能的结构（我选择了研究结构而不是源）以及最能匹配相关数据的模型。

在早些年，当我们交谈时，我会问很多问题，但我从来没有得到多少回应。我问一个问题，唐（Don）要么盯着窗外，看着帕萨迪纳市北部美丽的山景，要么抬头盯着天花板。在他有机会回答第一个问题之前，我会先想一想然后又问了一个问题。有时候，我决定让唐（Don）慢慢思索。这种方法效果要好得多。我暗自思忖，或许每次我问问题，他都需要重启大脑以处理最新的问题。现在，我发现自己在办公室里对学生们做着类似的事情，专注地思考手头的问题以提供最好的指导。

最终，我和唐（Don）会创造出一个或者多个可能的解决方案，之后我们会讨论为什么这个解决方案起或者不起作用，唐（Don）总是在他的工程记事本上画画，并把坏了的笔扔在他的地图盒后面。我一直认为我的想法是不错且可行的。在我们漫长的会议之后，我会进行模拟（此时通常是 1D 或 2D 的），当然，首先是我的想法。最终我意识到我的想法是不可行的，于是我对唐（Don）的结构进行了运算。让我惊讶的是，当时（但不是现在）唐（Don）的结构总是很好。唐（Don）通过观察和建模大量的数据学到了很多东西，这帮助他得出了适当的回答。有时候，这种回答要花上一段时间，而且不止一种方式。

在我研究生学习的早期，唐（Don）带我去新墨西哥州（New Mexico）参加一个空军会议。他竭尽全力把我介绍给重要人物，指导我，并在最初那晚的社交活动中不断地请我喝啤酒；他在杰克逊霍尔的一次会议上也这么做了。当活动接近尾声时，他暗示我们应该去吃晚餐，"去有好吃的的地方"。我们在附近逛了一会儿，我主要是跟着唐（Don），最后在一家有炸海鲜的地方停了下来，我们每人点了一大盘，又点了一些啤酒。吃到一半时，唐（Don）脱口而出说："你让我吃了这么多东西，我老婆会找我麻烦的。"第二天一早，我几乎看不清唐（Don）在晨跑时从我下榻的酒店窗外飞奔而过的画面。

在研究生阶段的后期，我进行了一次横跨太平洋的长途考察。差不多在同一时间，唐（Don）给我讲了一个故事，讲的是他在斯克里普斯期间进行的一次航行考察。那可能是在 20 世纪 60 年代的某个时候，全球定位系统还没有出现，当时的航行是在阿留申群岛及其周围区域。在航行中，他们遇到了唐（Don）描述为狂风暴雨的一场风暴，在船员不知情的情况下，这艘科考船被风暴带到岛链的另一边。那时唐（Don）说他再也不会坐游轮了。他可能是想在我出发之前给我一些指导和建议，谢谢你，唐（Don）。他还是很和善地让我离开了一段时间，这是一段很好的经历，我也可以集中精力完成工作和论文。

从加州理工学院毕业后，我在 AGU 与唐（Don）在下午晚些时候的海报会议上即兴讨论起了一个非常奇怪的数据。当然，唐（Don）当时穿着他的皮夹克。我向他描述了这个问题，并在一些纸片的背面画出了地震图。我知道它们长什么样，因为我已经盯着它们看了很长时间，甚至可能好几个月了。唐（Don）快速地看了一眼，说："我们为什么要看地震记录？因为它们很漂亮"，他想了一会儿，然后给了我一些可以尝试的模型，包括他和以前的学生在几十年前尝试过的模型。唐（Don）再一次接近了可能的模型，但还是一如既往地给予我指导和支持。但这一次，唐（Don）的模型与我提出的模型是相似的（Savage, 2012）。

我和唐（Don）之间还有一次互动是我记忆犹新的，那是发生在新墨西哥州的一次空军会议上。我刚刚结束了关于一个成像项目的演讲，在其他与会者提出了几个问题后，唐（Don）开始一个接一个地问我关于这个方法的问题，比如我观察到了什么，以及我是否相信这个结果。这似乎是一如既往的"唐（Don）很感兴趣，这是个有趣的问题，我们继续讨论吧。"提问持续了 20 分钟左右，就好像我们回到了唐（Don）的办公室，和他一起研究数据集。演讲结束后，很多人问我是否喜欢第二次"口试"。唐（Don）总是问最难的问题，但在某种程度上，这是为了找到问题或者数据集的根源。

谢谢你，唐（Don）。当我在迷雾中跌跌撞撞摸索的时候，你总是在那里向我伸出一只向导之手，"在森林里的每一棵树上都系上了黄丝带"。

参 考 文 献

Dreger D and Savage B (1999). Aftershocks of the 1952 Kern County, California, earthquake sequence. Bull Seismol Soc Am **89**(4): 1094–1108.

Grand SP and Helmberger DV (1984). Upper mantle shear structure of North America. Geophys J Int **76**(2): 399–438.

Savage B and Helmberger DV (2001). Kursk explosion. Bull Seismol Soc Am **91**(4): 753–759.

Savage B (2012). Seismic constraints on the water flux delivered to the deep Earth by subduction. Geology **40**(3): 235–238.

　　布赖恩·萨维奇目前是罗得岛大学地球科学系的地球科学教授，同时也是该系的主任。2004 年，在主要论文导师亨伯格教授的指导下，他在加州理工学院完成了博士学位。他主要致力于利用地震波波形数据成像板块规模的大陆构造，以更好地了解板块构造的形成、变形和稳定性。18 年来，他还是"地震分析程序包"（Seismic Analysis Code)的唯一开发者。他的主页是 https://web.uri.edu/geo/brian-savage/。

Chapter 15. My seismology journey with Donald V. Helmberger

Shengji Wei [*]

Asian School of the Environment/Earth Observatory of Singapore Nanyang Technological University, Singapore 639798, Singapore

[*]**Correspondence:** shjwei@gmail.com; shjwei@ntu.edu.sg

Citation: Wei SJ (2022). My seismology journey with Donald V. Helmberger. Earthq Sci 35(1): 54−57 doi: 10.1016/j.eqs.2022.01.010

My journey on the wiggles with Don started from February 2008, when I got an opportunity to visit the Caltech Seismolab as a visiting PhD student, which was made possible via Dr. Sidao Ni's recommendation. A previous student of Don, Sidao was a professor at the School of Earth and Space Sciences (ESS) at the University of Science and Technology of China (USTC) at that time. Sidao offered the "Computational Seismology" class at USTC where I learned a lot about the modern developments in seismology. I also met Sidao many times to discuss a wide range of research topics, I believe it is a style he inherited from his experiences with Don and other professors in Seismolab.

My first time seeing Don was in the printing room of the Seismolab, where I shook his hand and say hi to him, he told me that you speak good English. I was quite shocked, as I was barely able to say a complete sentence with my Chinese accent. Later on, we were joking that Don's English had been brought down so much by his Chinese students that an international student can easily impress him with speaking English. I was also wondering, maybe the seismograms are the best language that Don communicated with his students.

My first project with Don was to look into the seismograms produced by the 2008 $M_W6.0$ Nevada earthquake, through which I learned how to understand the seismograms in his unique ways. The USArray had been translated to the mid-western US at the time of the earthquake, hence hundreds of stations recorded the earthquake including the permanent stations in the western US. I ran the Cut-And-Paste code (Zhu LP and Helmberger, 1996; Zhao LS and Helmberger, 1994) using these seismograms to get the moment tensor solution. As a beginner in waveform seismology aiming for a robust point source focal mechanism solution of the earthquake, I discarded lots of "bad" fits and was quite happy with the nice waveform fits using a 1D velocity model. After telling me that these nice Pnl fits were the multiples of the Moho reflection phases and depth phases, Don quickly shifted his interests to those waveforms that I discarded. He asked me to organize the waveforms in various ways, and a few weeks later, out of these discarded waveforms that were recorded by the stations along the northwestern coast, he identified multi-pathing phases that sampled the subducting Juan de Fuca slab. At that moment, the $M_W7.9$ Wenchuan earthquake occurred and my interest and time was completely absorbed by the large earthquake source study. Thankfully, Dr. Risheng Chu continued analyzing the multi-pathing observations and eventually got them published (Chu RS et al., 2012).

Time flew quickly to the end of my one-year visit, I started several projects with Don in these 12 months, but none of them finished. Before I went back to USTC to wrap up my thesis, I told Don that if he has a postdoc position for me, I will for sure come back. Fortunately, he did. Now I look back to this process as a faculty member, I can not appreciate enough Don's trust, as I had only published one paper in the Chinese Journal of Geophysics that he could not read at the moment he offered me the position. This experience also later on shaped my way to select postdoc and student candidates at NTU.

I went back to the Seismolab on September 16, 2009, for my dream job to continue working with Don as a postdoc, mostly on large earthquake kinematic source study. That was a hectic period of earthquake source study in the lab, several damaging earthquakes occurred during my postdoc time, including El Mayor Cucapah earthquake in 2010 (Wei SJ et al., 2011), New Zealand earthquakes in 2010 and 2011 (Zhan ZW et al., 2011), Tohoku-Oki earthquake in 2011 (Wei SJ et al., 2012), Wharton Basin earthquake in 2012 (Wei SJ et al., 2013a), Brawley earthquake sequence in 2012 (Wei SJ et al., 2013b, 2015) and Sea of Okhotsk earthquake in 2013 (Wei SJ et al., 2013b). In these studies, I continued learning from Don on how to breakdown the complex waveforms produced by these earthquakes to make more sense from the inversion and modeling results. I also learned to find and appreciate the clean paths for earthquake source study at as high frequency as I could. Figure 1 is one of such examples (modified from Wei SJ et al., 2015), through which I realized 3D velocity models may not work well and path calibration is frequency dependent, and we still have a lot to learn on the Earth structure. In these projects, I also greatly benefitted from collaborations with Jean-Philippe Avouac, Rob Graves, Eric Fielding, Ken Hudnut and many other colleagues and visitors at the Seismolab. Coffee hours in the lab were the place that I could hear and participate in the most genuine scientific discussions, where Hiroo most frequently provided materials on earthquakes and stimulated a related discussion but many times ended up with something else. I gradually realized these benefits as I continued my academic career as a faculty, and I believe that coffee hour makes the Caltech Seismolab an unparalleled place for geoscience research.

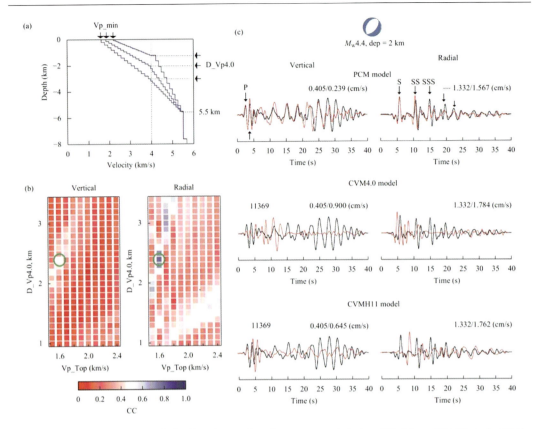

Fig. 1　Path calibration example for Brawley earthquake sequence study (modified from Wei SJ et al., 2015). (a) Representation of the parameterized velocity models. (b) Grid search result for the vertical and radial component. (c) 1Hz P-SV waveform (black) of the Mw4.4 calibration event and synthetics (red) calculated with the calibrated 1D model and 1D velocity models extracted from CVM4.0 (middle) and CVMH11.9 (bottom). Note the surface multiples and the surface waves in the data are well fitted by the synthetics.

Since I became a PI at the Earth Observatory of Singapore (EOS) and a faculty at NTU in 2014, the way that I work with my students and postdocs is deeply shaped by my experiences with Don. I like to meet frequently with my group members, trying to transfer as much as I know to them, but also learning from them. The idea of calibrating on the paths, cutting and pasting seismograms was further generalized to a Multiple Point Source MCMC-based inversion method (Shi QB et al., 2018); the high frequency waveform modeling/inversion experiences stimulated a project on trying to merge the gaps between back-projection and deterministic waveform analysis (Zeng HY et al., 2020).

In 2018, I learned that other places did not have a plan to arrange a retirement workshop for Don so I wrote a proposal to apply for some EOS internal grant for such a workshop. The workshop was held in August 2018, at the time that NTU implemented many new policies, including on the ways to use the approved budgets. With support from Kerry Sieh, who was the director of EOS and also a colleague of Don for many years at Caltech, we went through some key logistical difficulties and eventually made it happen. I also appreciate the great help from my secretary Linda Chua, this workshop would not happen without her detailed arrangements and encouragements. When everyone was in Singapore and I saw all the big smiles ((Figure 2), of course, some tears as well, and interesting and touching presentations, I felt that organizing the workshop is one of the most correct things that I have ever done.

Fig. 2　Helmberger academia family photo after the August, 2018 workshop in Nanyang Executive Center (NTU). Row 1 (left-to-right) Stephen Grand, Edward Garnero, John Vidale, Don Helmberger, Xiaodong Song, Charles Langston, Thorne Lay; Row 2, Ying Tan, Teh-Ru Alex Song, Ali Ozgun Konca, Zhongwen Zhan, Min Chen, Chen Ji, Sidao Ni, Brian Savage; Row 3, Xuhua Shi, Lianxing Wen, Daoyuan Sun, Justin Yen-Ting Ko, Voon Hui Lai; Liqing Jiao; Yongsheng Liu, Shengji Wei, Lupei Zhu; Row 4, Xin Wang, Yingyu Qi, Wardah Fadil, Muzli Muzli, Qibin Shi, Ping Tong, Xueyuan Huang, Farm Hui Jia, Shaolin Liu; Row 5, Hsin-Ying Yang; Jiayuan Yao, Hongyu Zeng, Weiwen Chen, Phyo Maung-Maung, Meng Chen, Chung-han Chan, Rishav Mallick, Priyamvada Nanjundiah.

Don's deep understanding and insights of waveform seismology do not fade away with his passing, instead, they become even more valuable in the era of big data. It is, however, also a great challenge to reconcile massive data processing and thorough digestion of the wiggles. At EOS, my research mostly focuses on SE Asia, where so many knowledge gaps exist, for instance, the Sagaing fault and Sumatran fault are similar to the San Andreas Fault, in terms of their potential large earthquakes and associated risks to huge population, but only a few tens of seismological papers have been published on these plate boundary type of faults in SE Asia. With usage of dense array and powerful computers, it is a great opportunity for modern seismology development in SE and hopefully, an extension of Don's legacy.

References

Chu RS, Schmandt B and Helmberger DV (2012). Juan de Fuca subduction zone from a mixture of tomography and waveform modeling. J Geophys Res: Solid Earth **117**(B3): B03304.

Shi QB, Wei SJ and Chen M (2018). An MCMC multiple point sources inversion scheme and its application to the 2016 Kumamoto M_w 6.2 earthquake. Geophysical Journal International **215**(2): 737–752.

Wei SJ, Fielding E, Leprince S, Sladen A, Avouac, JP, Helmberger D, Hauksson E, Chu RS, Simons M, Hudnut K, Herring T and Briggs R (2011). Superficial simplicity of the 2010 El Mayor-Cucapah earthquake of Baja California in Mexico. Nature Geoscience **4**(9): 615–618.

Wei SJ, Graves R, Helmberger D, Avouac JP and Jiang JL (2012). Sources of shaking and flooding during the Tohoku-Oki earthquake: a mixture of rupture styles. Earth Planet Sci Lett **333–334**: 91–100.

Wei SJ, Helmberger D and Avouac JP (2013a). Modeling the 2012 Wharton basin earthquakes off-Sumatra: Complete lithospheric failure. J Geophys Res: Solid Earth **118**(7): 3592–3609.

Wei SJ, Helmberger D, Zhan ZW and Graves R (2013b). Rupture complexity of the M_W 8.3 Sea of Okhotsk earthquake: Rapid triggering of complementary earthquakes? Geophys Res Lett **40**(19): 5034–5039.

Wei SJ, Avouac JP, Hudnut, KW, Donnellan A, Parker JW, Graves RW, Helmberger D, Fielding E, Liu Z, Cappa F and Eneva M (2015). The 2012 Brawley swarm triggered by injection-induced aseismic slip. Earth Planet Sci Lett **422**: 115–125.

Zeng HY, Wei SJ and Wu WB (2020). Sources of uncertainties and artefacts in back-projection results. Geophys J Int **220**(2): 876–891.

Zhan ZW, Jin BK, Wei SJ and Graves RW (2011). Coulomb stress change sensitivity due to variability in mainshock source models and receiving fault parameters: a case study of the 2010–201. Christchurch, New Zealand, earthquakes. Seismol Res Lett **82**(6): 800–814.

Zhao LS and Helmberger DV (1994). Source estimation from broadband regional seismograms. Bull Seismol Soc Am **84**(1): 91–104.

Zhu LP and Helmberger DV (1996). Advancement in source estimation techniques using broadband regional seismograms. Bull Seismol Soc Ame **86**(5): 1634–1641.

Shengji Wei is currently an associate professor at the Nanyang Technological University and a Principal Investigator at the Earth Observatory of Singapore. He was co-supervised by Prof. Helmberger from 2008.2 to 2009.2 during his visit to Caltech Seismolab and obtained his PhD from USTC in 2009. He then worked with Prof. Helmberger from 2009 – 2014 as a postdoc. His home page is: https://www.earthobservatory.sg/about-us/our-people/wei-shengji.

第 15 章　我和唐·亨伯格的地震学之旅

韦生吉

新加坡南洋理工大学，亚洲环境学院/地球观测中心

引用：　Wei SJ (2022). My seismology journey with Donald V. Helmberger. Earthq Sci 35(1): 54−57 doi: 10.1016/j.eqs.2022.01.010

　　我与唐（Don）的波形之旅始于 2008 年 2 月，当时在倪四道博士的推荐下，我有机会作为访问博士生到加州理工学院地震实验室进行访问。四道是唐（Don）以前的学生，当时是中国科学技术大学（USTC）地球和空间科学学院（ESS）的教授。四道在中国科学技术大学开设了"计算地震学"课程，我了解到了很多地震学的现代发展。我也多次和四道见面并且讨论广泛的研究课题，我相信这是他从与唐（Don）和其他教授在地震实验室的经历中继承下来的一种风格。

　　我第一次见到唐（Don）是在地震实验室的印刷室，我在那里和他握手打招呼，他告诉我我的英语说得很好。我很震惊，因为我用我的中国口音几乎说不出一个完整的句子。后来，我们开玩笑说唐（Don）的英语被他的中国学生拉低了许多，以至于一个国际学生说英语可以很容易地给他留下深刻印象。我还在想，也许地震图是唐（Don）与他的学生交流的最好的语言。

　　我与唐（Don）的第一个项目是研究 2008 年 Mw6.0 内华达地震产生的地震图，通过这个项目我学会了如何以他独特的方式理解地震图。在地震发生时，USArray 已经被转移到美国中西部,因此包括美国西部的永久台站在内的数百个台站记录了这次地震。我基于这些地震图运行了"剪切和粘贴"方法的代码（Zhu and Helmberger, 1996; Zhao and Helmberger, 1994）获得矩张量解。作为波形地震学的初学者，我的目标是获得地震的稳健点源震源机制解，我放弃了许多"糟糕"的拟合结果，并对使用一维速度模型得到的良好波形拟合感到非常满意。在告诉我这些漂亮的 Pnl 拟合是莫霍面反射相位和深度相位的组合后，唐（Don）很快将他的兴趣转移到了我舍弃的那些波形。他让我以不同方式整理这些波形，几周后，从西北海岸的台站记录的这些废弃波形中，他识别出了反应俯冲的胡安·德富卡板块的多路径震相。与此同时，Mw7.9 汶川大地震发生了，我的兴趣和时间完全被大震源研究所吸引。值得庆幸的是，储日升（Risheng Chu）博士继续分析了多路径观测结果并最终将其发表（Chu et. al., 2012）。

　　我一年的访问转瞬即逝，在这 12 个月里，我和唐（Don）开始了几个项目，但都没有完成。在我回到中国科学技术大学完成论文之前，我告诉唐（Don），如果他有适合我的博士后职位，我一定会回来的。幸运的是，他做到了。现在我作为一名教师回顾这一过程，我非常感激唐（Don）的信任，提供给我一个博士后职位，因为当时我只在

《地球物理学报》上发表了一篇他看不懂的论文。这段经历也造就了我后来在新加坡南洋理工大学选择博士后和学生的方式。

2009 年 9 月 16 日，为了我梦寐以求的工作，我回到地震实验室，作为一个博士后继续与唐（Don）工作，主要从事大地震的运动学研究。那是实验室震源研究的忙碌时期，在我博士后期间发生了几次破坏性地震，包括 2010 年的 El Mayor Cucapah 地震（Wei et al., 2011），2010 年和 2011 年的新西兰地震（Zhan et al., 2011），2011 年日本东北大地震（Wei et al., 2012），2012 年沃顿盆地地震（Wei et al., 2013a），2012 年布劳利地震序列（Wei et al., 2013b, 2015）和 2013 年鄂霍次克海地震（Wei et al., 2013b）。在这些研究中，我继续向唐（Don）学习如何分解这些地震产生的复杂波形，使反演和建模结果更加有意义。我还学会了在尽可能高的频率上为震源研究寻找和体会干净路径。图 1 就是这样的一个例子（修改自: Wei et al., 2015），通过这个例子我意识到三维速度模型可能无法起到很好的约束，路径校准依赖于频率，而且我们在地球结构方面还有很多需要学习的地方。在这些项目中，我也从与琼-菲利普·阿武阿克（Jean-Philippe Avouac）、罗布·格雷夫斯（Rob Graves）、埃里克·菲尔丁（Eric Fielding）、肯·赫德纳特（Ken Hudnut）以及地震实验室许多其他同事和访问学者的合作中受益匪浅。在实验室的咖啡时间，我可以听到并参与最真实的科学讨论，在这里博雄（Hiroo）最频繁地提供有关地震的材料并引发相关的讨论，但很多时候以其他内容结束。当我作为一名教师继续我的学术生涯时，我逐渐意识到这些好处，我相信咖啡时间使加州理工学院地震实验室成为一个无与伦比的地球科学研究场所。

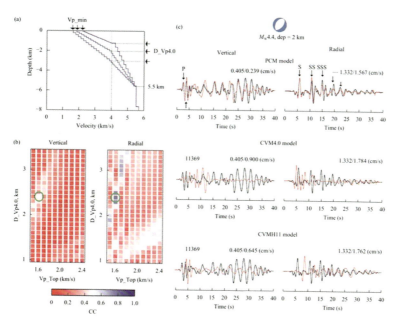

图 1　布劳利地震序列研究的路径校准例子（修改自: Wei et al., 2015）。（a）参数化的速度模型。（b）垂直和径向分量的网格搜索结果。（c）Mw4.4 校准事件的 1Hz P-SV 波形（黑色）和用校准后的 1D 模型、从 CVM4.0（中）以及 CVMH11.9（下）提取的 1D 模型计算的合成波形（红色）。注意数据中的多次表面波和表面波与合成波形拟合得非常好。

　　自从 2014 年我成为新加坡地球观测站 （EOS） 的 PI 和南洋理工大学的教师以来，我与学生和博士后的合作方式深深地受到了我与唐（Don）的经历的影响。我喜欢经常与我的小组成员见面，试着把我所知道的东西尽可能多地传授给他们，同时也向他们学习。路径校准、剪切和粘贴地震图的想法被进一步推广为基于多点源 MCMC 反演方法（Shi et al., 2018）；高频波形建模/反演经验激发了一个尝试合并反投影和确定性波形分析之间的空缺的项目（Zeng et. al., 2020）。

　　在 2018 年，我了解到其他地方没有为唐（Don）安排退休研讨会的计划，于是我写了一份提案，申请一些 EOS 内部拨款来资助这样的研讨会。研讨会于 2018 年 8 月举行，当时南洋理工大学实施许多新政策，包括如何使用已批准的预算。在 EOS 主任、唐（Don）在加州理工学院多年的同事克里·西（Kerry Sieh）的支持下，我们克服了一些关键的后勤困难并最终实现了这个目标。我也很感谢我的秘书琳达·周（Lind Chua）的大力帮助，没有她的精心安排和鼓励，这次研讨会是不可能举行的。当大家都在新加坡的时候，我看到了所有人灿烂的笑容（图 2），当然也有一些泪水，以及有趣和感人的演讲，我觉得组织研讨会是我做过的最正确的事情之一。

图 2　2018 年 8 月在南洋行政中心（南洋理工大学）举办的研讨会结束后，亨伯格（Helmberger）学术家庭合影。第一排（从左到右）斯蒂芬·格兰德（Stephen Grand），爱德华·加内罗（Edward Garnero），约翰·维达莱（John Vidale），唐·亨伯格（Don Helmberger），宋晓东（Xiaodong Song），查尔斯·兰斯顿（Charles Langston），索恩·莱（Thorne Lay）；第二排，谭英（Ying Tan），宋德儒（Teh-Ru Alex Song），阿里·孔贾（Ali Ozgun Konca），詹中文（Zhongwen Zhan），陈敏（Min Chen），纪晨（Chen Ji），倪四道（Sidao Ni），布赖恩·萨维奇（Brian Savage）；第三排，石许华（Xuhua Shi），温联星（Lianxing Wen），孙道远（Daoyuan Sun），郭彦廷（Justin Yen-Ting Ko），赖文慧（Voon Hui Lai），焦利青（Liqing Jiao），刘永生（Yongsheng Liu），韦生吉（Shengji Wei），朱露培（Lupei Zhu）；第四排，王新（Xin Wang），齐樱宇（Yingyu Qi），法迪勒（Wardah Fadil），木子李（Muzli），施其斌（Qibin Shi），童平（Ping Tong），黄雪源（Xueyuan Huang），范惠佳（Farm Hui Jia），刘少林（Shaolin Liu）；第五排，杨欣颖（Hsin-Ying Yang），姚家园（Jiayuan Yao），曾红玉（Hongyu Zeng），陈伟文（Weiwen Chen），朴蒙蒙（Phyo Maung-Maung），陈蒙（Meng Chen），詹中翰（Chung-han Chan），马利克（Rishav Mallick），普利亚（Priyamvada Nanjundiah）。

唐（Don）对波形地震学的深刻理解和洞察并没有随着他的去世而消失，反而在大数据时代变得更有价值。然而，协调海量数据处理和彻底洞悉波形也是一个巨大的挑战。在 EOS，我的研究主要集中在东南亚，那里存在许多知识空白，例如，就潜在的大地震和对大量人口的相关风险而言，实皆断层和苏门答腊断层与圣安德烈斯断层相似，但关于东南亚板块边界型断层的地震学论文仅有几十篇。通过布设密集台阵和使用功能强大的计算机，这对东南亚地区的现代地震学发展是一个巨大的机遇，也有望成为唐（Don）遗志的延伸。

参 考 文 献

Chu RS, Schmandt B and Helmberger DV (2012). Juan de Fuca subduction zone from a mixture of tomography and waveform modeling. J Geophys Res: Solid Earth **117**(B3): B03304.

Shi QB, Wei SJ and Chen M (2018). An MCMC multiple point sources inversion scheme and its application to the 2016 Kumamoto M_w 6.2 earthquake. Geophysical Journal International **215**(2): 737–752.

Wei SJ, Fielding E, Leprince S, Sladen A, Avouac, JP, Helmberger D, Hauksson E, Chu RS, Simons M, Hudnut K, Herring T and Briggs R (2011). Superficial simplicity of the 2010 El Mayor-Cucapah earthquake of Baja California in Mexico. Nature Geoscience **4**(9): 615–618.

Wei SJ, Graves R, Helmberger D, Avouac JP and Jiang JL (2012). Sources of shaking and flooding during the Tohoku-Oki earthquake: a mixture of rupture styles. Earth Planet Sci Lett **333–334**: 91–100.

Wei SJ, Helmberger D and Avouac JP (2013a). Modeling the 2012 Wharton basin earthquakes off-Sumatra: Complete lithospheric failure. J Geophys Res: Solid Earth **118**(7): 3592–3609.

Wei SJ, Helmberger D, Zhan ZW and Graves R (2013b). Rupture complexity of the M_W 8.3 Sea of Okhotsk earthquake: Rapid triggering of complementary earthquakes? Geophys Res Lett **40**(19): 5034–5039.

Wei SJ, Avouac JP, Hudnut, KW, Donnellan A, Parker JW, Graves RW, Helmberger D, Fielding E, Liu Z, Cappa F and Eneva M (2015). The 2012 Brawley swarm triggered by injection-induced aseismic slip. Earth Planet Sci Lett **422**: 115–125.

Zeng HY, Wei SJ and Wu WB (2020). Sources of uncertainties and artefacts in back-projection results. Geophys J Int **220**(2): 876–891.

Zhan ZW, Jin BK, Wei SJ and Graves RW (2011). Coulomb stress change sensitivity due to variability in mainshock source models and receiving fault parameters: a case study of the 2010–201. Christchurch, New Zealand, earthquakes. Seismol Res Lett **82**(6): 800–814.

Zhao LS and Helmberger DV (1994). Source estimation from broadband regional seismograms. Bull Seismol Soc Am **84**(1): 91–104.

Zhu LP and Helmberger DV (1996). Advancement in source estimation techniques using broadband regional seismograms. Bull Seismol Soc Ame **86**(5): 1634–1641.

韦生吉目前是南洋理工大学副教授，新加坡地球观测站责任研究员。他于 2008 年 2 月～2009 年 2 月访问加州理工学院地震实验室期间，由亨伯格（Helmberger）教授共同指导，并于 2009 年获得中国科学技术大学博士学位。2009~2014 年，他作为博士后与亨伯格（Helmberger）教授一起工作。他的主页是 https://www.earthobservatory.sg/about-us/our-people/wei-shengji。

Chapter 16. Deep diving with Donald V. Helmberger

Daoyuan Sun [*]

Laboratory of Seismology and Physics of Earth's Interior, School of Earth and Space Sciences, University of Science and Technology of China, Hefei 230026, China

[*]**Correspondence:** sdy2014@ustc.edu.cn

Citation: Sun DY (2022). Deep diving with Donald V. Helmberger. Earthq Sci 35(1): 58−60 doi: 10.1016/j.eqs.2022.01.008

It has been more than a year since Don left us. He left us so suddenly. We planned to have a phone call after he settled down at his new house. However, it never happened. Although he had some medical issues persistently in his last year, he had been so dedicated to science that he kept working on multiple papers about Earth's deep interior. Our unfinished paper is about to provide an alternative explanation of the anomalous SPdKS+SKPdS, which has been routinely used to image the Ultralow Velocity Zone (ULVZ). I am so grateful to Don that he brought me into the deep Earth, taught me how to read seismograms, and always inspired and supported me as my family.

Joining the Seismo Lab in 2003 as a graduate student, I started with a project with Tom Ahrens and Paul Asimow on both preheating shock wave experiments and thermodynamics calculation for MgO-FeO-SiO$_2$ system under lower mantle conditions. The Seismo Lab is a unique place in having an open environment and advocating interdisciplinary research. Students have to choose two distinct projects, a requirement for the PhD oral examination. That was how I came to know Don while I was looking for my second project.

Don knew that I was working on experiments for lower mantle studies, so he convinced me to work on an oral project of studying the African Large Low Shear Velocity Province (LLSVP, preferred to be called a "Superplume" at that time) following Sidao Ni's work. Because I had no experience in seismology at all, he had the greatest patience to show me all the literature in his magic filing cabinets and guide me to plot seismograms. To make sure I understood what he was talking about, he always wrote notes down and marked what's important on the plot of seismograms. I got lucky to pass the oral exam and the committee's suggestion was to take more classes of thermodynamics. However, like many other Chinese students who also worked with Tom and Don at the same time, we eventually gravitated to

Don as our thesis advisor. "Oral exam" plus the "coffee hour" provides two luxurious, intense, and career-impacting experiences for first-year graduate students. With the absolute freedom to explore and try different things, students not only learn broad knowledge, but also learn how to be creative and cooperative.

In 2004, a breakthrough in the study of the core-mantle boundary (CMB) was the discovery of the post-perovskite phase, which directly supports the D" discontinuity as a phase boundary. In fact, in an earlier paper in 1999, Igor Sidorin, Mike Gunris, and Don Helmberger (Sidorin et al., 1999) had proposed this idea from seismological observation, in which a solid-solid phase transition can explain well the observed topography of the D" discontinuity. Don was so excited by the new mineralogical evidence. Then, my first paper with Don (Sun et al., 2006) was to look at lower mantle triplication data sampling Central America and attempted to reexamine the idea of the phase boundary. We found that a phase boundary model can indeed explain the observed Scd phase. However, the existence of strong lateral variations suggests significant effects of presence of slab debris on phase changes. For most of my thesis work, I tried to include more data to provide a new mapping from the tomographic model to the lower mantle phase boundary by including chemical differences.

Working with Don was such an easy job. All you need to do is to feed him with a load of seismograms and wait for him to put different marks on the wiggles. Then you repeat this process the next day. Don was indeed an artist, drawing all kinds of lines on the seismograms and then telling you what happened in the Earth. Don was very creative and full of ideas for explaining observed seismic images. Once we made a 3D image of ULVZ (Figure 1). Don instantly linked the figure to the Alps (or the San Gabriel Mountain outside his window) and the Tour de France, which makes the interpretation of "Rolling hills on the core-mantle boundary" so easy and vivid (Sun et al., 2013). During the period when finite-frequency tomography and banana-donut kernel developed, Don was preparing a talk at SEDI. To explain what we thought about the banana-donut kernel, we simply split a banana and scanned it for the slides (Figure 2). "Seismology is fun", Don always said.

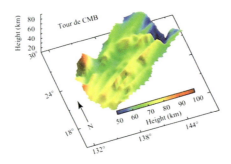

Fig. 1　A 3D image of ULVZ was named "Tour de CMB" by Don. The original manuscript including this figure was not accepted because of some oversimplified assumptions. Later, a revised manuscript (Sun et al., 2013) was published.

Fig. 2　Don gave a talk showing the banana-donut kernel using a "real" example at the 11th SEDI meeting held in Kunming, China in 2008.

The good collaboration between Don, Mike Gurnis, and Jennifer Jackson, as well as the cooperation among many students, made the Seismo Lab the best and most exciting place in the world to study the Earth's deep interior. It is not about having a product line. There were always some group discussion going on by exchanging ideas among seismology, geodynamics, and mineral physics, which were simply driven by the curiosity of understanding the D" layer, ULVZ, and LLSVP. Don always encouraged me from the beginning to participate in the discussion and express my ideas, which helped me a lot to better explain the wiggles to others and to gain a broad understanding of the deep Earth.

Don just loved the seismological data. He always tried to look at individual waveform records one by one. When you saw the huge paper-record drawers in his office, you would understand why he is the master of seismograms. He just knows every wiggle. Don had shown that all you need to be a first-class seismologist is a pencil, a ruler, and of course tons of paper (some may not like this idea). He taught me the best way to compare two seismograms by scanning one on a transparent film and overlaying them against the glass window. It definitely works!

Of course, Don had his idea on big data. When USArray data was available for the first time, Don was so excited, just like a child seeing boxes of candy. He urged me to plot every record. 700 stations! For the whole month, Don's office was all covered with plots on A4 papers from the table to the floor, with Don's notes and tape stitching the papers. During the whole month, he marked too many strange waveforms and found too many interesting structures, and we became lost in piles of seismograms. Then he said, "we need a colored map". That is where the idea of "multi-path detector" (Sun et al., 2009; Sun and Helmberger, 2011) comes from, which allows us to focus on a group of stations with the most waveform distortion and detect sharp edges in a systematic and efficient way. However, Don always went back to those stations with complicated waveforms and marked them with all kinds of notes again, whereupon the magic started again.

Don had a special gift for training students. He spent so much time with students and respected every student as an individual. There was always a line for students waiting to talk to him. I was once selected as one of the "night owls" in the division, so it was unlikely that Don would find me in the office in the morning. However, he was very patient and never complained. But I did see his "See me" notes on my computer screen almost every day (Figure 3). Only after I graduated did I realize that this was his way of pushing me forward, but in a gentle, motivating, and caring way.

Fig. 3　Don's "See me" notes. Only a small portion of the notes is shown. The left is the lecture notes from Don's "Advanced Seismology" class showing a Cagniard path.

After I graduated from Caltech in 2009, I went to the DTM, Carnegie Institution of Science, and then the University of Southern California (USC) as a postdoc. We made phone calls regularly and worked on different papers (Sun DY et al., 2010; Sun DY and Helmberger, 2011). During this time, we were quite interested in the SPdKS+SKPdS phase to study the structure of ULVZ. We found that Generalized Ray Theory (GRT) code and the old finite-difference (FD) code is not ideal for this problem. Don encouraged me to spend time rewriting the finite-difference code. Subsequently, Dunzhu Li further refined source excitation and out-of-plane geometric spreading correction and implemented the code on the GPU (Li DZ et al., 2014). The two-dimensional FD code has been widely used among different groups for both global and regional small-scale studies. Don is the pioneer in using the GRT to study the deep Earth. He knew all the details of the original F77 code. Whenever I wanted to modify the code and got lost in multiple "GOTO" statements, Don could clearly point out the problems I was encountering. Don also liked to promote new numerical codes, such as FD and SPECFEM. In particular, we later realized that the 3D effect is so important and the original GRT code has limits. However, the GRT code was still Don's favorite. After taking Don's "Advanced Seismology" class five times, I do realize that the GRT is the key to understanding "waveform modelling", where each wiggle is related to a specific ray. Don always told me that "modelling is not about fitting the data exactly". Instead, you must understand how the wave propagates and what is the sensitivity of the model parameter. "Data never lie".

When I was at USC, I started working with Meghan Miller on the shallow mantle. Since I still lived in Pasadena and Meghan Miller also had a visiting office in the Seismo Lab, I always stayed at Caltech on Fridays and weekends. Don had shown great interest in our work and had continued to offer great insights. He always rated my work "five stars" and telling me "what a brilliant idea", which gave me a lot of confidence. In 2014, I moved back to China and had a faculty position at the University of Science and Technology of China. Over the phone, Don told me so many things, big and small, about surviving in academia. But the most important thing is to "keep doing good science", Don used to say. He was so happy about every little achievement I had made.

Don is the most modest guy I have ever met. He always put his students first. He always inspired and took good care of his students and the people around him. He not only trained me to be a seismologist, but also mentored me in many different aspects of science and life. Don always said, "Earth is so complicated", "After I die, I prefer to go to the deep Earth and see what the hell is going on there". We know that Don is definitely up in heaven, taking care of everyone as he always does. My students and I will keep working on the deep Earth and keep studying the wiggles that we know will make Don happy and proud.

References

Li DZ, Helmberger D, Clayton RW and Sun DY (2014). Global synthetic seismograms using a 2-D finite-difference method. Geophys J Int **197**(2): 1166–1183.

Sidorin I, Gurnis M and Helmberger DV (1999). Evidence for a ubiquitous seismic discontinuity at the base of the mantle. Science **286**(5443): 1326–1331.

Sun DY, Song TRA and Helmberger D (2006). Complexity of D″ in the presence of slab-debris and phase changes. Geophys Res Lett **33**(12): L12S07.

Sun DY, Helmberger D, Ni SD and Bower D (2009). Direct measures of lateral velocity variation in the deep Earth. J Geophys Res: Solid Earth **114**(B5): B05303.

Sun DY, Helmberger D and Gurnis M (2010). A narrow, mid-mantle plume below Southern Africa. Geophys Res Lett **37**(9): L09302.

Sun DY and Helmberger D (2011). Upper-mantle structures beneath USArray derived from waveform complexity. Geophys J Int **184**(1): 416–438.

Sun DY, Helmberger DV, Jackson JM, Clayton RW and Bower DJ (2013). Rolling hills on the core-mantle boundary. Earth Planet Sci Lett **361**: 333–342.

Daoyuan Sun, professor at the University of Science and Technology of China. He received his bachelor's degree in solid geophysics from the University of Science and Technology of China in 2000. In 2009, he got his Ph.D. degree from Caltech under the supervision of Professor Don Helmberger. His doctoral dissertation was entitled "Seismic Structure of the Lower Mantle". After graduation, he conducted postdoctoral research at the Department of Terrestrial Magnetism of the Carnegie Institution of Washington (Carnegie Postdoctoral Fellow) from 2010 to 2011 and the Department of Earth Sciences of the University of Southern California from 2012 to 2014. His research focuses on imaging the deep interior of the Earth, seismic wave propagation theory and computation, and the interior of other planets and the moon. He serves as the editor of the GRL at present.

第 16 章　跟随唐(Don)悠游于地球深处

孙道远

中国科学技术大学，地球和空间科学学院，地震学与地球内部物理实验室，安徽合肥

引用：Sun DY (2022). Deep diving with Donald V. Helmberger. Earthq Sci 35(1): 58–60 doi: 10.1016/j.eqs.2022.01.008

唐（Don）已经离开我们一年多了，一切是如此突然。我本打算等他在新房子安顿好后打个电话给他，然而，这将永远不会发生。尽管唐（Don）在生命的最后一年里有些疾病，他仍旧致力于科学工作并撰写多篇有关地球深部的论文。我们未完成的论文提供了通常用于对超低速区（ULVZ）进行成像的异常 SPdKS+SKPdS 震相的另一种解释。我非常感谢唐（Don）将我领进地球深处的世界，教我看地震图，并像家人一样一直激励和支持着我。

2003 年我作为研究生加入了地震实验室，在汤姆·阿伦斯（Tom Ahrens）和保尔·阿西莫（Paul Asimow）指导下开展了一个在下地幔条件下 MgO-FeO-SiO$_2$ 系统的预加热冲击波实验和热力学计算的项目。地震实验室的独特性体现在其拥有着开放的氛围并且提倡跨学科研究。这里的博士生资格考试需要选择两个不同的课题，也就是在寻找第二个课题的时候我认识了唐（Don）。

唐（Don）知道我通过实验研究下地幔，所以他说服我做的课题是接着倪四道的工作继续研究非洲大尺度剪切波低速体（LLSVP，当时也被称为"超级地幔柱"）。由于我完全没有地震学背景，他非常耐心地展示给我他那奇妙的文件柜里的文献，并指导我绘制地震图。为了确保我能跟上他在说什么，他总是帮我写下来，并在地震图上标出重要的内容。我很幸运地通过了资格考试，委员会的建议是多修些热力学课程。然而，像其他许多同时选了汤姆（Tom）和唐（Don）的中国学生一样，唐（Don）最终成为了我们的论文指导老师。"资格考试"加上"咖啡时间"为一年级研究生提供了奢侈、高强度且受益终身的经历。这里的学生完全拥有探索和尝试不同事物的自由，不仅可以学习广泛的知识，还可以学习如何变得有创造力和具有合作精神。

2004 年，后钙钛矿相的发现是研究核幔边界（CMB）研究的一大突破，这也直接支持了 D″不连续面是一个相变界面的观点。事实上，在此前 1999 年发表的一篇论文中，伊戈尔·西多林（Igor Sidorin）、迈克·歌尼斯（Mike Gurnis）和唐·亨伯格（Don Helmberger）（Sidorin et al.，1999）提出了这一想法，认为固态相变可以很好地解释地震学观测到的 D″不连续面的起伏。唐（Don）为新的矿物学证据而激动不已。于是，我与唐（Don）的第一篇论文（Sun et al.，2006）就是研究中美洲下地幔三重震相的数据，

并试图重新审视相变界面对应 D″不连续面的想法。我们发现相变界面模型确实可以解释观测到的 Scd 震相。然而，其强烈的横向变化表明俯冲板片残留的存在剧烈影响了相变过程。我的博士论文中大部分内容则是试图通过引入化学差异，利用更多数据建立从层析成像模型到下地幔相变界面起伏的新映射关系。

与唐（Don）一起工作是如此"轻松"。你只需要给他提供大量的地震图，然后等着他在上面做上不同的标记，然后第二天重复这个步骤。唐（Don）绝对是个艺术家，他在地震图上画出各种各样的线条然后告诉你地球内部发生了什么。唐（Don）富有创造力，对于解释观测到的地震学图像充满灵感。有一次我们得到一幅 ULVZ 的三维图像（图1），唐（Don）马上从这幅图联想到阿尔卑斯山（或窗外的圣加布里埃尔山）和环法自行车赛道，这使得解释"核幔边界上的起伏的山丘"瞬间变得轻松和生动（Sun et al.，2013）。在有限频层析成像和香蕉-甜甜圈敏感核理论出现时，唐（Don）正在准备在一个 SEDI 演讲。为了更好地解释我们对香蕉-甜甜圈敏感核的认识，我们真的切开并扫描一根香蕉来制作幻灯片（图2）。"地震学很好玩"，唐（Don）总是这样说。

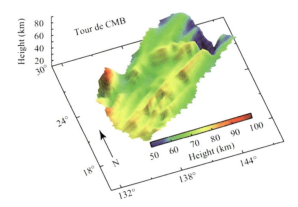

图1　ULVZ 的 3D 图像被唐（Don）命名为"Tour de CMB"。由于有一些过于简单的假设，包括该图在内的原始手稿未被接收。后来，修订稿（Sun, 2013）在 2013 年出版。

图2　唐(Don)于 2008 年在中国昆明举行的第 11 届 SEDI 会议上用"真实"示例展示了香蕉-甜甜圈敏感核。

唐（Don）、迈克·歌尼斯（Mike Gurnis）和珍妮弗·杰克逊（Jennifer Jackson）之间的良好合作，以及许多学生间的合作，使地震实验室成为了世界上研究地球深部的最好和最激动人心的地方。然而这里并不只是一个生产线。地震学、地球动力学和矿物物理学之间的交叉碰撞使得讨论不断地激发出火花，而这一切仅仅是出于对 D″层、ULVZ 和 LLSVP 的好奇。唐（Don）从一开始就一直鼓励我参与讨论并发表观点，让我可以更好地向他人解释地震图并增加我对地球深处的了解。

唐（Don）喜欢地震数据，他总是尝试逐个查看单道波形记录。当你亲眼看到他办公室里装满纸质地震图的巨大抽屉时，你就会理解为什么他被称为地震图大师。他了解地震图中的每一个波形。你可以从唐（Don）身上看到，要成为一流的地震学家，你只需要一支铅笔、一把尺子，当然再加上成吨的白纸（有些人可能不喜欢这个做法）。他传授给我比较两组地震图的最佳方法，就是把其中一组扫描到透明胶片上再将它们叠在玻璃窗上。这方法绝对好用！

当然，唐（Don）对大数据也有自己的看法。USArray 数据公开的第一时间，唐（Don）兴奋得像一个孩子看到糖果盒一样。他催我赶紧把每条记录画出来。700 个台站啊！整整一个月，唐（Don）的办公室从桌子到地板都被画着波形的 A4 纸堆满，纸被胶带粘着，并布满他的笔记。一整个月，他标记了太多异常的波形，发现了太多有趣的结构，我们渐渐迷失在成堆的地震图中。然后他说，"我们需要一张彩图"。这就是"多路径检测器"（Sun et al., 2009; Sun and Helmberger, 2011）的想法的由来，它使我们能专注于波形变化最剧烈的一组台站，并系统地有效检测尖锐边界。然后，唐（Don）又总是回归到那些波形复杂的台站，再次用各种记号标记它们，于是"魔法"又开始了。

唐（Don）有带学生的特殊天赋。他花很多时间和学生在一起，并且尊重每个学生，总有学生等着和他说话。我曾经被选为系里的"夜猫子"之一，所以早上唐（Don）经常在办公室找不到我。然而，他非常有耐心并且从不埋怨。我几乎每天都能在我的电脑屏幕上看到他的"来找我"的便条（图 3）。当我毕业后，我才意识到这是他鞭策我的方式，但是以一种温和、激励和关怀的方式。

图 3　唐（Don）的"来找我"便条。只展示了一小部分。左边是唐（Don）的《高级地震学》课程中展示卡尼亚尔路径（Cagniard path）的讲义。

2009 年从加州理工学院毕业后，我先后在卡内基科学研究所地球磁场系和南加州大学进行博士后研究。唐（Don）和我仍定期通电话并继续合作（Sun et al., 2010; Sun and Helmberger, 2011）。此间，我们对 SPdKS+SKPdS 震相非常感兴趣，因此用它来研究 ULVZ 的结构。我们发现广义射线理论（GRT）的代码和旧版的有限差分（FD）代码在这个问题上的效果并不理想。唐（Don）鼓励我花时间重写有限差分代码。随后，李墩柱改进了震源激发和大圆面外几何扩散校正，并实现了 GPU 版本的代码（Li et al., 2014）。该二维 FD 代码已在不同研究组中广泛使用，用于全球和区域小尺度研究。唐（Don）是使用 GRT 研究地球深部的先驱。他知道原始 F77 代码的所有细节。每当我想修改代码但迷失在多重"GOTO"语句中时，唐（Don）都可以马上指出我遇到的问题。唐（Don）同样喜欢推广新的数值计算代码，例如 FD 和 SPECFEM。尽管在后来工作中，我们意识到 GRT 代码的局限性，3D 效应不能被忽略。然而，GRT 代码仍然是唐（Don）的最爱。在听了五遍唐（Don）的《高级地震学》课程后，我终于意识到 GRT 是理解"波形模拟"的关键：每个波形都与特定的射线相关。唐（Don）总是告诉我，"波形模拟并非是精准拟合数据"。更重要的是去了解波的传播方式以及对模型参数的敏感性。"数据从不撒谎"。

我在南加州大学做博士后时和梅根·米勒（Meghan Miller）一起研究浅部地幔。当时我仍然住在帕萨迪纳，且梅根·米勒（Meghan Miller）在加州理工学院的地震实验室也有一间访问办公室，因此我在周五和周末总是待在那 。唐（Don）对我们的工作表现出极大的兴趣，并持续提供很棒的建议。他总是给我的工作打"五颗星"，并告诉我这是"多么棒的想法"，这也给了我很大的信心。2014 年，我回到中国，在中国科学技术大学任职。在电话里，唐（Don）提点我很多关于如何在学术界生存的大大小小的事情，但最重要的是"坚持做好的科学"。他对我取得的每一个小成就都很高兴。

唐（Don）是我见过的最谦虚的人。他总是把学生放在第一位，鼓励并照顾他的学生和他身边的人。他不仅将我培养成一名地震学家，还在科学和生活的许多不同方面指导我。唐（Don）总说，"地球好复杂啊"，"我死后，我想去地球深处看看到底是怎么回事"。我想，唐（Don）一定是去了天堂，像生前一样关照着每个人。我和我的学生将继续研究地球深部，并继续研究地震图上的波形，我们知道唐（Don）会为此感到高兴和自豪的。

参 考 文 献

Li DZ, Helmberger D, Clayton RW and Sun DY (2014). Global synthetic seismograms using a 2-D finite-difference method. Geophys J Int **197**(2): 1166–1183.

Sidorin I, Gurnis M and Helmberger DV (1999). Evidence for a ubiquitous seismic discontinuity at the base of the mantle. Science **286**(5443): 1326–1331.

Sun DY, Song TRA and Helmberger D (2006). Complexity of D″ in the presence of slab-debris and phase changes. Geophys Res Lett **33**(12): L12S07.

Sun DY, Helmberger D, Ni SD and Bower D (2009). Direct measures of lateral velocity variation in the deep Earth. J Geophys Res: Solid Earth **114**(B5): B05303.

Sun DY, Helmberger D and Gurnis M (2010). A narrow, mid-mantle plume below Southern Africa. Geophys Res Lett **37**(9): L09302.

Sun DY and Helmberger D (2011). Upper-mantle structures beneath USArray derived from waveform complexity. Geophys J Int **184**(1): 416–438.

Sun DY, Helmberger DV, Jackson JM, Clayton RW and Bower DJ (2013). Rolling hills on the core-mantle boundary. Earth Planet Sci Lett **361**: 333–342.

孙道远，中国科学技术大学教授、博士生导师。2000 年获中国科学技术大学固体地球物理学士学位，2009 年获加州理工学院博士学位。博士期间师从唐·亨伯格教授，博士论文题目为"下地幔地震结构"。2010~2011 年和 2012~2014 年先后于华盛顿卡内基学院地球磁场系（卡内基博士后）和南加州大学地球科学进行博士后研究。主要从事地球深部地震学结构成像、地震波传播理论和计算、其他行星及月球内部结构等方面的研究。现为国际期刊 GRL 主编。

Chapter 17. A grand master of seismology and mentoring

Zhongwen Zhan [*]

Seismological Laboratory, California Institute of Technology, Pasadena, CA 91125, USA

[*]**Correspondence:** zwzhan@caltech.edu

Zhan ZW (2022). A grand master of seismology and mentoring. Earthq Sci 35(1): 61−62 doi: 10.1016/j.eqs.2022.01.011

I joined Don Helmberger's group in the summer of 2008, after getting a Master's degree in China from Sidao Ni, another graduate student of Don's. I was very excited, because Don has a giant academic family tree and I thought I would become Don's last student, which is quite an honor in the Chinese culture, so-called the "final apprentice". I was wrong! Don had another seven students after me and the final apprentice honor went to Voon-Hui Lai. Over Don's long career, he had scores of students, many of whom are now big names in academia, especially in the United States and in China, because Don mentored a number of Chinese students.

I often wonder how Don could be so successful in training students and obviously I could not figure it out. But emotionally, one Chinese word often comes to my mind, that is "Shi Fu". It may translate to "mentor", but I am not sure that captures it very well. It has two characters, Shi and Fu, both very simple. Shi means teacher. Don was of course a great teacher. Well, I do not necessarily mean the Advanced Seismology class that I had to take three times to understand. In fact, after returning to the Caltech Seismo Lab in 2015, I co-taught the class a few times with Don and had to substantially update the materials. But Don taught us what maybe the most important thing in seismology: to love the wiggles. I am sure all his students had the experience of printing pages and pages of seismograms and looking at them one by one in Don's office (e.g., Figure 1). Don absolutely loved them. Whenever I did not finish what I promised to do, I would just bring seismograms and Don would not remember to ask about the actual work. One of the most important tools to learn initially was "pssac" or "pssac2", developed by previous students in Don's group, to plot seismograms beautifully with GMT. Fortunately, I learned those tools with Sidao in China already so the transition into Don's group was not too difficult.

Fig. 1   Don Helmberger and the author reading seismograms together.

The second character in "Shi Fu" is "Fu". "Fu" means father and I think it is appropriate here because Don's students all respect and love him from the bottom of their hearts. Everyone probably has a different reason. For me, Don gave me so much trust and support to explore, more than what I feel I deserved. Even for the topics that he was not particularly interested in, he would still try his best to support me. My Master's thesis was about ambient noise correlations, and Don could not care less about seismic noise. But instead of trying to convince me to stop working on noise, he put a lot of time to help me write my first paper in seismology about retrieving body waves from noise (Zhan ZW et al., 2010). Later Don suggested that I use ambient noise correlations to calibrate path effects and study earthquakes better (Zhan ZW et al., 2011), as a compromise of our research interests, which eventually moved me out of noise to several real earthquake projects (e.g., Zhan ZW et al., 2012, 2014a, b). However, Don's attempt to guide me into deep Earth seismic modeling never went too far, partially because he was never very insistent. The hardest push you can expect from Don is a small sticker note on your screen that only has three words: "See me, Don". On the other hand, whenever I talked to Don, I felt more confident, lifted, and on the edge of discovering something important from the wiggles so I wanted to work hard on the projects. This was even true in that summer of 2008, when my English was much worse. Don seemed to have the magic power to communicate with me with no problem. In fact, I think Don's amazing skills with students was probably key to his long productive career, even after he could not play with data directly on next generation computers. Don always tried as much as he could to help the careers of his students and kept the connections going for years, sometimes decades. When I returned to the Seismo Lab in 2015 as a faculty member, he introduced me to many external funding opportunities, and we wrote several proposals together. In fact, the moment-tensor paper from the Air Force project Don and I co-PI-ed is about to be published (Jia Z et al., 2022). Maybe it is the last paper of Don's.

　　Don was a great teacher and mentor, but he cared and gave more love to his students than he had to, and we loved him back. In some Kungfu movies they translate 师父 to "Master". Certainly, Don was a grand master of seismology and at the same time, a grand master of mentoring. I will always remember him, miss him, and my time with him will keep inspiring myself to be a better mentor in the future.

References

Jia Z, Zhan Z and Helmberger DV (2022). Bayesian differential moment tensor inversion: theory and application to the North Korea nuclear tests. Earth ArXiv, doi: 10.31223/X5TH01

Zhan ZW, Ni SD, Helmberger DV and Clayton RW (2010). Retrieval of Moho-reflected shear wave arrivals from ambient seismic noise. Geophys J Int **182**(1): 408–420.

Zhan ZW, Wei SJ, Ni SD and Helmberger D (2011). Earthquake centroid locations using calibration from ambient seismic noise. Bull Seismol Soc Am **101**(3): 1438–1445.

Zhan ZW, Helmberger D, Simons M, Kanamori H, Wu WB, Cubas N, Duputel Z, Chu RS, Tsai VC, Avouac JP, Hudnut KW, Ni SD, Hetland E and Culaciati FHO (2012). Anomalously steep dips of earthquakes in the 2011 Tohoku-Oki source region and possible explanations. Earth Planet Sci Lett **353–354**: 121–133.

Zhan ZW, Kanamori H, Tsai VC, Helmberger DV and Wei SJ (2014a). Rupture complexity of the 1994 Bolivia and 2013 Sea of Okhotsk deep earthquakes. Earth Planet Sci Lett **385**: 89–96.

Zhan ZW, Helmberger DV, Kanamori H and Shearer PM (2014b). Supershear rupture in a M_w 6.7 aftershock of the 2013 Sea of Okhotsk earthquake. Science **345**(6193): 204–207.

　　Zhongwen Zhan is currently Professor of Geophysics at the Seismological Laboratory, California Institute of Technology. He completed his PhD at Caltech in 2013 with Prof. Helmberger and returned to Caltech as Assistant Professor in 2015 after two years of post-doctoral research at the Scripps Institution of Oceanography, University of California, San Diego. He is a recipient of the Keiiti Aki Young Scientist Award and the Macelwane Medal from the American Geophysical Union and is a Fellow of the AGU.

第 17 章　伟大的地震学家和学术导师

詹中文

美国加州理工学院地震实验室

引用：Zhan ZW (2022). A grand master of seismology and mentoring. Earthq Sci 35(1): 61–62 doi: 10.1016/j.eqs.2022.01.011

　　我在 2008 年夏天加入了唐·亨伯格（Don Helmberger）的研究组，此前我在中国从唐（Don）的另一名研究生倪四道老师那里得了硕士学位。我十分激动，因为唐（Don）桃李满天下，我想我将成为他的最后一个学生，这在中国文化中是一个相当大的荣誉，被称为"关门弟子"。但我错了！唐（Don）在我之后还有另外七名学生，最终荣誉归于赖文慧（Voon Hui Lai）。在唐（Don）的漫长学术生涯中，他培养了大量学生，其中许多人现在是学术界的大人物，特别是在美国和中国，因为唐（Don）也指导了许多中国学生。

　　我经常想知道唐（Don）如何能够如此成功地培养学生，显然我无法弄清楚。但从情感上，我经常想到一个中文词，那就是"师父"，在英文中它可能翻译为"导师"，但我不确定这是否能很好地表达这个词的含义。它有两个字，"师"和"父"，都非常简单，"师"是老师的意思。唐（Don）当然是一个伟大的老师。好吧，我不是特指我必须听三遍才能理解的高等地震学课程。事实上，在 2015 年回到加州理工学院地震实验室后，我与唐（Don）共同教授了几次课程，并不得不大幅更新课程材料。但唐（Don）教会了我们地震学中最重要的事情：热爱波形。我相信他的所有学生有这样的经历：打印出一页又一页的地震图并在唐（Don）的办公室一张一张地查看（如图 1）。唐（Don）绝对喜欢它们。每当我没有完成我承诺要完成的工作时，我就会把地震图带来，而唐（Don）往往会忘记问我实际工作。最初要学习的最重要的工具之一是"pssac"或"pssac2"，这是由唐（Don）研究组以前的学生开发的，用于在 GMT 里绘制漂亮的地震图。幸运的是，我在中国的时候就已经和倪四道学习了这些工具，所以过渡到唐（Don）的研究组并不困难。

　　"师父"的第二个字是"父"，"父"是父亲的意思，我觉得用在这里很合适，因为唐（Don）的学生们都从心底里尊敬和爱戴他。每个人可能都有不同的原因。对我来说，唐（Don）给了我如此多的信任和支持去探索，比我觉得我应得的多得多。即便是他并不特别感兴趣的话题，他还是会尽力支持我。我的硕士论文是关于背景噪声互相关的，而唐（Don）对地震噪声丝毫不关心。但他并没有试图说服我停止研究噪声，而是投入大量时间帮助我写了第一篇关于从背景噪声中提取体波的地震学论文（Zhan et al.,

2010）。后来唐（Don）建议我用背景噪声的互相关来校准路径效应，并更好地研究地震（Zhan et al., 2011），作为我们研究兴趣的折中，这最终使我把注意力从噪声中转移出来，参加了几个天然地震项目（例如 Zhan et al., 2012，2014a，2014b）。然而，唐（Don）试图引导我进入地球深部地震建模的尝试并没有走得太远，部分原因是他从来没有非常坚持。你可以从唐（Don）那里获得的最强的催促是你屏幕上的一个小贴纸，只有三个字："See me, Don（来找我，唐）"。另一方面，每当我与唐（Don）交谈的时候，我都会感觉更加自信、更加振奋，并感到几乎就能从波形的起伏中获得重要发现，这使我想在这些项目上努力工作。甚至在 2008 年的那个夏天也是如此，当时我的英语要差得多，而唐（Don）似乎拥有可以毫无障碍地与我交流的魔力。事实上，我认为唐（Don）在学生培养方面的惊人能力可能是他长期高效的学术生涯的关键，即使他无法直接在下一代计算机上处理数据。唐（Don）总是尽其所能地为他学生的职业生涯提供帮助并持续数年甚至数十年保持联系。当我在 2015 年作为教员回到地震实验室时，他向我介绍了许多外部资助的机会，我们一起写了几个提案。事实上，唐（Don）和我共同负责的来自空军项目的矩张量论文即将发表（Jia et al., 2022）。也许这是唐（Don）的最后一篇论文。

图 1　唐·亨伯格（Don Helmberger）和作者在一起看地震图

唐（Don）是一位伟大的教师和导师，但他对学生的关心和付出的爱远远超过了他作为老师所必需的，而我们也爱他。在一些功夫电影中，人们把"师父"翻译成"大师"。当然，唐（Don）是一位地震学的大师，同样也是一位善于指导的大师。我将永远记住他，怀念他，和他共度的那段时光将不断激励我自己在未来成为更好的导师。

参 考 文 献

Jia Z, Zhan Z and Helmberger DV (2022). Bayesian differential moment tensor inversion: theory and application to the North Korea nuclear tests. Earth ArXiv, doi: 10.31223/X5TH01

Zhan ZW, Ni SD, Helmberger DV and Clayton RW (2010). Retrieval of Moho-reflected shear wave arrivals from ambient seismic noise. Geophys J Int **182**(1): 408–420.

Zhan ZW, Wei SJ, Ni SD and Helmberger D (2011). Earthquake centroid locations using calibration from ambient seismic noise. Bull Seismol Soc Am **101**(3): 1438–1445.

Zhan ZW, Helmberger D, Simons M, Kanamori H, Wu WB, Cubas N, Duputel Z, Chu RS, Tsai VC, Avouac JP, Hudnut KW, Ni SD, Hetland E and Culaciati FHO (2012). Anomalously steep dips of earthquakes in the 2011 Tohoku-Oki source region and possible explanations. Earth Planet Sci Lett **353–354**: 121–133.

Zhan ZW, Kanamori H, Tsai VC, Helmberger DV and Wei SJ (2014a). Rupture complexity of the 1994 Bolivia and 2013 Sea of Okhotsk deep earthquakes. Earth Planet Sci Lett **385**: 89–96.

Zhan ZW, Helmberger DV, Kanamori H and Shearer PM (2014b). Supershear rupture in a M_w 6.7 aftershock of the 2013 Sea of Okhotsk earthquake. Science **345**(6193): 204–207.

　　詹中文目前是加州理工学院地震学实验室的地球物理学教授。他于 2013 年在加州理工学院跟随亨伯格教授完成博士学位，在加州大学圣迭戈分校斯克里普斯海洋研究所进行了两年的博士后研究后，于 2015 年回到加州理工学院担任助理教授。他是美国地球物理联合会安艺敬一青年科学家奖和迈克尔文奖章获得者，同时也是美国地球物理联合会会士。

Chapter 18. Exploring Earth's boundaries with Donald V. Helmberger

Voon Hui Lai [*]

Research School of Earth Sciences, The Australian National University, ACT 2601, Australia

[*]**Correspondence:** voonhui.lai@anu.edu.au

Citation: Lai VH (2022). Exploring Earth's boundaries with Donald V. Helmberger. Earthq Sci 35(1): 63−66
doi: 10.1016/j.eqs.2022.01.014

Seismic waveform modeling is one of the most powerful tools for understanding Earth's structure, since it allows waveforms to be quantitatively predicted using physical source representations and a velocity model. In the late 1960s, Don Helmberger developed the foundations of generalized ray theory (GRT) using the Cagniard-de Hoop method (Helmberger, 1968). This advance ushered in a new era of computing synthetic seismograms at local to teleseismic distances in applications ranging from studying strong motions generated by earthquakes to modeling Earth's interiors from basin to core. Over the intervening period, rapid improvements in computational power could have seen semi-analytical methods such as GRT superseded by large-scale numerical waveform simulations. Instead, the insights and intuition afforded by GRT on how the seismic waveforms are affected by source and structural effects have proven invaluable. In essence, our models of the seismic source and Earth's structure are only as good as our understanding of the input seismic data.

As his final PhD student, I have heard many legendary stories of how Don teased out subtle differences in seismic waveforms to discover important structures and dynamics within the Earth. I will be forever grateful that I got to witness this act first-hand by exploring three very different problems with Don. Our first adventure together involved investigating the poorly understood lower crust and upper mantle structure along North American - Pacific plate boundary, not bottom-up, but rather from north to south (Lai et al., 2017). SH waves generated by earthquakes in the Mendocino triple junction and recorded at the Southern California Seismic Network are sensitive to the sharp lateral variation of velocity across the plate boundary (Figure 1). We were able to model anomalous travel times across the region using 3D waveform simulations, confirming the presence of a strong oceanic upper mantle buttressed against a weaker continental margin crust that localizes plate boundary deformation and accounts for the observed asymmetric strain rates.

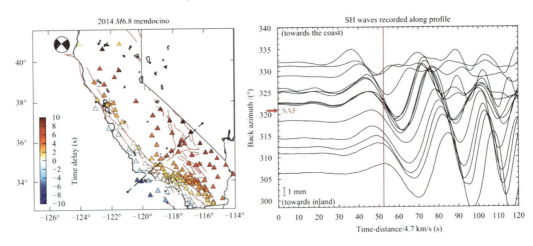

Fig. 1   Time delay observed in Californian seismic network from a Mendocino event (modified from Lai et al., 2017). (left) Map shows the measured time shifts between the observed long period (30–50 s) SH waves for the 2014 M6.8 Mendocino event and synthetics from the 1D 'Gil7' model. Cooler color indicates the observed waves arrive earlier than predicted by 1-D synthetics and vice-versa. (right) Azimuthal record section of broadband SH waves recorded by stations along the profile (see map) from the event, plotted with reduced time (distance/4.7 km/s). The red arrow marks where the San Andreas Fault intersects the profile. SH waves arrived at the coast earlier than at the eastern border of California by 14 seconds. This time difference can be explained with a sharp velocity change in the lower crust-upper mantle across the plate boundary, which is not present in the current 3-D community velocity models

Our second adventure began when we noticed that, in the rupture study of regional earthquakes near Los Angeles Basin by Lui et al. (2016), the shaking duration of long-period waves (> 2 seconds) was anomalously long for earthquakes occurring at shallow depths (Figure 2). Using beamforming analyses and 3D waveform simulations of carefully selected local events, we were able to identify that the shaking duration is depth-dependent and is a path effect caused by the local sedimentary basin. To better predict the long duration of shaking, we needed to improve our velocity models, paying particular attention to shallow heterogeneities and the attenuation structure (Lai et al., 2020).

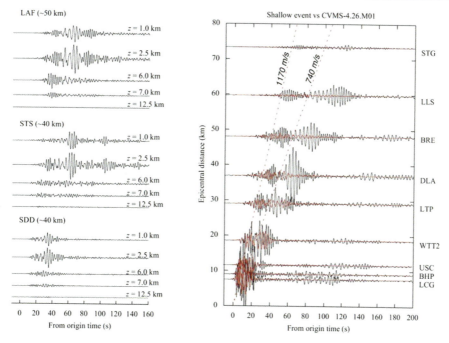

Fig. 2　Depth-dependent shaking duration at Los Angeles Basin (modified from Lai et al., 2020). (left) Tangential velocity waveforms for five local events with depths ranging between 1.0 and 12.5 km occurring just outside the Los Angeles Basin. Stations LAF and STS which are within the basin show an additional ~50 s of shaking but not SDD which has a travel path completely outside the basin. (right) Record section shows the comparison between tangential velocity data (in black) for a shallow event and the 3-D synthetics (in red) generated for the Community Velocity Model CVM-S.4.26.M01. The current 3-D model can predict the initial arrivals but not the late strong shaking which requires shallow heterogeneities and improved attenuation model

For our final adventure, I was drawn into the deep Earth when Don showed me record sections of S-diffracted phases exhibiting strange multipathing behavior and we started brainstorming all the possible reasons to explain the multipathing. Upon closer investigation, we found that, in the region where Sdiff multipathing occurs, there is a coincident, rapid variation in differential ScS-S travel times that can only be explained by complex interaction between an ultra-low velocity zone and a subducted slab at the very edge of the Pacific Large Low Shear Velocity Province (Lai et al., 2022). Many previous studies in this region have only focused on a single seismic phase but with Don's expertise across all seismic waves, we were able to combine multiple phases to shed light on such complicated structural variation, which cannot be observed by ScS or Sdiff alone. This discovery is particularly exciting, as the interaction between these structural anomalies may be responsible for promoting upwelling and it occurs near the predicted source location of the Hawaiian hotspot plume (Figure 3).

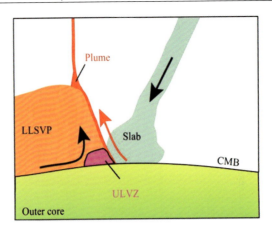

Fig. 3　Schematic cartoon showing the ULVZ-slab interaction near the edge of the Pacific LLSVP (reproduced from Lai et al. (2022)). The modeling of Sdiff multipathing and ScS-S differential travel times suggests a ULVZ structure driven towards the edge of the Pacific LLSVP while potentially pushed by a subducted slab, a configuration that may trigger plume generation due to strong thermal instabilities

Apart from a keen eye for seismic wiggles, Don imparted many great lessons to me on how to become a truly well-rounded scientist. He understood that science cannot be undertaken in a vacuum. From early on, he actively paired me with different researchers both within and outside the Seismo Lab in order to gain new skills, learn how to collaborate, and most importantly, develop different perspectives on analyzing and interpreting data. He was very encouraging when I decided to put these new skills into practice by starting my own research collaborations with other faculty members. In these projects, I soon found myself scrutinizing the waveforms so closely – holding record sections up against the lights – just the way he used to during our afternoon discussions. His constant reminders to separately identify the effects of source and structure on seismic waveforms helped me to avoid many interpretation pitfalls when I was analyzing the source dynamics of debris flows and caldera collapse. His example of seeking out collaboration encouraged me to make new connections, which greatly expanded my scientific network and opened my mind to many exciting new developments in the broader geophysics field.

Don's boundless enthusiasm and selflessness in mentoring has transformed many generations of seismologists, including myself. Despite already having a long list of major discoveries under his belt, he was constantly thinking (while staring out at the San Gabriel Mountains, and later a giant world map after he moved office) about how we can better image the Earth, especially the boundaries, at higher resolution. There are still so many unanswered questions to be studied, for instance the effect of anisotropy on waveforms in oceanic crust and the deep Earth, which would have kept him and will keep many of us busy for a long time. During my last phone call with him, after teasing my incapability to adapt to the cold Canberran winter (he grew up in northern Minnesota), he asked, "Are you having fun looking at the waveforms?" and I proudly replied, "I am!" "Great. Keep having fun!", he responded. I smiled then, and I smile now knowing that deep down, I will continue to do so in his spirit and to his honor.

References

Helmberger DV (1968). The crust-mantle transition in the Bering Sea. Bull Seismol Soc Am **58**(1): 179–214.

Lai VH, Helmberger DV, Dobrosavljevic VV, WuW, Sun D, Jackson JM and Gurnis M (2022). Strong ULVZ and slab interaction at the northeastern edge of the Pacific LLSVP favors plume Generation. Geochemistry, Geophysics, Geosystems **23**: e2021GC010020, https://doi.org/10.1029/2021GC010020

Lai VH, Graves RW, Wei SJ and Helmberger D (2017). Evidence for strong lateral seismic velocity variation in the lower crust and upper mantle beneath the California margin. Earth Planet Sci Lett **463**: 202–211.

Lai VH, Graves RW, Yu CQ, Zhan ZW and Helmberger DV (2020). Shallow basin structure and attenuation are key to predicting long shaking duration in Los Angeles basin. J Geophys Res **125**(10): e2020JB019663.

Lui SKY, Helmberger D, Yu JJ and Wei SL (2016). Rapid assessment of earthquake source characteristics. Bull Seismol Soc Am **106**(6): 2490–2499.

Voon Hui Lai is currently a postdoctoral fellow at the Research School of Earth Sciences, Australian National University (ANU-RSES). She completed her Ph.D. in Geophysics at Caltech in 2020 with Prof. Don Helmberger and Prof. Zhongwen Zhan as her primary thesis advisors. At Caltech, she co-authored several papers with Don on modelling complex waveforms observed in sedimentary basins and lowermost mantle. At ANU-RSES, she uses Distributed Acoustic Sensing (DAS), a new generation fiber-optics based seismic array, to perform high resolution subsurface imaging and source characterizations.

Her webpage can be found at: https://vhlai-seis.github.io/.

第 18 章　与唐·亨伯格一起探索地球的边界

赖文慧

澳大利亚国立大学地球科学研究院，ACT 2601，澳大利亚

引用：Lai VH (2022). Exploring Earth's boundaries with Donald V. Helmberger. Earthq Sci 35(1): 63−66 doi: 10.1016/j.eqs.2022.01.014

地震波形建模是了解地球结构最强大的工具之一，因为它借助物理上的震源表示方法和速度模型对波形进行定量预测。在 20 世纪 60 年代后期，唐·亨伯格（Don Helmberger）使用卡尼亚尔−德胡普方法（Helmberger，1968）发展了广义射线理论（GRT）的基础。这一进展开创了计算从区域到远震距离的合成地震图的新时代，其应用范围包括研究地震产生的强烈运动和建立从盆地到地核的地球内部模型。在这期间，随着计算能力的迅速提高，可以看到虽然诸如 GRT 这样的半分析方法被大规模数值波形模拟所取代，但是 GRT 提供的关于地震波形如何受震源和结构影响的理解和直观表示被证明是非常宝贵的。从本质上讲，我们对震源和地球结构的模型只有在了解了输入的地震数据后才会有更好的认识。

作为他最后的博士生，我听过许多关于唐（Don）如何从地震波形的细微差异中发现地球内部重要结构和动力学特征的传奇故事。我将永远感激我能够通过与唐（Don）一起探索三个截然不同的问题，从而亲眼见证他是怎么做的。我们的第一次的"冒险"是关于沿着北美-太平洋板块边界调查其下方知之甚少的下地壳和上地幔结构，不是自下而上，而是从北到南（Lai et al.，2017）。由 Mendocino 三岔点地震所产生的，并在南加州地震台网被记录到的 SH 波对整个板块边界速度的急剧横向变化很敏感（图 1）。我们能够使用 3D 波形模拟对该地区的异常旅行时进行建模，确认了强度较大的海洋上地幔的存在，这部分地幔支撑在较弱的大陆边缘地壳上，该地壳定位了板块边界变形并解释了观察到的不对称应变率。

当我们注意到这一点时，我们的第二次"冒险"开始了，在 Lui 等人（2016）的洛杉矶盆地附近区域地震的破裂研究中，长周期波的震动持续时间（> 2 秒）对于发生在浅层深度的地震来说异常长（图 2）。通过使用 beamforming 分析和对精心挑选的局部事件进行的 3D 波形模拟，我们能够确定震动持续时间与深度有关，并且反映了由局部沉积盆地引起的路径效应。为了更好地预测长时间的震动，我们需要改进速度模型，特别是浅层非均一性和衰减结构（Lai et al.，2020）。

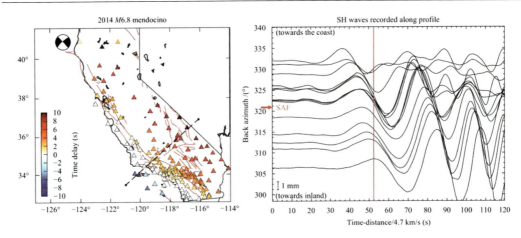

图 1　在加利福尼亚地震台网中观察到的 Mendocino 事件的时间延迟（修改自 Lai et al., 2017）。（左）地图显示了观测到的 2014 年 M6.8 Mendocino 事件的长周期（30～50 秒）SH 波与一维"Gil7"模型的合成波之间的测量时间偏移。较冷的色调表示观察到的波比一维合成波预测的更早到达，反之亦然。（右）沿特定剖面（见地图）排布的台站记录的来自这一事件的宽频带 SH 波，按方位角绘制的记录剖面，以动校正时间（距离除以 4.7 km/s）绘制。红色箭头标志着圣安地列斯断层与剖面相交的地方。SH 波到达海岸的时间比加州东部边界的时间早 14 秒。这个时间差可以用跨越板块边界的下地壳−上地幔的急剧速度变化来解释，这在目前的三维公共速度模型中是不存在的。

　　在我们的最后一次"冒险"中（Lai et al., 2022），当唐（Don）向我展示了表现出奇怪的多路径行为的 S 衍射相位的记录部分时，我被地球深处所吸引，我们开始集思广益，想出所有可能的原因来解释多路径 。经过仔细调查，我们发现，在 Sdiff 多路径发生的区域，存在着 ScS-S 差分旅行时间一致的快速变化，这只能用太平洋大型低剪切速度省最边缘的超低速区和俯冲板块之间的复杂相互作用来解释。该地区之前的许多研究仅关注单个地震相位，但凭借唐（Don）在各种地震波方面的专业知识，我们能够将多个相位结合起来以阐明这种复杂的结构变化，而仅 ScS 或 Sdiff 无法观察到这些变化。这一发现特别令人兴奋，因为这些结构异常之间的相互作用可能是促进上升流的原因，并且它发生在人们预测的夏威夷热点地幔柱的源位置附近（图 3）。

　　Sdiff 多路径和 ScS-S 差分旅行时间的建模表明 ULVZ 结构被推向太平洋 LLSVP 的边缘，同时可能受到俯冲板片的推动，这种构造可能因强烈的热不稳定性而引发地幔柱的生成。

　　除了对地震波动的敏锐眼光外，唐（Don）还向我传授了许多关于如何成为真正全面的科学家的重要经验。他明白科学不能闭门造车。从一开始，他就积极地让我与地震实验室内外的不同研究人员交流，以获得新技能，学习如何合作，最重要的是，在分析和解释数据方面形成不同的观点。当我决定将这些新技能付诸实践，与系里的其他教师开始自己的研究合作时，他也总是鼓励我。在这些项目中，我很快发现自己在仔细检查波形——把记录部分对着灯光——就像他在我们下午的讨论中经常做的那样。他不断提醒我分别识别震源和结构对地震波形的影响，这帮助我在分析泥石流和火山口塌陷的震源动力学时避免了许多解释误区。他寻求合作的例子鼓励我与其他人建立新的联系，这

极大地扩展了我的学术社交网络，并使我在更广泛的地球物理学领域的许多令人兴奋的
新发展方面开阔了眼界。

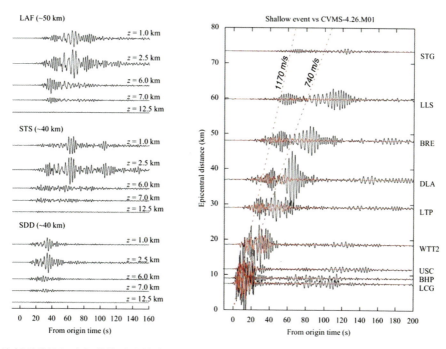

图 2　洛杉矶盆地深度相关的震动持续时间（修改自 Lai et al., 2020）。（左）五个恰好在洛杉矶盆地
外的局部事件的切向速度波形，震源深度介于 1.0 和 12.5 km 之间。位于盆地内的 LAF 和 STS 站显示
了额外的约 50 秒的震动，但 SDD 没有，它的地震波行进路径完全在盆地之外。（右图）波形记录显
示了一个浅层事件的切向速度数据（黑色）和与由公共速度模型 CVM-S.4.26.M01 生成的三维合成数据
（红色）之间的比较。

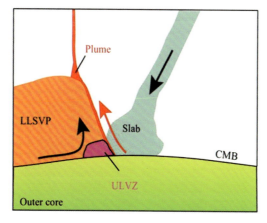

图 3　显示太平洋 LLSVP 边缘附近的 ULVZ 与俯冲板片相互作用的示意图。（修改自 Lai et al., 2022）

　　唐（Don）的无限热情和无私的指导，改变了许多代的地震学家，包括我自己。尽
管他已经有了一长串的重大发现，但他一直在思考（在盯着 San Gabriel 山的时候，以及

后来他搬了办公室后的巨大世界地图），我们如何能以更高的分辨率更好对地球进行成像，尤其是边界。还有很多悬而未决的问题有待研究，例如各向异性对海洋地壳和地球深处波形的影响，这将使他和我们中的许多人在很长一段时间内花大量时间进行研究。在我与他的最后一次电话中，在嘲笑我没有能力适应堪培拉的寒冷冬天（他在明尼苏达州北部长大）之后，他问道："你看波形的时候开心吗？"我自豪地回答："是的！"
"太好了。继续玩吧！"，他回答。我当时笑了，现在的我也笑了，我知道在内心深处，我将继续带着他的精神和荣誉走下去。

参 考 文 献

Helmberger DV (1968). The crust-mantle transition in the Bering Sea. Bull Seismol Soc Am **58**(1): 179–214.

Lai VH, Helmberger DV, Dobrosavljevic VV, WuW, Sun D, Jackson JM and Gurnis M (2022). Strong ULVZ and slab interaction at the northeastern edge of the Pacific LLSVP favors plume Generation. Geochemistry, Geophysics, Geosystems **23**: e2021GC010020, https://doi.org/10.1029/2021GC010020

Lai VH, Graves RW, Wei SJ and Helmberger D (2017). Evidence for strong lateral seismic velocity variation in the lower crust and upper mantle beneath the California margin. Earth Planet Sci Lett **463**: 202–211.

Lai VH, Graves RW, Yu CQ, Zhan ZW and Helmberger DV (2020). Shallow basin structure and attenuation are key to predicting long shaking duration in Los Angeles basin. J Geophys Res **125**(10): e2020JB019663.

Lui SKY, Helmberger D, Yu JJ and Wei SL (2016). Rapid assessment of earthquake source characteristics. Bull Seismol Soc Am **106**(6): 2490–2499.

赖文慧目前是澳大利亚国立大学地球科学研究院（ANU-RSES）的博士后研究员。她于2020年在加州理工学院获得了她的地球物理学博士学位，主要论文导师是唐·亨伯格（Don

Helmberger）教授和詹中文教授。在加州理工学院，她与唐（Don）共同撰写了多篇关于在沉积盆地和最下层地幔中观察到的复杂波形建模的论文。在 ANU-RSES，她使用分布式声学传感器（DAS），一种基于光纤的新一代地震阵列，来进行高分辨率的地下成像和震源特征分析。她的主页是 https://vhlai-seis.github.io/。

Chapter 19. Donald V. Helmberger, the master mentor: Testimonials from former international students

Xiaodong Song [1,*], Sidao Ni [2], Ying Tan [3], Alex Song [4], Risheng Chu [5], Daoyuan Sun [6], Shengji Wei [7], Semechah Lui [8], Voon Hui Lai [9]

1. Institute of Theoretical and Applied Geophysics, School of Earth and Space Sciences, Peking University, Beijing 100871, China (xiao.d.song@gmail.com)

2. State Key Laboratory of Geodesy and Earth's Dynamics, Innovation Academy of Precision Measurement Science and Technology, Chinese Academy of Sciences, Wuhan 430077, China (sdni@whigg.ac.cn)

3. Chevron Technical Center, Houston TX 77002, USA (ying.tan@chevron.com)

4. Department of Earth Sciences, University College London, London WC1E 6BT, United Kingdom (alex.song@ucl.ac.uk)

5. State Key Laboratory of Geodesy and Earth's Dynamics, Innovation Academy of Precision Measurement Science and Technology, Chinese Academy of Sciences, Wuhan 430077, China (chur@asch.whigg.ac.cn)

6. Laboratory of Seismology and Physics of Earth's Interior, School of Earth and Space Sciences, University of Science and Technology of China, Hefei 230026, China (sdy2014@ustc.edu.cn)

7. Asian School of the Environment/Earth Observatory of Singapore, Nanyang Technological University, Singapore 639798, Singapore (shjwei@gmail.com)

8. Department of Earth Sciences, University of Toronto, Toronto, ON, M5S 3B1, Canada (semechah.lui@utoronto.ca)

9. Research School of Earth Sciences, The Australian National University, ACT 2601, Australia (voonhui.lai@anu.edu.au)

[*]**Correspondence:** Contact any author at email provided.

Citation: Song XD, Ni SD, Tan Y, Song A, Chu RS, Sun DY, Wei SJ, Lui S and Lai VH (2022). Donald V. Helmberger, the master mentor: Testimonials from former international students. Earthq Sci 35(1): 67−70 doi: 10.1016/j.eqs.2022.01.003

Don trained many Ph.D. students over the ~5 decades of his career, at least 45 were advised or co-advised according to a Caltech account. A large number were international students including a high percentage of Chinese students. The contributors to this article graduated over a time span of 26 years, and we are now distributed in 6 countries across 14 time zones, yet we represent only a small fraction of his former students and postdocs.

Don had a natural talent for mentoring that attracted us deeply. Below are direct testimonies from us to that effect. It is easy to see common threads regarding his mentoring style. First, Don spent a lot of time with students. Second, he loved to look at data and to show students how to appreciate them. Third, he had a magical touch that is hard to describe. The following words come easily to our minds when thinking about him: insightful, inspirational, patient, humorous, magical, supportive, caring, and generous.

I

Don loved to look at data (seismograms). Digital stations were still sparse in the early 1990s. He would go down to the basement to find film chip records and bring up a pile of paper-copy seismograms. He spent tons of time with students (in his office, or at football games and beer hours). Often there was a line of students waiting outside his office to talk to him or we would find "See me, Don" notes on our desks or computer screens. Thus, I was very happy to grab a chance to move into an office obliquely opposite to his so that I could see whether he was available without leaving my office. We would look over seismograms, codes, figures, and manuscripts in great details. He would hold up seismograms (synthetic and observed) and see how they match or mismatch. After some 30 years, these are the most vivid pictures that come up from my memory.

He had the magic of inspiration, out of his wisdom and humor, but also of modesty, kindness, and generosity.

II

Don was an inspirational mentor and a true seismologist with expertise for deciphering the secrets of earthquakes, interior of the Earth, as well as nuclear tests. His virtuosity in uncovering the above secrets is best demonstrated in his deep love of various seismic signals (wiggles, or seismic phases) in seismograms. I started my graduate study examining old seismograms on microfilms archived in the basement of the Seismo Lab, and Don taught me how to use the archaic instruments for reading the microfilms and how to understand and decipher the seismic phases in the seismograms. I would say, Don was much like the famous computer genius Alan Turing who cracked German secret codes during World War II. Don cracked the secret codes in seismograms and discovered many important features inside the Earth. Inspired by Don, I also become addicted to deciphering the seismic wiggles.

I much cherished "See me, Don" notes on my desk. Each note led to valuable opportunity for me to learn from Don and to share my progress with him.

III

Don was a fantastic advisor, the best one a student could wish for. He not only taught me how to solve the mysteries of the Earth from seismograms but also made sure I was having fun doing it. Don spent a lot of time working closely with his students. He closely monitored our well-being and academic progress and provided timely guidance. He set high standards for himself and his students. During my early days in graduate school, I felt some pressure from time to time, especially when Don put a yellow sticker with a sad face and a short message "can I see u?" on my computer after I had missed our regular catch-up sessions. Later, with hindsight, I started to appreciate his effort and to see the benefit of his approach. My officemate Chen Ji once joked that he was jealous about Don's daily reminder and mother-hen approach for me. Don certainly knew who would need a little bit more help there. Besides seismology, Don also taught me wisdom of life, and corrected my English pronunciations of letters like "r" and "n". I really liked his jokes; it just sometimes took me a while to figure them out. I enjoyed working with Don and really appreciate his patience and encouragement, especially when things did not go as expected. From time to time, I reminded myself what Don had taught me: "you need to get up and try again wherever you fall" or "some little birds, they never know how high they could fly, cause they never try"... We had stayed in touch since I graduated, and every time I called Don, I felt I was so welcome. It was always great to hear his excited and joyful voice. Don had been like a family member for me, and I know many of his students feel the same way. Don's fatherly care will live with us forever.

IV

I cherish every minute I had with Don. Perhaps some people just have that kind of charisma. Don was not loud and he almost always had a smile on his face, probably because another good idea came to his mind or perhaps he just finished another look at some seismograms. Normally, I sat next to Don in his office, we discussed a bit and next thing you know, he started looking at Mt Wilson, and soon after, we both were looking at Mt Wilson. For me, these short episodes of silence, sometimes they could be quite long, actually brought a peace of mind and clarity to me, and all of a sudden, we would come to a new understating about the story behind the seismograms. The idea may not work the next time, but the inspiration was always there, and Don seemed to have a magic touch to make people around him better. In a way, Don invited us to see the world through his lens. The inspiration comes each time when I see Mt. Wilson.

I consider myself incredibly lucky that I had seemingly a lot of time with Don during the 7 years I spent at the Seismo Lab since the summer of 2000. After a few long years and a move to the UK, we finally saw each other again in 2018 in Singapore. For some reason, seeing Don always brought a big smile to my face. I will always remember the humor and wisdom, the affection and the kindness from him.

V

I first met Don in November 2006 at the Earthscope/USArray Imaging Science and CIG Seismology Workshop in Washington University in St. Louis. Prof. Lupei Zhu, my PhD advisor and Don's former student, invited him to stop by Saint Louis University for suggestions on our ongoing project. His profound knowledge of seismology, particularly waveform modeling, fascinated me, and I was determined to follow his path into the limitless universe of seismic wiggles.

In April 2008, I was lucky enough to join the Seismo Lab as Don's post-doc. Since then, we collaborated frequently and published 13 papers together, mostly on earthquake sources and upper mantle velocity structures from waveform modeling. Don was like a magician. He could turn many ordinary things into magic tools for seismic waveform modeling. I would show him observed and synthetic waveforms along different distance profiles for various azimuths. On each profile, he would draw many straight lines using a large ruler, marking arrivals of major seismic phases (apparent velocity of these phases can be inferred from the slopes of the lines). He also marked on a sticky note to tell different arrivals. Occasionally, he would copy a distance profile onto a transparency and align with other profiles to see the azimuthal variations. These seemingly small tricks enlightened me. I often use the same tricks in meeting with my students.

VI

Don was so humble and always proud of his students. Once, I asked him why he could train so many great students. He smiled and said, "Let them play in the sandpit freely and nicely". He was so good at identifying the distinct personalities of different students and treating them uniquely but equally. In any case, he was always supportive, caring, and believed everybody should be able to become the master to understand the wiggles.

I heard that there was always a line of students outside Don's office. I was lucky that I did not need to wait in line. From that point of view, I was not a very good student. Don always came to my office and put a note of "see me" on my computer screen. Sometimes, he would draw a smiling face instead. It was always a joyful and cherished moment to sit with Don in his office. Seeing Don plotting lines on the seismograms, waiting for him to reboot from a sudden stop, and enjoying the view of Mount Wilson and day dreaming with him has been the greatest memory.

Don's class of "Advanced Seismology" is notoriously hard. I know Don had prepared the lectures and class notes so seriously and brought piles of papers for everybody. He always went to the classroom before the class and wrote down equations on the blackboard. However, his class was just so difficult. However, every time I sat in that class, I learned something new.

"This is a wild goose chase", was sometimes the verdict after we studied some problems for several months and decided to "put it in a folder". However, such folders never stopped Don and us from studying more wiggles.

VII

Don had a unique charisma to attract students to work with him to get into his world of understanding the seismograms. When we identified phases in the seismogram, we sometimes bet on the solutions to verify our speculations and of course, I lost almost all the wagers. It is no question that strong curiosity had driven his life-long addiction to the seismograms. In one of the many conversations we had, he said that after I die, I will go to the bottom of the mantle and see what the hell is going on there. He also expressed several times in coffee hours and seminars that he is a dreamer in doing science. His genuine curiosity infected many of his students through countless meetings, which is one of the reasons that the Seismo Lab has a very high student ratio staying in academia after graduation. Don cared a lot about his students, not only for their work but also their life. He wanted his students to be happy in doing what they do, which he considered as the most important reason to eventually keep them in academia.

VIII

Don was one of the first professors I met at Caltech, and he gave me a warm welcome to the world of seismology. I am always inspired by his sharpness in extracting interesting waveform features and generating countless research ideas around them. One of Don's favorite things to do was to study seismograms on paper or transparency films. I am sure many of his students have had experience spending hours printing seismograms before their meetings with Don. Although tree lovers might not appreciate this, I would always look forward to spending fun afternoons sitting next to Don to go over the wiggles together. I would walk into his office with a few questions, and ended up walking out with way more!

As a mentor, Don showed tremendous support and care through the ups and downs of my research career. Don was a man with few words, but his small gestures (a hidden thumbs-up during my qualifying exam) and unique sense of humor (telling me how much I should pay him for therapy time while I was getting ready for my defense) were the little magical things he did that kept me going. Don's office door was always open; the energy and time he dedicated to his students is something for which I will always be grateful. It has been a true blessing to have worked under Don's wings during my years at Caltech. I will miss him and the lessons he taught me in seismology and in life.

IX

Don is my greatest inspiration in my academic journey to become both an exceptional seismologist and an outstanding mentor. It is well known that Don had a very keen eye for seismograms and it seems almost magical to see how he identified anomalies from plain looking wiggles. However, as I have been able to meet many of his previous students over time, I am more amazed by Don's innate ability to cultivate each student, as we all have different personalities and background, to become the best scientist we can be. The journey of doing good science is difficult and peppered with failures, and Don was there with me, giving his time and knowledge with no holding back. He showed that there is always time to look at record sections, how to let go of wrong interpretations and start over, how not to be afraid to ask silly questions, and most importantly how to build confidence in our scientific capability. I will miss our afternoon discussions, where we poured over record sections and stared out the window at the mountains, thinking of models to explain the waveform anomaly, try them, and repeat again. "Praise from the praise-worthy is beyond all rewards." I will always be grateful for his patience in me as I am finding my footing in science; his trust in me by affirming my big or small achievements, whether it is finding an earthquake with good waveforms or winning grants; and last but not least, his confidence in me to pursue open questions about our Earth (even if it's without him).

Xiaodong Song is currently Chair Professor at School of Earth and Space Sciences, Peking University. He received his M.S. degree in 1991 and Ph.D. degree in 1994 at Caltech with Prof. Helmberger as thesis advisor. He then joined Lamont-Doherty Earth Observatory of Columbia University as a postdoc fellow and later as Associate Research Scientist and Storke-Doherty Lecturer. He subsequently served on the faculty of Department of Geology at University of Illinois at Urbana-Champaign from 1999 to 2020 before relocating to Beijing, China. His work on the inner core differential rotation was named as a breakthrough of the year by Science magazine (1996). He received Doornbos Prize by the Studies of Earth Deep Interior Committee of the International Union of Geophysics and Geodesy (1996), Outstanding Overseas Young Scientist Award by the Natural Science Foundation of China (1998), Solid Earth Distinguished Lectureship by the Asia Oceania Geosciences Society (AOGS) (2016). He currently serves as the Editor-in-Chief of Earthquake Science. His webpage can be found at: http://geophy.pku.edu.cn/people/songxiaodong/english/index.html.

Professor Sidao Ni is a seismologist at the Innovation Academy for Precision Measurement Science and Technology (APM), Chinese Academy of Sciences. He serves as deputy Director of the APM, and director of the State Key Laboratory of Geodesy and Earth's Dynamics. Dr. Ni's expertise is in waveform seismology. He received his undergraduate (1993) and master's (1996) degrees from the University of Science and Technology of China (USTC) under the supervision of Prof. Guoming Xu, and his Ph.D. degree from the California Institute of Technology (Caltech) in 2001 under the supervision of Prof. Don V Helmberger. Then he worked as research scientist at the SeismoLab until 2004. After his return to China, he worked at the University of Science and Technology of China before joining Institute of Geodesy and Geophysics of the Chinese Academy of Sciences. He was awarded the Distinguished Young Investigator from National Science Foundation of China and the Hundred Talents Program from the Chinese Academy of Sciences. He has been principal investigator of National Key Basic Research Project of China (973 Program) of the Ministry of Science and Technology, key projects of the National Science Foundation of China, and received Natural Science Award of Hubei Province, the Science and Technology Award of the Chinese Geophysical Society, the ZhuLi-Yuehua Outstanding Teacher Award of Chinese Academy of Sciences .

Ying Tan is currently a senior geophysicist with Chevron Technical Center in Houston, TX. She completed her Ph.D. at Caltech in 2006 with Prof. Helmberger as her primary thesis advisor.

Alex Song is currently Associate Professor of Earth Sciences, University College London (UCL). He completed his Ph.D. at Caltech in 2006 with Prof. Helmberger as his primary thesis advisor. After two years as a Carnegie Fellow in the Department of Terrestrial Magnetism (DTM) at the Carnegie Institution for Sciences, he serves as a scientist in Japan Agency for Marine-Earth Science and Technology (JAMSTEC) for 4 years before joining UCL. His webpage can be found at: https://www.ucl.ac.uk/earth-sciences/people/academic/dr-teh-ru-alex-song/.

Risheng Chu, Ph.D., Professor of Geophysics at Innovation Academy for Precision Measurement Science and Technology, Chinese Academy of Sciences. He received his bachelor degree from University of Science and Technology in 2002, and Ph.D. from Saint Louis University in 2008. He then moved to Seismological Laboratory at California Institute of Technology as a post-doctoral researcher, and then a staff scientist till 2013, under supervision of Prof. Helmberger. He was awarded the First Prize for Natural Science in Hubei Province in 2018 and Fu Chengyi Award for Outstanding Young Scientists of the Chinese Geophysical Union in 2021. His research is focused on earth's internal structures and earthquake source properties. He is PI of several projects from Ministry of Science and Technology and the National Natural Science Foundation of PRC. He has published more than 70 research papers in high-profile journals, e. g., Nature Geoscience, EPSL, JGR. He is now acting as secretary of Hubei Province Geophysical Society, deputy president of Hubei Province Seismological Society, and member of editorial boards for National Science Review, Earthquake Science, Earthquake Research Advances, and Acta Seismologica Sinica.

Daoyuan Sun, professor at the University of Science and Technology of China. He received his bachelor's degree in solid geophysics from the University of Science and Technology of China in 2000. In 2009, he got his Ph.D. degree from Caltech under the supervision of Professor Don Helmberger. His doctoral dissertation was entitled "Seismic Structure of the Lower Mantle". After graduation, he conducted postdoctoral research at the Department of Terrestrial Magnetism of the Carnegie Institution of Washington (Carnegie Postdoctoral Fellow) from 2010 to 2011 and the Department of Earth Sciences of the University of Southern California from 2012 to 2014. His research focuses on imaging the deep interior of the Earth, seismic wave propagation theory and computation, and the interior of other planets and the moon. He serves as the editor of the GRL at present.

Shengji Wei is currently an associate professor at the Nanyang Technological University and a Principal Investigator at the Earth Observatory of Singapore. He was co-supervised by Prof.

Helmberger from 2008.2 to 2009.2 during his visit to Caltech Seismolab and obtained his PhD from USTC in 2009. He then worked with Prof. Helmberger from 2009 – 2014 as a postdoc. His home page is: https://www.earthobservatory.sg/about-us/our-people/wei-shengji.

Semechah Lui is currently an assistant professor of applied geophysics at University of Toronto Mississauga. She completed her Ph.D. at Caltech in 2017 with Prof. Helmberger as her supervisor. Prior to joining UTM, she was a postdoctoral fellow working with Prof. Paul Young of University of Toronto and Prof. Yihe Huang of University of Michigan. Semechah's research webpage can be found at sites.google.com/view/skylui.

Voon Hui Lai is currently a postdoctoral fellow at the Research School of Earth Sciences, Australian National University (ANU-RSES). She completed her Ph.D. in Geophysics at Caltech in

2020 with Prof. Don Helmberger and Prof. Zhongwen Zhan as her primary thesis advisors. At Caltech, she co-authored several papers with Don on modelling complex waveforms observed in sedimentary basins and lowermost mantle. At ANU-RSES, she uses Distributed Acoustic Sensing (DAS), a new generation fiber-optics based seismic array, to perform high resolution subsurface imaging and source characterizations.

Her webpage can be found at: https://vhlai-seis.github.io/.

第 19 章　唐·亨伯格，桃李满天下的一代宗师：来自他过去的国际学生的感言

宋晓东 [1]，倪四道 [2]，谭英 [3]，宋德儒 [4]，储日升 [5]，孙道远 [6]，韦生吉 [7]，吕家欣 [8]，赖文慧 [9]

1 北京大学地球与空间科学学院，理论与应用地球物理研究所，北京 100871，中国

2 中国科学院精密测量科学与技术创新研究院，大地测量与地球动力学国家重点实验室，武汉 430077，中国

3 雪佛龙技术中心，路易斯安那街 1500 号，得克萨斯州休斯敦 77002，美国

4 伦敦大学学院，地球科学系，WC1E 6BT，英国伦敦

5 中国科学院精密测量科学与技术创新研究院，大地测量与地球动力学国家重点实验室，武汉 430077

6 中国科学技术大学，地球和空间科学学院，地震与地球内部物理实验室，合肥，230026，中国

7 南洋理工大学，亚洲环境学院/新加坡地球观测研究所，新加坡

8 多伦多大学，地球科学系，加拿大多伦多

9 澳大利亚国立大学，地球科学研究学院，澳大利亚 ACT 2601

引用：Song XD, Ni SD, Tan Y, Song A, Chu RS, Sun DY, Wei SJ, Lui S and Lai VH (2022). Donald V. Helmberger, the master mentor: Testimonials from former international students. Earthq Sci 35(1): 67−70 doi: 10.1016/j.eqs.2022.01.003

　　唐（Don）培养了许多博士。根据加州理工学院的记录，在大约 50 年的职业生涯中，他单独或者与他人共同指导的学生至少有 45 人。这其中有很多是国际学生，而且很大一部分是中国学生。这篇文章的作者们毕业时间最远相隔 26 年，现在散布在跨越了 14 个时区的 6 个国家，但我们也只是代表他以前的学生和博士后的一小部分。

　　唐（Don）与生俱来的指导才能，始终深深地吸引着我们。我们记忆中对他的指导风格的一些共有印象，能很好地证明他的这种才能。首先，唐（Don）花了很多时间和学生在一起；其次，他喜欢查看数据并向学生展示如何分析它们；第三，他的魅力难以形容。在怀念他的时候，我们很容易想到以下几个词：洞察力、发人深省、耐心、幽默、神奇、支持、关怀和慷慨。

一

　　唐（Don）喜欢看数据（地震图）。在 20 世纪 90 年代初期，数字地震台仍然很少。

他会去地下室寻找胶片记录，并拿出一堆纸质地震图。他的大把时间都用来和学生在一起（在他的办公室，或者在橄榄球比赛和啤酒时间）。经常有学生排着队在他的办公室外等着和他说话，在我们的桌子或电脑屏幕上也常会出现"见我，唐（Don）"的字条。因此，我很高兴抓住了机会搬到他斜对面的办公室，这样我不用离开办公室就可以看到他是否有空。我们会仔细地查看地震图、代码、图像或是手稿，不放过一个细节。他会举起合成的和观测的地震图，看看它们有多么地匹配或者不匹配。在 30 年后，这仍是我记忆中最生动的画面。

他有启发灵感的魔力，这种魔力来自他的智慧和幽默，也来自他的谦虚、善良和慷慨。

二

唐（Don）致力于利用地震波破解地震、核试验以及地球奥秘，他是真正的地震学大师，也是一位卓越的导师。他终生与地震图上的波形信号打交道，在震相波形的识别、测量与拟合等研究方面形成了高深的洞察力，达到了一览众山小的高超境界。二十多年来，我慢慢意识到，唐（Don）在地震学界的位置，犹如计算机学界中的阿兰·图灵（Alan Turing）。在第二次世界大战中，图灵破解了德国的密码机。而唐（Don）则是破解地震波密码的高手，在地球科学研究中做出了一系列突破性的发现。他高超的洞察力穿透了地壳、地幔以及地核，对全球地震学的发展，做出了巨大的贡献。

1996 年，我到加州理工学院学习，第一项科研任务是从地震实验室地下室的胶片库中查找、扫描地震图。唐（Don）不仅手把手教我使用古老的胶片机，还耐心讲解如何识别和研究震相波形，把我这个懵懂的地震学初学者带入了地震学研究的殿堂。现在回想起来，唐（Don）谆谆教导我时候的音容笑貌，依然历历在目。在我攻读博士期间，经常在办公桌上看到唐（Don）留给我的"来找我，唐（Don）"的留言条，然后我赶快去找他，或者汇报工作，或者请教困惑。对于这些留言条，我特别的怀念，因为每个留言条都给了我宝贵的机会，能够近距离地得到这位世界级的地震大师指导。

三

唐（Don）是一位出色的导师，是学生所希望的最好的那种。他不仅教我如何从地震图上解开地球的奥秘，同时还努力确保我乐在其中。唐（Don）花了很多时间与他的学生紧密合作。他密切关注我们的幸福感和学业进展，并及时提供指导。他为自己和他的学生设定了很高的标准。在读研究生的初期，我时不时会感到一些压力。尤其是当我错过了我们的常规进度交流时间的时候，唐（Don）会在我的电脑前贴上一张带有悲伤表情和"我能见你吗？"的黄色贴纸。事后回想，我才逐渐开始懂得他的用心并看到这种方法的好处。我的同办公室室友纪晨（Chen Ji）曾经开玩笑说，他嫉妒唐（Don）每天对我的提醒，还有唐（Don）对我如同鸡妈妈一般的教育方式。唐（Don）当然知道如何因材施教。除了地震学，唐（Don）还教导我生活的智慧，并纠正了我的"r"和"n"等字母的英文发音。我真的很喜欢他讲的笑话，只是有时我得花点功夫才能找到笑点。我很享受和唐（Don）一起工作的过程，也十分感谢他的耐心和鼓励，尤其是当事情不如预想般顺利的时候。我时常想起唐（Don）教我的话："无论在哪里跌倒，你都要站起来再试一次"，还有"有的小鸟，他们永远不知道自己能飞多高，因为他们从不尝试"……

毕业之后，我跟唐（Don）一直保持着联系。每次给他打电话，他都待我特别热情。他那兴奋而快乐的声音给你的感觉总是那么棒。唐（Don）对我来说就像家人一般，我知道他的许多学生也有同样的感受。唐（Don）那父亲般的关怀将永远伴随着我们。

四

我珍惜和唐（Don）在一起的每分每秒，也许有些人就是有这种魅力。唐（Don）的声音不大，脸上几乎总是挂着微笑，可能是因为他又想到了一个好主意，或是他刚刚又看了一些地震图。情况往往是这样的：在唐（Don）的办公室里，我坐在他的旁边，我们讨论了点什么，接下来，他也许会开始眺望威尔逊山，就这么过了一会儿，我也会开始眺望。对我来说，这些或短或长的沉默，确实能给我带来了内心的平静和思路的清晰。往往是突然之间，对地震图背后故事的新认识会在我们脑中闪现。这个想法下一次可能行不通，但灵感一直都在，而唐（Don）似乎有一种可以让周围的人变得更好的魔力。某种程度上来说，唐（Don）是在带着我们通过他的镜头看世界。每次看到威尔逊山，我仿佛就有了灵感。

自 2000 年夏天开始，我在地震实验室度过了 7 年，能有很多时间跟唐（Don）在一起，这让我感到无比幸运。经过几年的漫长岁月之后，我又搬到了英国，2018 年我们终于在新加坡相见。不知为何，看到唐（Don）总是让我脸上露出灿烂的笑容。我将永远铭记他的幽默和智慧，亲情和善意。

五

2006 年 11 月，我在圣路易斯华盛顿大学的 Earthscope/USArray 成像科学和 CIG 地震学研讨会上第一次见到了唐（Don）。他是受我的博士生导师也是他以前的学生朱露培（Lupei Zhu）教授的邀请，到圣路易斯大学就我们正在进行的项目提出建议。他对地震学，尤其是波形建模方面的渊博知识，让我着迷，于是我决心跟随他的道路进入地震波的无限宇宙。

2008 年 4 月，我有幸作为唐（Don）的博士后加入地震实验室。从那时起，我们经常合作并一起发表了 13 篇论文，主要是关于用地震震源和波形建模方法得到的上地幔速度结构。唐（Don）就像一个魔术师，他可以将许多普通的东西变成地震波形建模的神奇工具。我会向他展示沿不同距离剖面针对各种方位角得到的实际波形与合成波形。在每个剖面上，他会用一把大尺子画出许多直线，标记主要地震震相的到时（这些震相的视速度可以从线的斜率推断出来）。他还在便利贴上做标记，以显示不同的到时。有时，他会将距离剖面复制到透明胶片上，并与其他剖面对齐以查看方位角变化。这些看似不起眼的小技巧让我大开眼界。在与学生面谈时，我经常使用相同的技巧。

六

唐（Don）非常谦虚，总是为他的学生感到骄傲。有一次，我问他为什么能培养出这么多优秀的学生。他笑着说："让他们在沙坑里自由自在地玩耍。"他非常擅长发现每个学生的独特个性，并以独特又平等的方式对待他们。无论如何，他总是支持、关心他人，并相信每个人都应该能成为理解地震波的大师。

我听说唐（Don）的办公室外面总是排着长队。我很幸运，我不需要排队等候。从这个角度来看，我不是一个很好的学生。唐（Don）总是来我的办公室，在我的电脑屏幕上放一张"来找我"的字条。有时，他会在字条上画一张笑脸。和唐（Don）一起坐在他的办公室里的时光总是快乐而珍贵。看唐（Don）在地震图上画线，等他从突然的停顿中重新继续，与他一起欣赏威尔逊山的景色，甚至和他一起做白日梦，都是我最美好的回忆。

唐（Don）的"高级地震学"课程是出了名的难。我知道唐（Don）非常认真地准备了上课内容和课堂笔记，并为每个人带来了成堆的论文。他总是在课前去教室，在黑板上写下公式。然而，他的课实在是太难了。不过，只要坐在那里听课，我就总能学到一些新东西。

"这完全是在白费力气"，有时是我们把一个问题研究了几个月并决定"把它放在一个文件夹中"之后的结论。然而，这样的文件夹从未阻止唐（Don）和我们研究更多的地震图。

七

唐（Don）有一种独特的魅力，可以吸引学生与他一起工作，进入他理解地震图的世界。当我们尝试确定地震图中的震相时，我们有时会对不同的答案押注，然后再验证我们的猜测，当然，我几乎输掉了所有的赌注。毫无疑问，强烈的好奇心驱使他终生沉迷于地震图中。有一次在我们聊天的时候，他说："在我死后，我会去地幔的底部，看看那里到底发生了什么。"他还在咖啡时间和研讨会上多次表示，他是科学研究中的梦想家。在与学生们无数次的交流中，他真挚的好奇心也感染了他的许多学生，这也是从地震实验室毕业后留在学术界的学生比例非常高的原因之一。唐（Don）非常关心他的学生，不仅关心他们的工作，也关心他们的生活。他希望他的学生在做事情时感到快乐，他认为这是最终让学生们留在学术界的最重要原因。

八

唐（Don）是我在加州理工学院遇到的第一批教授之一，他热烈地欢迎我进入地震学的世界。在提取有趣的波形特征并围绕它们产生无数研究想法的方面，他的敏锐总是给我许多启发。唐（Don）最喜欢做的事情之一是研究纸上或透明胶片上的地震图。我敢肯定，唐（Don）的许多学生在与他会面之前都曾花费数小时打印地震图。虽然这可能不讨树木爱好者喜欢，但我总是期待与唐（Don）一起遍览波形，度过一个个有趣的下午。我会带着几个问题走进他的办公室，结果带着更多的问题走出来！

作为导师，唐（Don）在我研究生涯的起起落落中给予了我巨大的支持和关怀。唐（Don）是一个话不多的人，但一些有魔力的小事，比如他的某些不起眼的手势（在我的资格考试中偷偷竖起的大拇指）和独特的幽默感（在我准备答辩时，告诉我应该为他给我"治疗"的时长付多少钱）帮助我坚持了下来。唐（Don）的办公室门一直开着；他为学生付出的精力和时间，我将永远感激不尽。在加州理工学院的这些年里，能在唐（Don）的翅膀呵护下工作实在是我的福分。我会想念他以及他在地震学和生活中给我的教导。

九

在努力成为卓越的地震学家和杰出的导师的学术旅程中，唐（Don）的存在是最能鼓舞到我的。众所周知，唐（Don）对地震图有非常敏锐的眼光。他总是能令人不可思议地从看似普通的波动中识别异常。然而，随着时间的推移，我认识了许多他以前的学生，此时的我更惊讶于唐（Don）与生俱来的培养每个学生的能力。尽管我们都有不同的个性和背景，唐（Don）能使我们尽可能地成为最好的科学家。做好科学的旅程是艰难的，是充满了失败的。而唐（Don）始终和我在一起，毫不犹豫地付出了他的时间和知识。他的存在向我们表明，研究波形记录总是有时间的，他教导我们如何放弃错误的解释并重新开始，如何不害怕提出愚蠢的问题，最重要的是如何建立对我们科学能力的信心。我会想念我们的下午讨论，在那里我们倾注心血于波形记录，我们凝视着窗外的群山，我们思索着解释波形异常的模型，进行尝试，不断往复。"值得称赞之人的称赞胜过一切奖励。"当我在科学中寻找立足点时，我永远感谢他对我的耐心；无论是发现具有良好波形的地震还是获得资助，他总是通过肯定我这些或大或小的成就来表达对我的信任；最后但同样重要的一点是，即使没有亲自参与，他对我在地球的开放性问题中的探索也充满信心。

　　宋晓东现任北京大学地球与空间科学学院讲席教授，国家级人才计划专家。于 1994 年在加州理工学院获得博士学位，亨伯格教授是他的论文导师。随后，他加入哥伦比亚大学拉蒙特-多尔蒂地球观测站，做博士后，后来担任副研究员和讲师。他于 1999 年加入伊利诺伊大学厄巴纳-香槟分校地质系，从助理教授到终身正教授工作20多年，于2020年全职回国。他在内核差速旋转方面的工作被《科学》杂志（1996）评为年度十大突破之一。他曾获得国际地球物理和大地测量学联合会（IUGG）地球深部内部研究委员会多恩斯博斯奖（1996），中国自然科学基金委海外杰出青年基（B 类）（1998），亚洲大洋洲地球科学学会（AOGS）固体地球杰出讲座（2016）。目前担任国际英文期刊《地震科学》主编。他的主页是：http://geophy.pku.edu.cn/people/songxiaodong/。

　　倪四道，中国科学院精密测量科学与技术创新研究院研究员、副院长，大地测量与地球动力学国家重点实验室主任，主要从事波形地震学研究。本科（1993）及硕士（1996）毕业于中国科学技术大学，导师为徐果明教授。2001 年博士毕业于美国加州理工学院，随后在加州理工学院地震实验室从事研究工作，科研及论文指导导师为唐·亨伯格教授。2004 年回国工作，先后任职于中国科学技术大学、中国科学院测量与地球物理研究所，入选了国家基金委杰出青年科学基金、中国科学院百人计划等人才计划，主持了科技部 973 项目、国家基金委重点项目等科研项目，获得了湖北省自然科学一等奖、中国地球物理学会科学技术奖（一等）、中国科学院先进工作者、中国科学院朱李月华优秀教师等奖励。

　　谭英目前是得克萨斯州休斯敦雪佛龙技术中心的一名高级地球物理学家。她于 2006 年在加州理工学院获得博士学位，亨伯格教授是她的主要论文导师。

宋德儒目前是伦敦学院大学（UCL）地球科学专业的副教授。他于 2006 年在加州理工学院完成博士学位，亨伯格教授是他的主要论文导师。在卡内基科学研究所地磁系担任了两年的卡内基博士后，他又在日本海洋地球科学与技术机构（JAMSTEC）担任了四年的研究员，之后加入了伦敦学院大学。个人主页：https://www.ucl.ac.uk/earth-sciences/people/academic/dr-teh-ru-alex-song/。

储日升，中国科学院精密测量科学与技术创新研究院研究员、博士生导师。2002 年毕业于中国科学技术大学，获地球物理学士学位；2008 年获得美国圣路易斯大学地球物理博士学位；随后赴加州理工学院地震实验室跟随亨伯格教授从事博士后研究，2013 年成为研究科学家。2018 年获得湖北省自然科学一等奖，2021 年获中国地球物理学会傅承义青年科技奖。主要从事地球内部结构和地震震源性质研究，主持了科技部和国家自然科学基金委等项目。在 Nature Geoscience、EPSL、JGR 等期刊上发表论文 70 多篇，担任湖北省地球物理学会秘书长、湖北省地震学会副理事长，兼任 National Science Review 首届地学编辑工作组成员和 Earthquake Science Earthquake Research Advances《地震学报》等期刊编委。

孙道远，中国科学技术大学教授、博士生导师。2000 年获中国科学技术大学固体地球物理学士学位，2009 年获加州理工学院博士学位。博士期间师从唐·亨伯格教授，博士论文题目为"下地慢地震结构"。2010~2011 年和 2012~2014 年先后于华盛顿卡内基学院地球磁场系（卡内基博士后）和南加州大学地球科学进行博士后研究。主要从事地球深部地震学结构成像、地震波传播理论和计算、其他行星及月球内部结构等方面的研究。现为国际期刊 GRL 主编。

韦生吉目前是南洋理工大学副教授，新加坡地球观测站责任研究员。他于 2008 年 2 月~2009 年 2 月访问加州理工学院地震实验室期间，由亨伯格教授共同指导，并于 2009 年获得中国科学技术大学博士学位。2009~2014 年，他作为博士后与亨伯格教授一起工作。他的主页是 https://www.earthobservatory.sg/about-us/our-people/wei-shengji。

　　吕家欣目前是加拿大多伦多大学密西沙加分校（UTM）应用地球物理学的助理教授。她于 2017 年在加州理工学院完成博士学位，亨伯格教授是她的导师。在加入 UTM 之前，她作为博士后与多伦多大学的保罗·杨教授和密歇根大学的黄一荷教授一起工作。她的主页网址是：sites.google.com/view/skylui。

　　赖文慧目前是澳大利亚国立大学地球科学研究院（ANU-RSES）的博士后研究员。她于 2020 年在加州理工学院获得了她的地球物理学博士学位，主要论文导师是唐·亨伯格教授和詹中文教授。在加州理工学院，她与唐共同撰写了多篇关于在沉积盆地和最下层地幔中观察到的复杂波形建模的论文。在 ANU-RSES，她使用分布式声学传感器（DAS），一种基于光纤的新一代地震阵列，来进行高分辨率的地下成像和震源特征分析。她的主页是 https://vhlai-seis.github.io/。

Responsible Editor: Han Peng and Cui Yan

This book is in memory of Professor Donald V. Helmberger, an extraordinary seismologist and mentor of graduate students and young researchers pursuing the field of seismology. The book includes two forwards and a preface by distinguished colleagues along with 19 articles by a subset of his former students, reproduced in English and Chinese. The articles from his students identify many of the break-through discoveries that they participated in and convey the scientific philosophy and mentoring approach that Professor Helmberger followed throughout his career. The success of his mentoring is also reflected in the impressive academic and research careers of the numerous students that he supervised. The discipline of seismology now employs extensive seismic waveform modeling as a critical approach to constraining Earth structure from the inner core to the crust, as well as rapid quantification of earthquake space-time rupture behavior. The articles provide testimonials of Professor Helmberger's humble, inquisitive mind, and his great enthusiasm for understanding the wiggles of seismic recordings that endeared him to his graduate students and colleagues. The book is suitable for a wide spectrum of readers: undergraduate and graduate students, young researchers, and research advisers in geophysics and beyond.

ISBN 978-7-03-074369-5